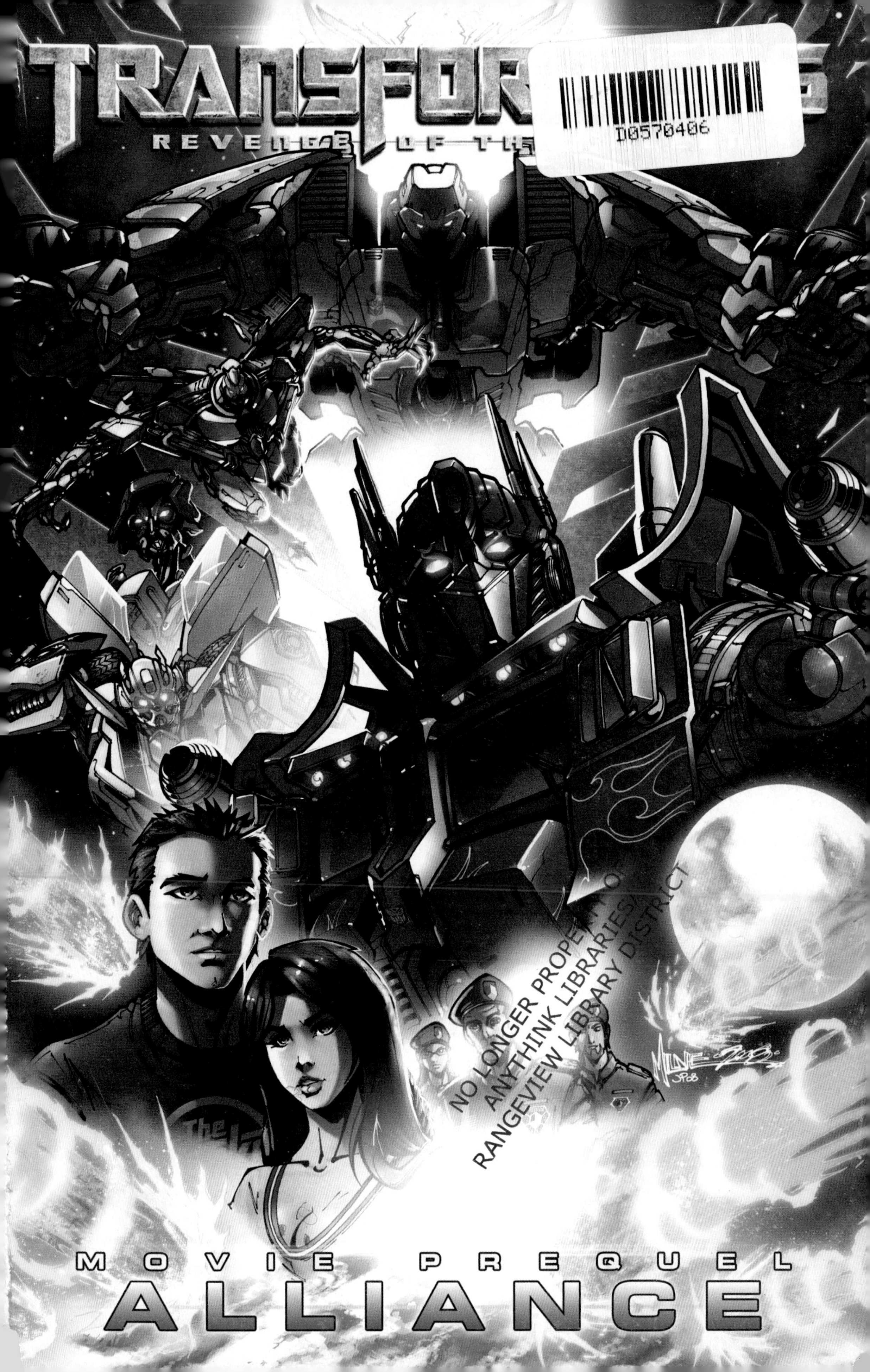
MOVIE PREQUEL
ALLIANCE

TRANSFORMERS: REVENGE OF THE FALLEN:
ALLIANCE

WRITTEN BY: **CHRIS MOWRY**

ART BY: **ALEX MILNE**

COLORS BY: **JOSH PEREZ & KRIS CARTER**

LETTERS BY: **CHRIS MOWRY & NEIL UYETAKE**

ORIGINAL SERIES EDITS BY: **DENTON J. TIPTON & ANDY SCHMIDT**

COLLECTION EDITS BY: **JUSTIN EISINGER & MARIAH HUEHNER**

COLLECTION DESIGN BY: **CHRIS MOWRY**

Special thanks to Hasbro's Aaron Archer, Michael Kelly, Amie Lozanzki, Val Roca, Ed Lane, Michael Provost,
Erin Hillman, Samantha Lomow, and Michael Verecchia for their invaluable assistance.

Licensed by:

ISBN: 978-1-60010-456-5
12 11 10 09   2 3 4 5

IDW Publishing
Operations:
Ted Adams, Chief Executive Officer
Greg Goldstein, Chief Operating Officer
Matthew Ruzicka, CPA, Chief Financial Officer
Alan Payne, VP of Sales
Lorelei Bunjes, Dir. of Digital Services
AnnaMaria White, Marketing & PR Manager
Marci Hubbard, Executive Assistant
Alonzo Simon, Shipping Manager

Editorial:
Chris Ryall, Publisher/Editor-in-Chief
Scott Dunbier, Editor, Special Projects
Andy Schmidt, Senior Editor
Justin Eisinger, Editor
Kris Oprisko, Editor/Foreign Lic.
Denton J. Tipton, Editor
Tom Waltz, Editor
Mariah Huehner, Associate Editor

Design:
Robbie Robbins, EVP/Sr. Graphic Artist
Ben Templesmith, Artist/Designer
Neil Uyetake, Art Director
Chris Mowry, Graphic Artist
Amauri Osorio, Graphic Artist
Gilberto Lazcano, Production Assistant

DREAMWORKS PICTURES   Paramount   www.IDWPUBLISHING.com

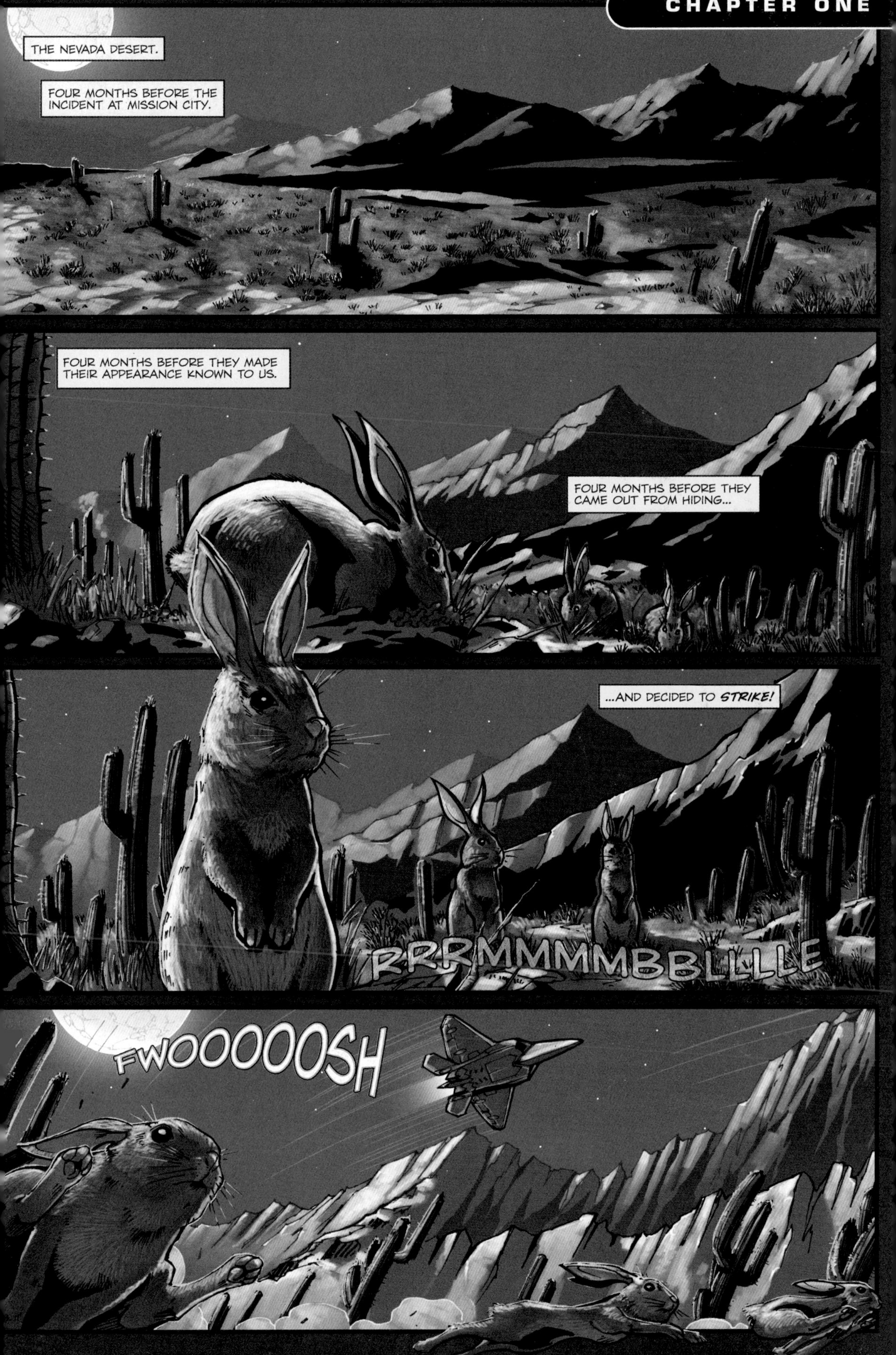
THE NEVADA DESERT.
FOUR MONTHS BEFORE THE INCIDENT AT MISSION CITY.
FOUR MONTHS BEFORE THEY MADE THEIR APPEARANCE KNOWN TO US.
FOUR MONTHS BEFORE THEY CAME OUT FROM HIDING...
...AND DECIDED TO *STRIKE!*
RRRMMMMMBBLLLLE
FWOOOOOSH

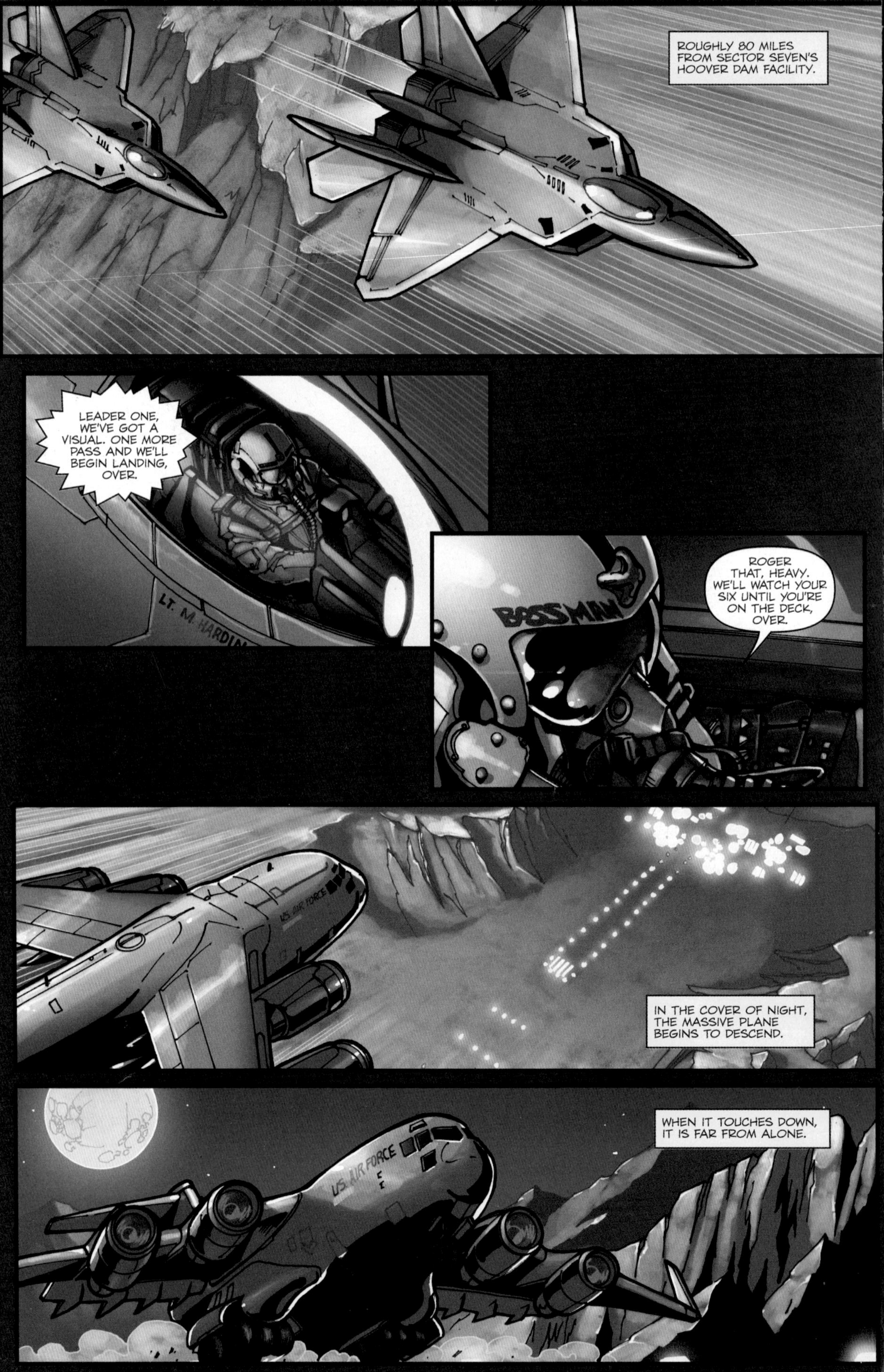
ROUGHLY 80 MILES FROM SECTOR SEVEN'S HOOVER DAM FACILITY.
LEADER ONE, WE'VE GOT A VISUAL. ONE MORE PASS AND WE'LL BEGIN LANDING, OVER.
LT. M. HARDIN
BASSMAN
ROGER THAT, HEAVY. WE'LL WATCH YOUR SIX UNTIL YOU'RE ON THE DECK, OVER.
U.S. AIR FORCE
IN THE COVER OF NIGHT, THE MASSIVE PLANE BEGINS TO DESCEND.
WHEN IT TOUCHES DOWN, IT IS FAR FROM ALONE.
U.S. AIR FORCE

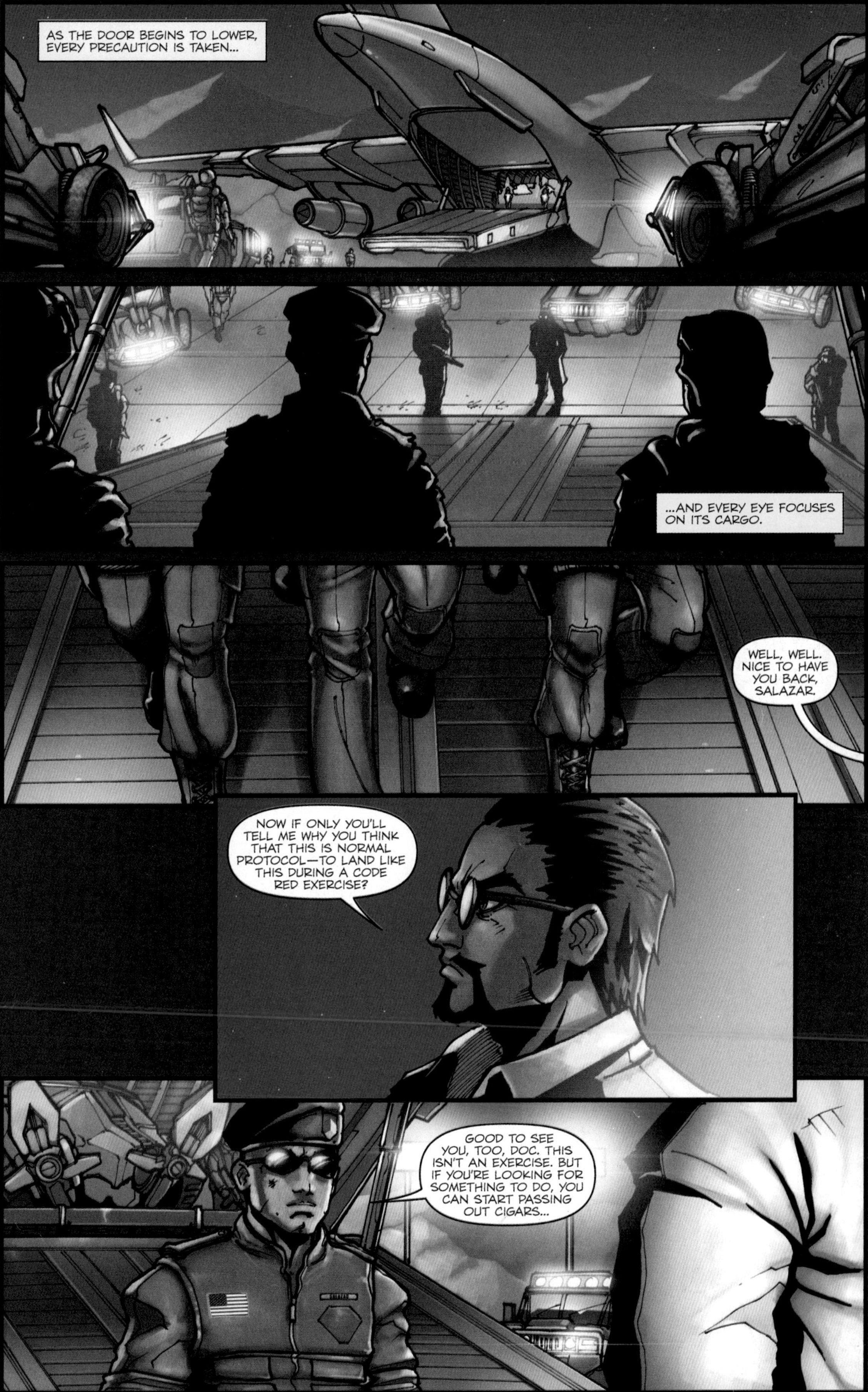
AS THE DOOR BEGINS TO LOWER, EVERY PRECAUTION IS TAKEN...
...AND EVERY EYE FOCUSES ON ITS CARGO.
WELL, WELL. NICE TO HAVE YOU BACK, SALAZAR.
NOW IF ONLY YOU'LL TELL ME WHY YOU THINK THAT THIS IS NORMAL PROTOCOL—TO LAND LIKE THIS DURING A CODE RED EXERCISE?
GOOD TO SEE YOU, TOO, DOC. THIS ISN'T AN EXERCISE. BUT IF YOU'RE LOOKING FOR SOMETHING TO DO, YOU CAN START PASSING OUT CIGARS...

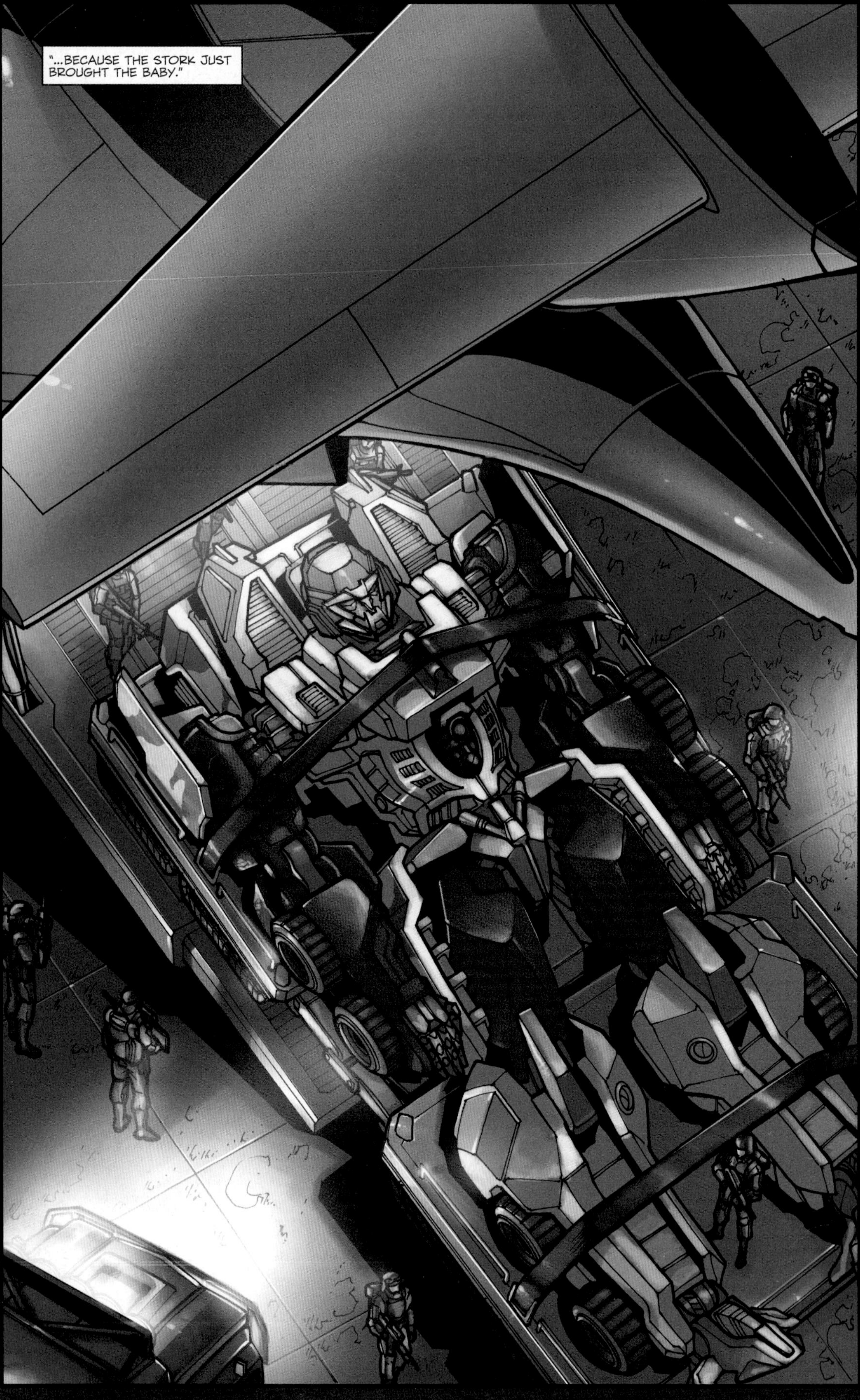
"...BECAUSE THE STORK JUST BROUGHT THE BABY."

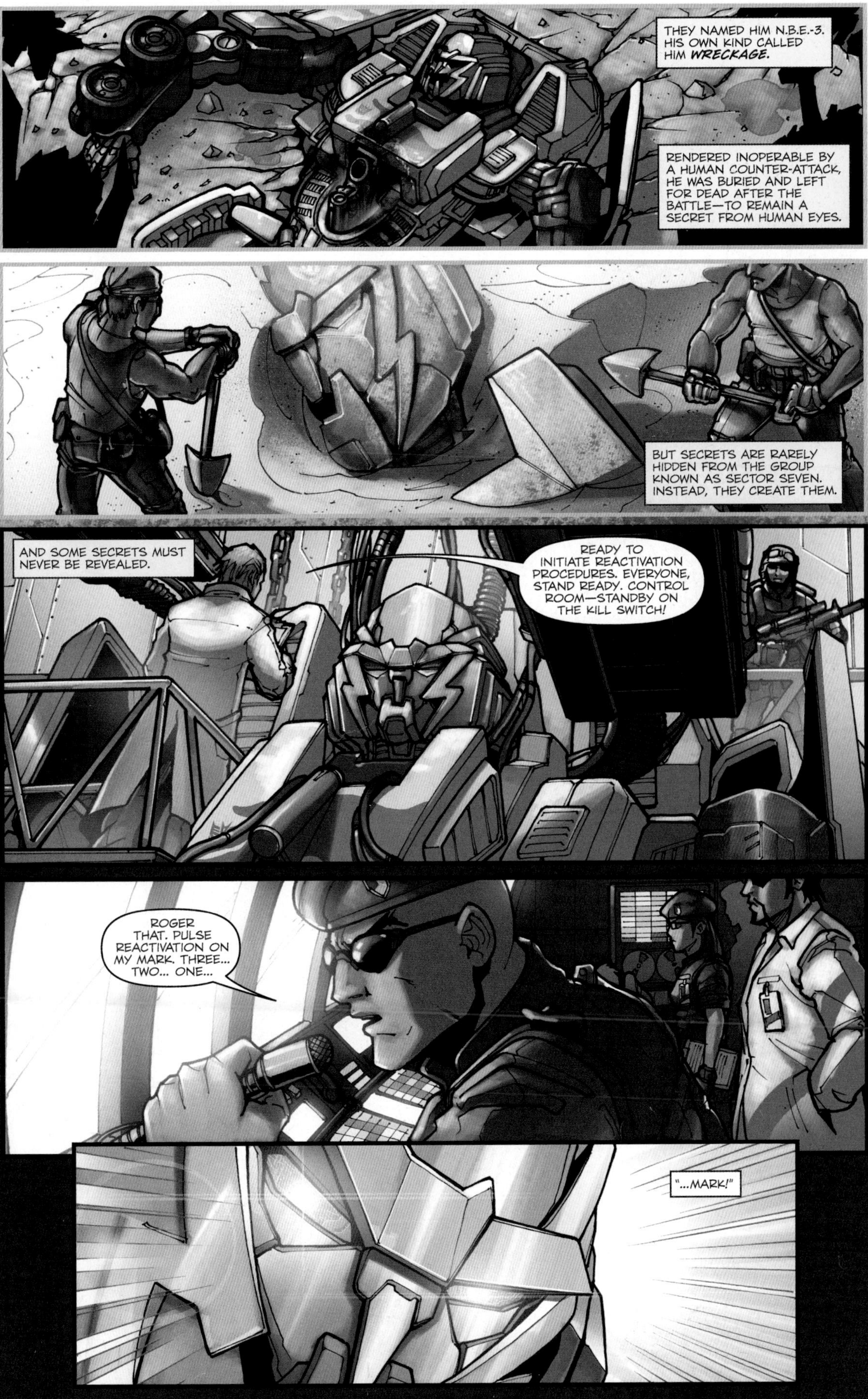
THEY NAMED HIM N.B.E.-3. HIS OWN KIND CALLED HIM WRECKAGE.
RENDERED INOPERABLE BY A HUMAN COUNTER-ATTACK, HE WAS BURIED AND LEFT FOR DEAD AFTER THE BATTLE—TO REMAIN A SECRET FROM HUMAN EYES.
BUT SECRETS ARE RARELY HIDDEN FROM THE GROUP KNOWN AS SECTOR SEVEN. INSTEAD, THEY CREATE THEM.
AND SOME SECRETS MUST NEVER BE REVEALED.
READY TO INITIATE REACTIVATION PROCEDURES. EVERYONE, STAND READY. CONTROL ROOM—STANDBY ON THE KILL SWITCH!
ROGER THAT. PULSE REACTIVATION ON MY MARK. THREE... TWO... ONE...
"...MARK!"

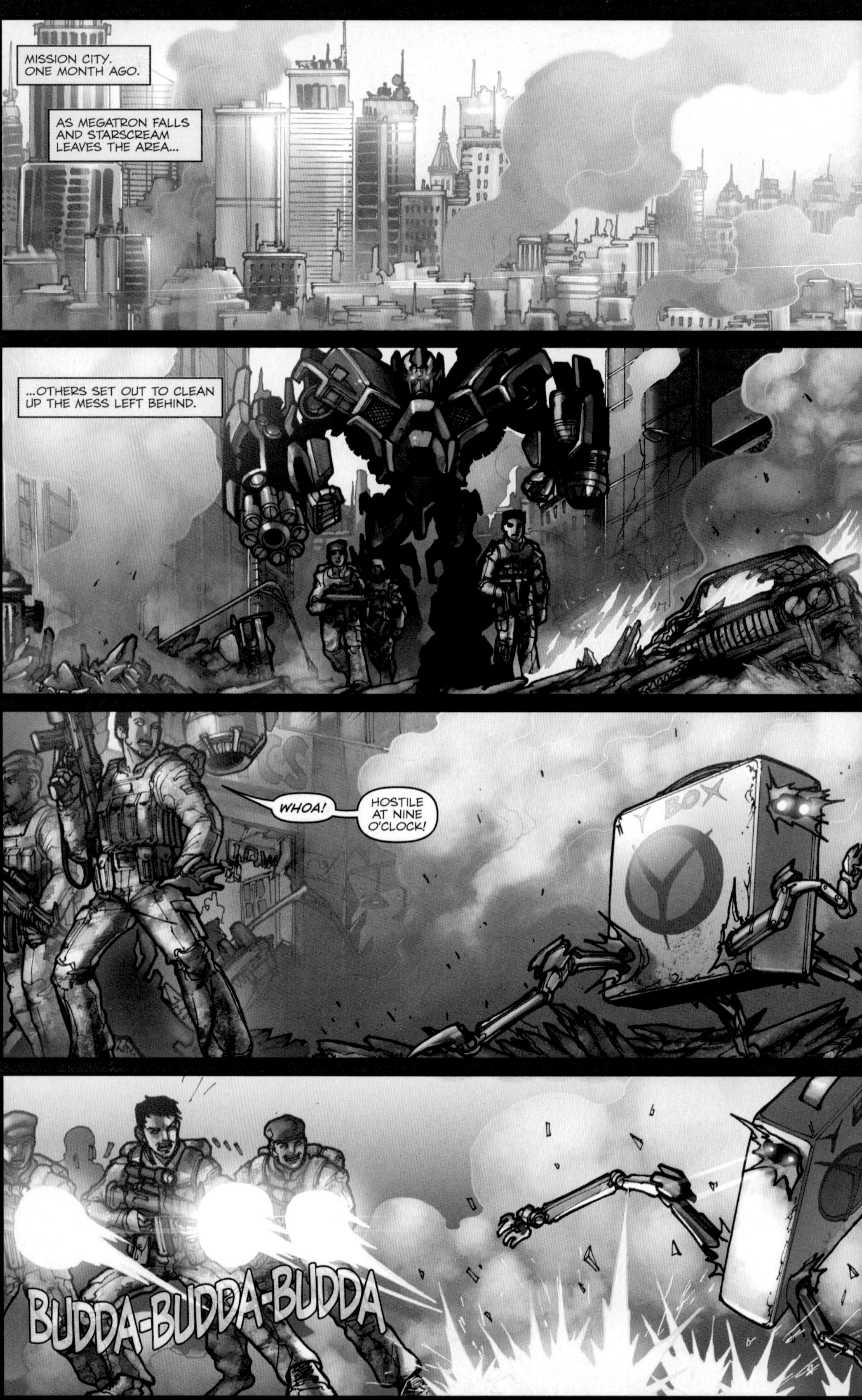

MISSION CITY. ONE MONTH AGO.
AS MEGATRON FALLS AND STARSCREAM LEAVES THE AREA...
...OTHERS SET OUT TO CLEAN UP THE MESS LEFT BEHIND.
WHOA!
HOSTILE AT NINE O'CLOCK!
BUDDA-BUDDA-BUDDA

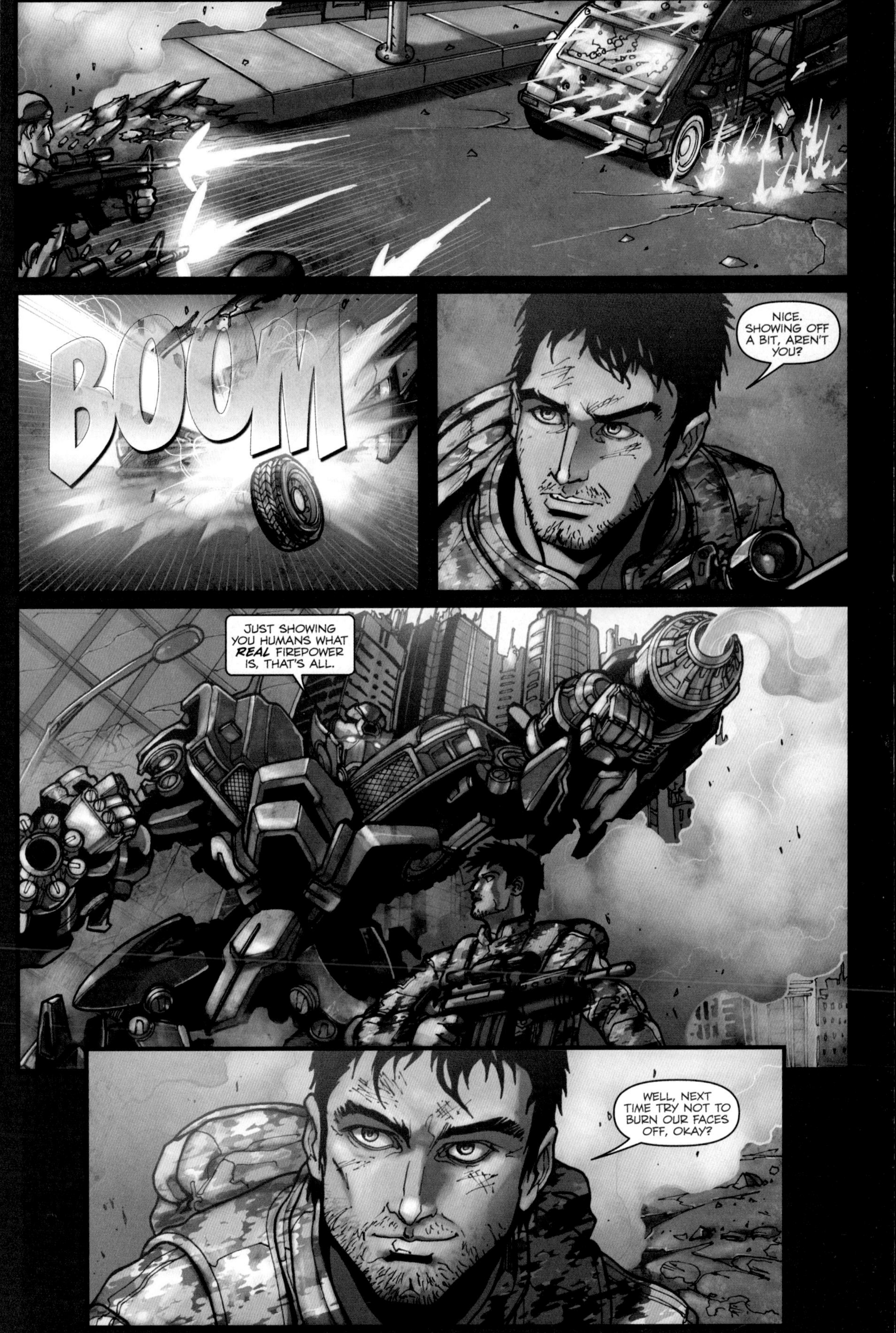
BOOM
NICE. SHOWING OFF A BIT, AREN'T YOU?
JUST SHOWING YOU HUMANS WHAT REAL FIREPOWER IS, THAT'S ALL.
WELL, NEXT TIME TRY NOT TO BURN OUR FACES OFF, OKAY?

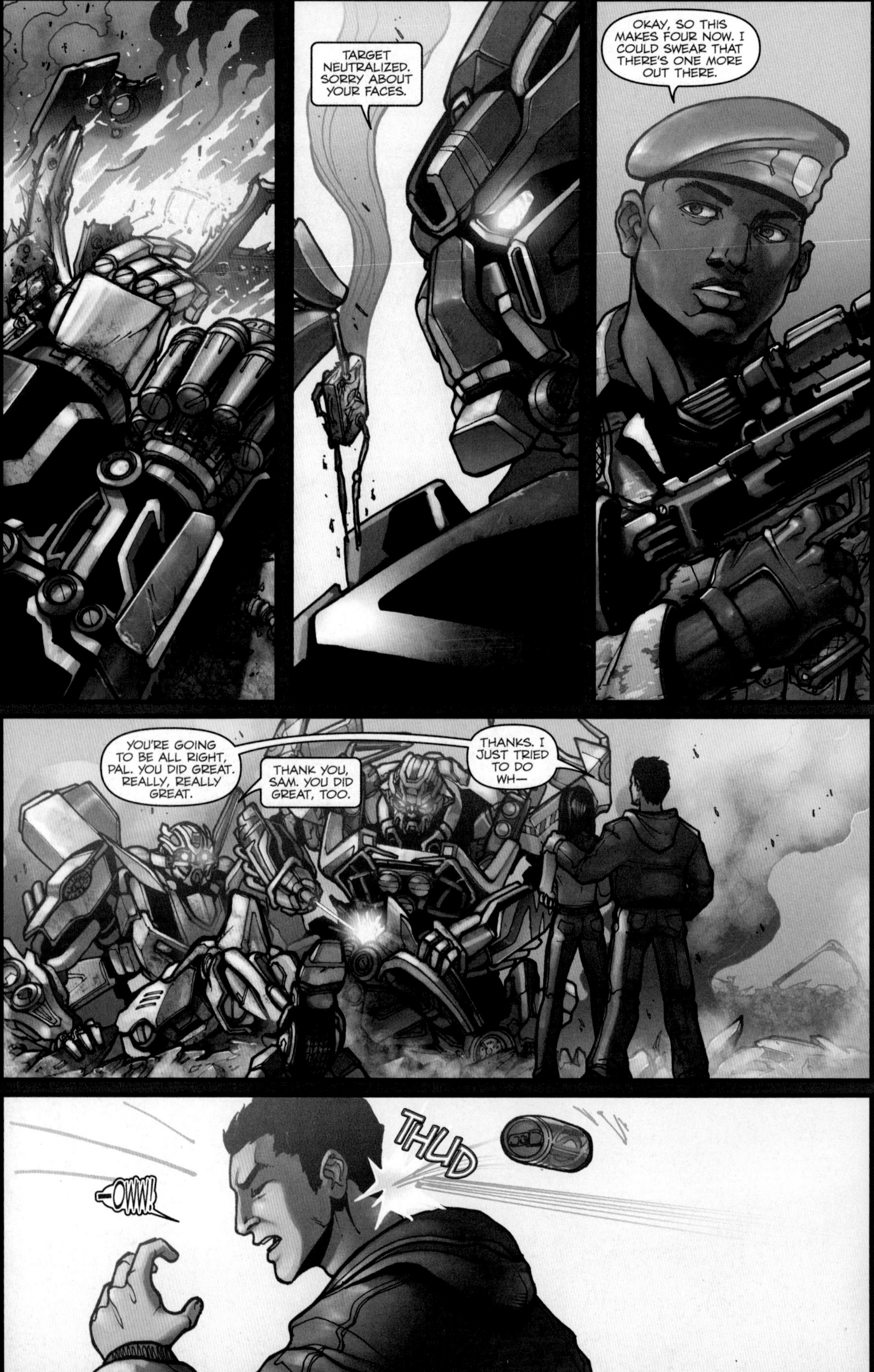

TARGET NEUTRALIZED. SORRY ABOUT YOUR FACES.
OKAY, SO THIS MAKES FOUR NOW. I COULD SWEAR THAT THERE'S ONE MORE OUT THERE.
YOU'RE GOING TO BE ALL RIGHT, PAL. YOU DID GREAT. REALLY, REALLY GREAT.
THANK YOU, SAM. YOU DID GREAT, TOO.
THANKS. I JUST TRIED TO DO WH—
THUD
OWW!

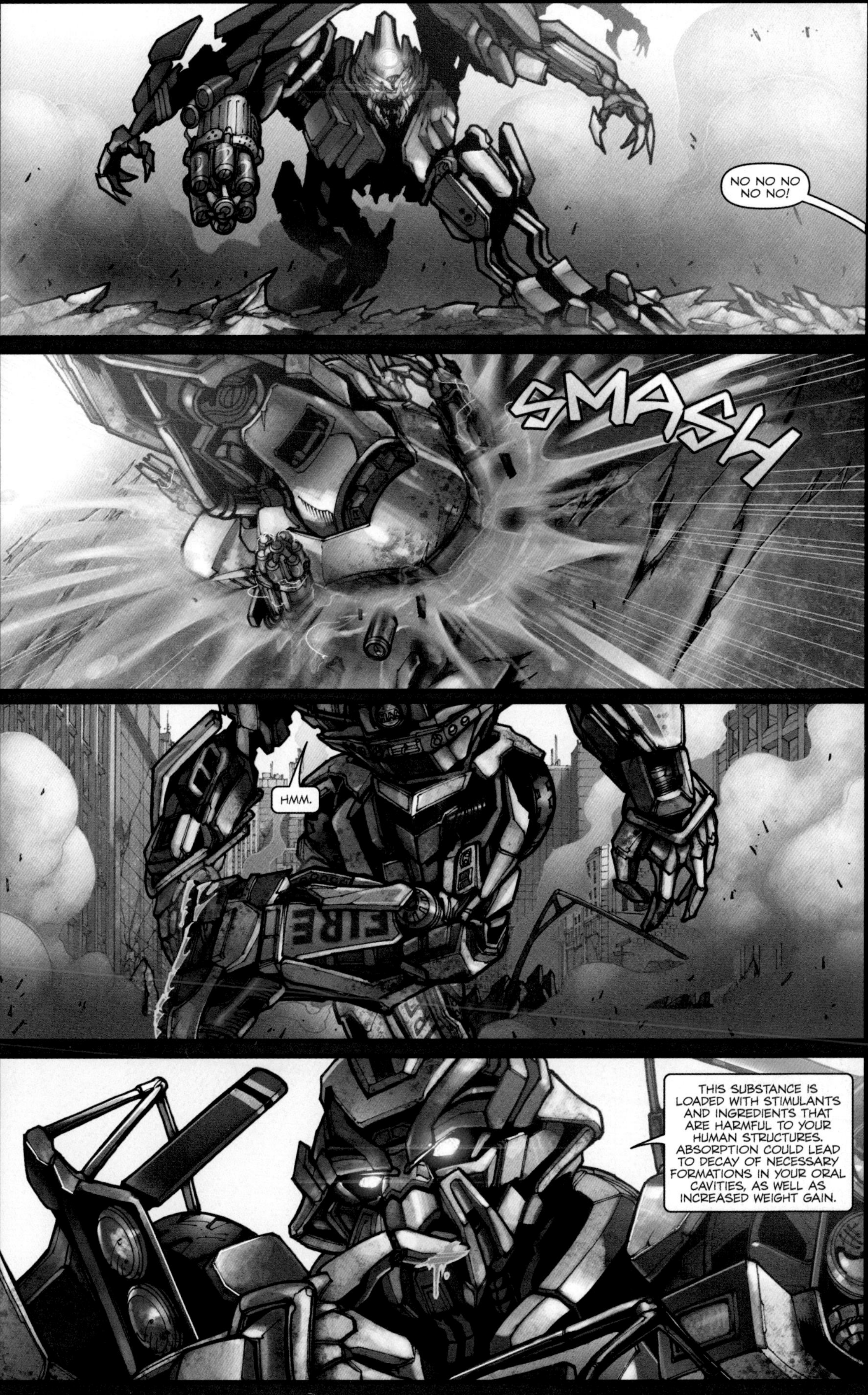
NO NO NO
NO NO!
SMASH
HMM.
FIRE
THIS SUBSTANCE IS LOADED WITH STIMULANTS AND INGREDIENTS THAT ARE HARMFUL TO YOUR HUMAN STRUCTURES. ABSORPTION COULD LEAD TO DECAY OF NECESSARY FORMATIONS IN YOUR ORAL CAVITIES, AS WELL AS INCREASED WEIGHT GAIN.

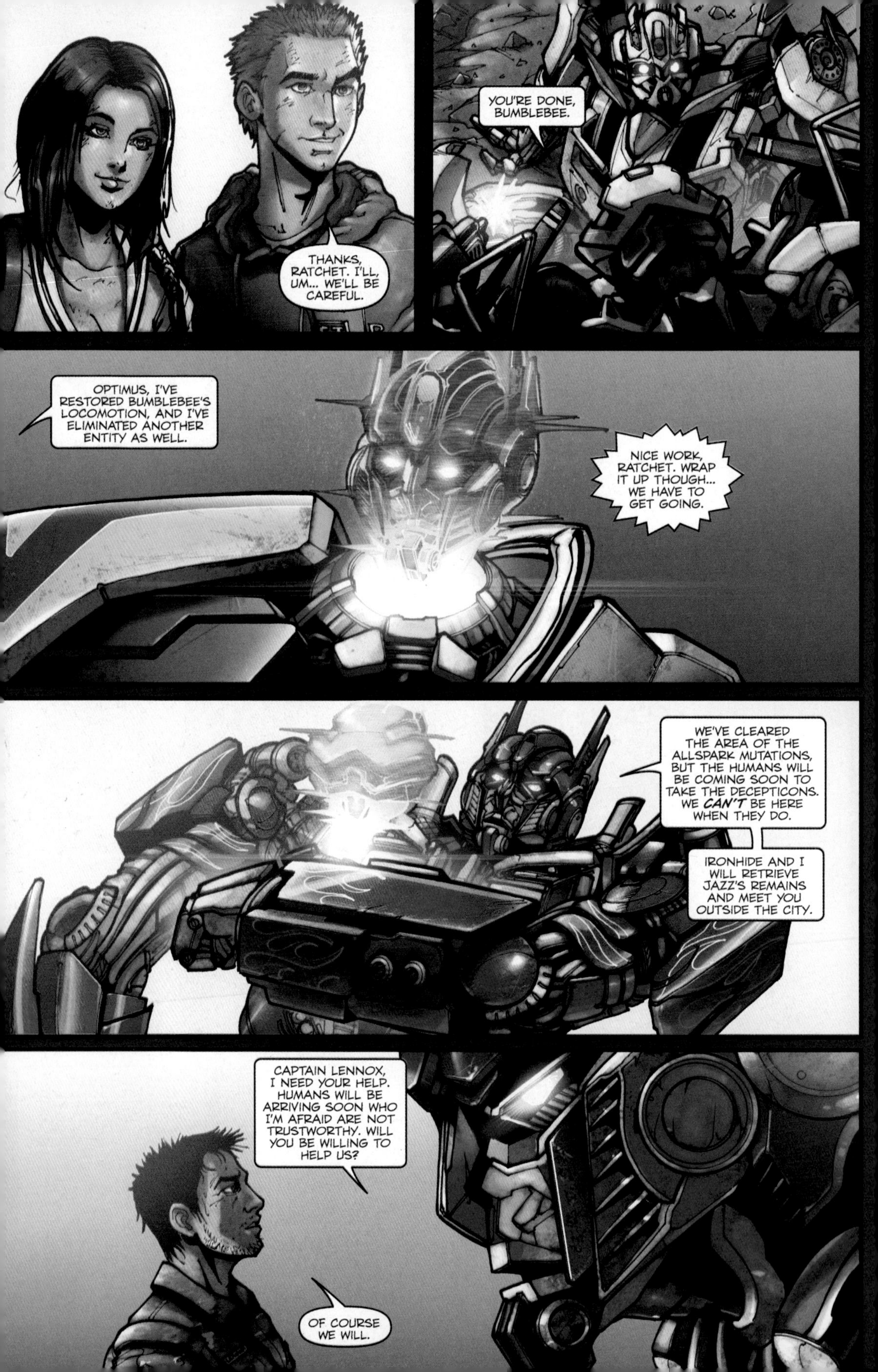

THANKS, RATCHET. I'LL, UM... WE'LL BE CAREFUL.
YOU'RE DONE, BUMBLEBEE.
OPTIMUS, I'VE RESTORED BUMBLEBEE'S LOCOMOTION, AND I'VE ELIMINATED ANOTHER ENTITY AS WELL.
NICE WORK, RATCHET. WRAP IT UP THOUGH... WE HAVE TO GET GOING.
WE'VE CLEARED THE AREA OF THE ALLSPARK MUTATIONS, BUT THE HUMANS WILL BE COMING SOON TO TAKE THE DECEPTICONS. WE *CAN'T* BE HERE WHEN THEY DO.
IRONHIDE AND I WILL RETRIEVE JAZZ'S REMAINS AND MEET YOU OUTSIDE THE CITY.
CAPTAIN LENNOX, I NEED YOUR HELP. HUMANS WILL BE ARRIVING SOON WHO I'M AFRAID ARE NOT TRUSTWORTHY. WILL YOU BE WILLING TO HELP US?
OF COURSE WE WILL.

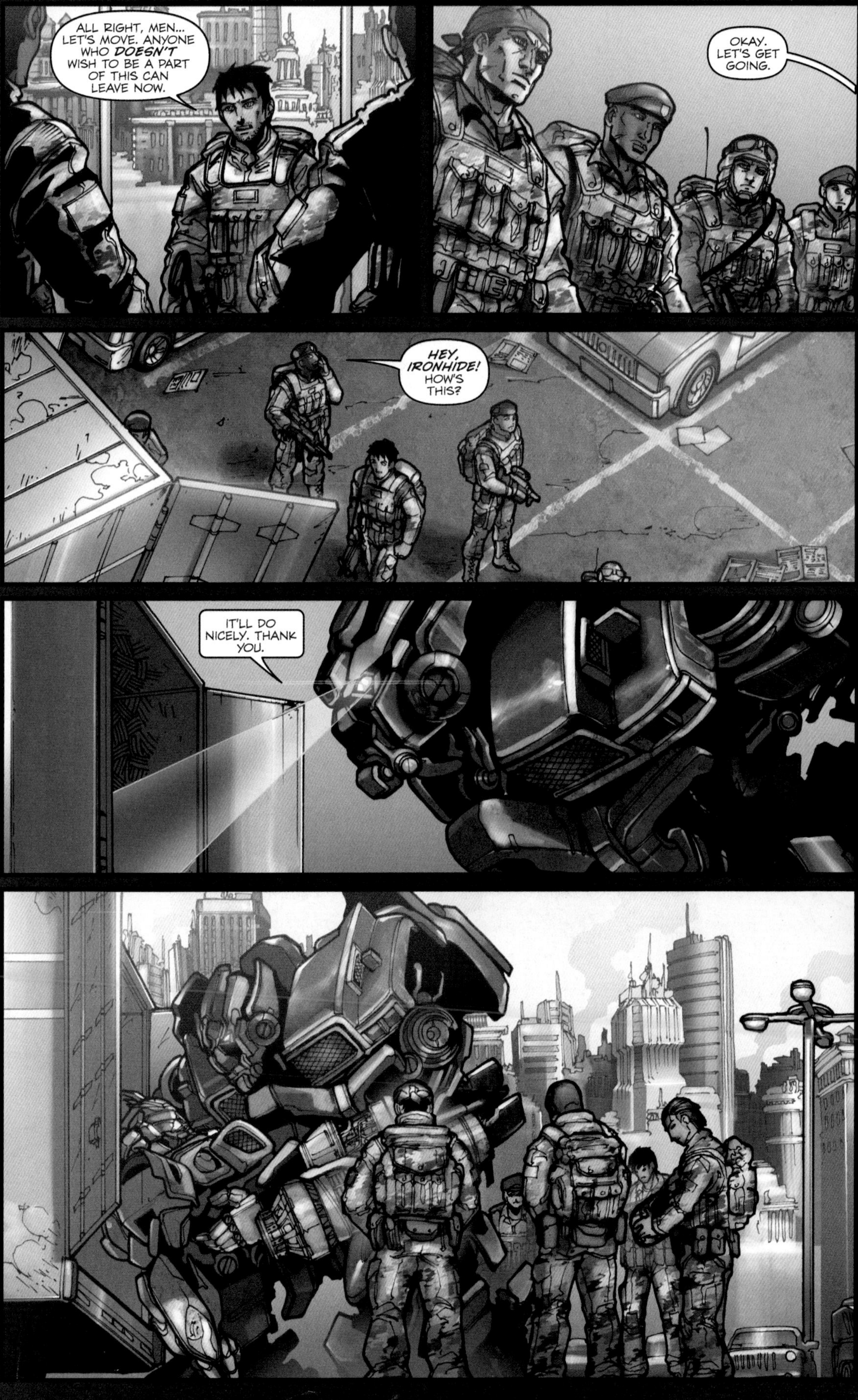
ALL RIGHT, MEN... LET'S MOVE. ANYONE WHO *DOESN'T* WISH TO BE A PART OF THIS CAN LEAVE NOW.
OKAY. LET'S GET GOING.
HEY, IRONHIDE! HOW'S THIS?
IT'LL DO NICELY. THANK YOU.

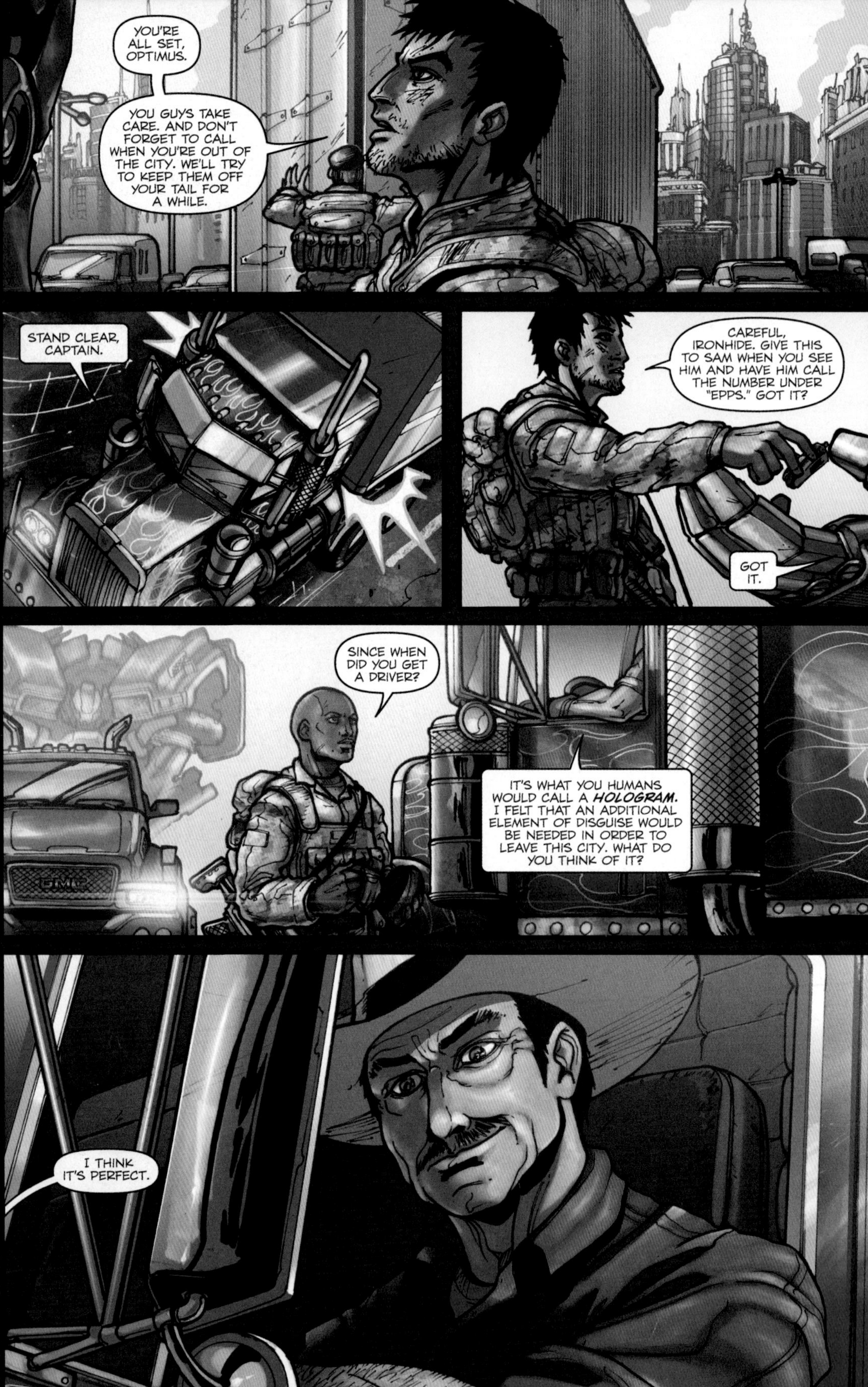
YOU'RE ALL SET, OPTIMUS.
YOU GUYS TAKE CARE. AND DON'T FORGET TO CALL WHEN YOU'RE OUT OF THE CITY. WE'LL TRY TO KEEP THEM OFF YOUR TAIL FOR A WHILE.
STAND CLEAR, CAPTAIN.
CAREFUL, IRONHIDE. GIVE THIS TO SAM WHEN YOU SEE HIM AND HAVE HIM CALL THE NUMBER UNDER "EPPS." GOT IT?
GOT IT.
SINCE WHEN DID YOU GET A DRIVER?
IT'S WHAT YOU HUMANS WOULD CALL A ***HOLOGRAM.*** I FELT THAT AN ADDITIONAL ELEMENT OF DISGUISE WOULD BE NEEDED IN ORDER TO LEAVE THIS CITY. WHAT DO YOU THINK OF IT?
I THINK IT'S PERFECT.

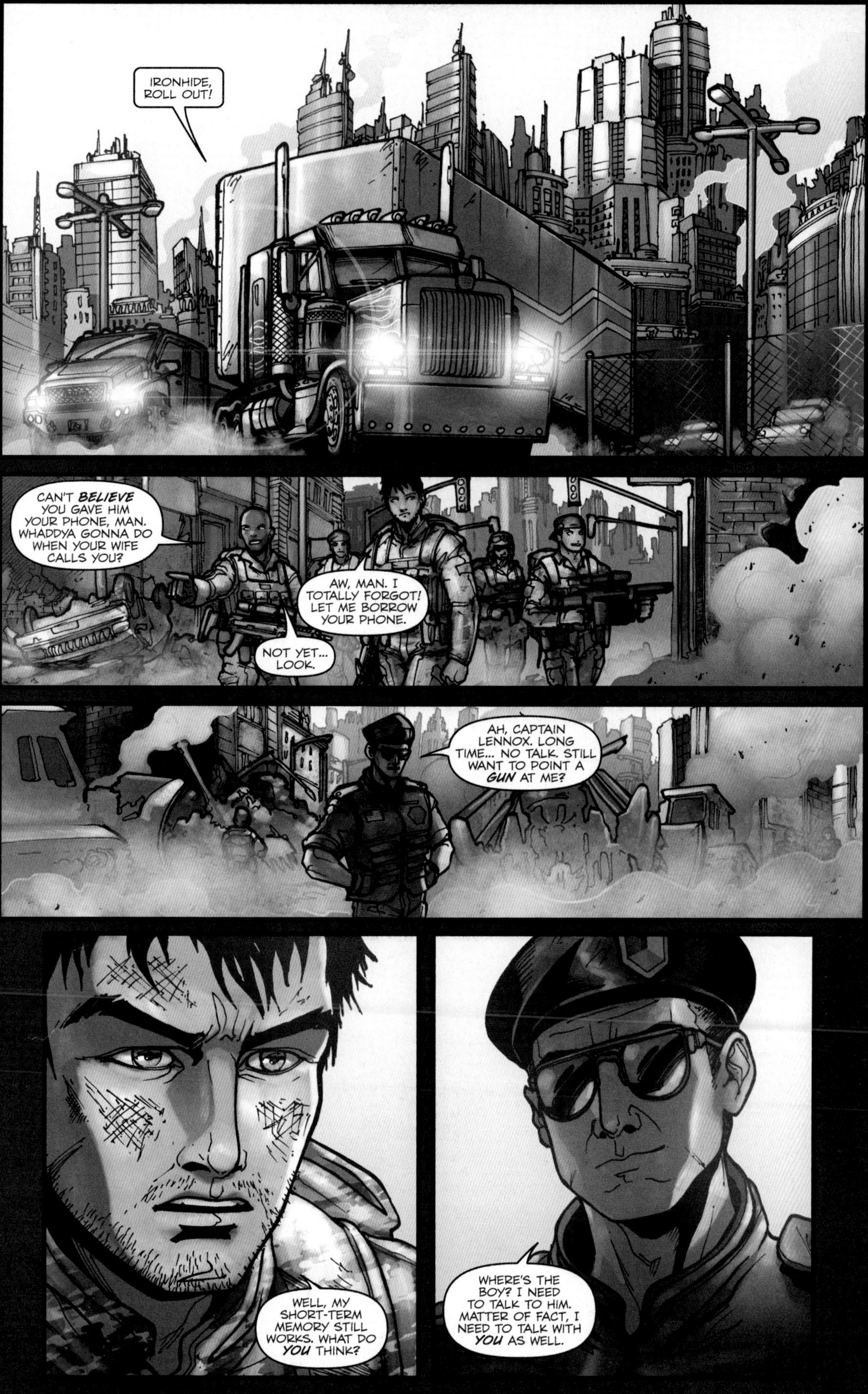
IRONHIDE, ROLL OUT!
CAN'T BELIEVE YOU GAVE HIM YOUR PHONE, MAN. WHADDYA GONNA DO WHEN YOUR WIFE CALLS YOU?
AW, MAN. I TOTALLY FORGOT! LET ME BORROW YOUR PHONE.
NOT YET... LOOK.
AH, CAPTAIN LENNOX. LONG TIME... NO TALK. STILL WANT TO POINT A GUN AT ME?
WELL, MY SHORT-TERM MEMORY STILL WORKS. WHAT DO YOU THINK?
WHERE'S THE BOY? I NEED TO TALK TO HIM. MATTER OF FACT, I NEED TO TALK WITH YOU AS WELL.

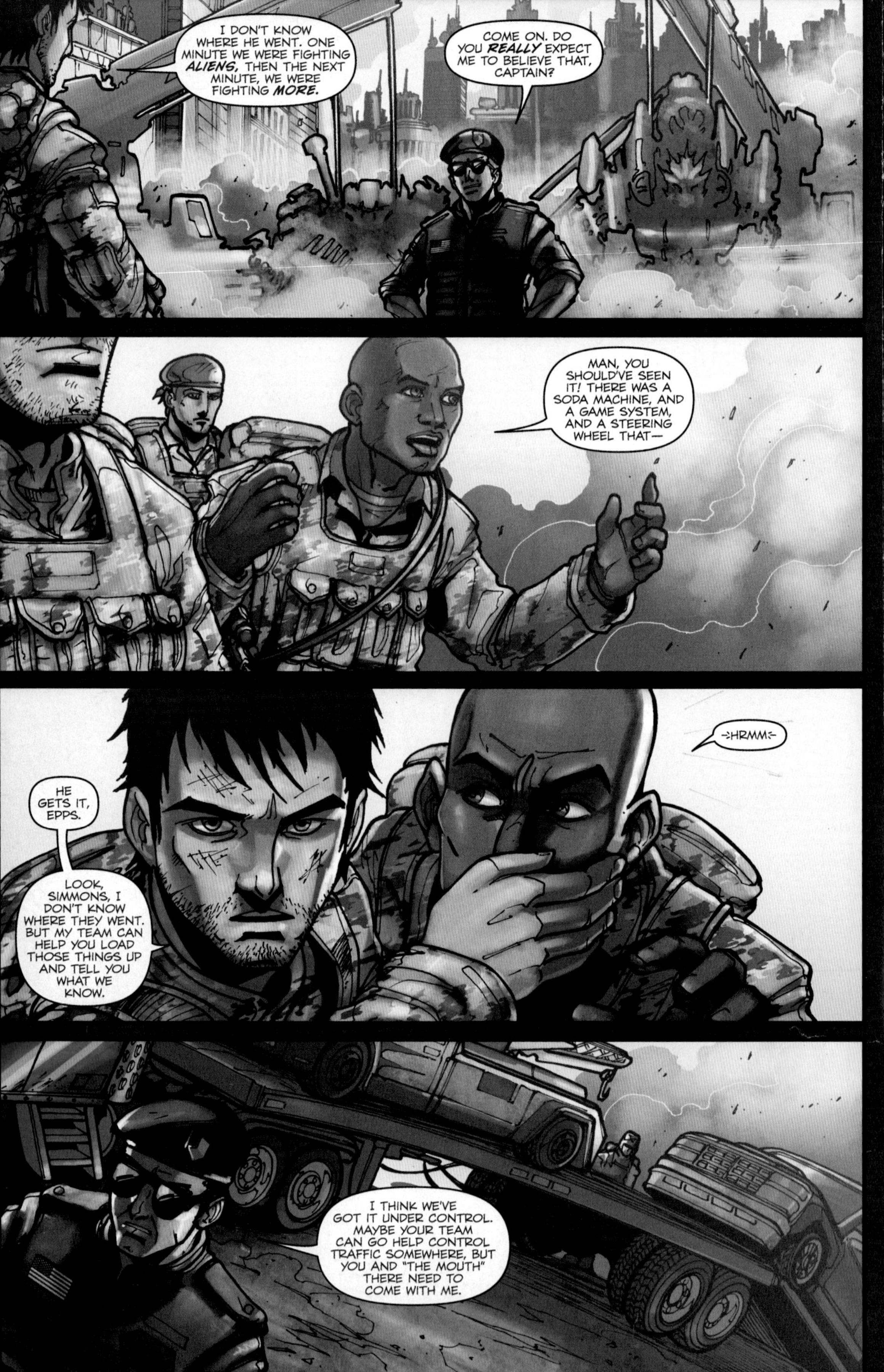
I DON'T KNOW WHERE HE WENT. ONE MINUTE WE WERE FIGHTING *ALIENS,* THEN THE NEXT MINUTE, WE WERE FIGHTING *MORE.*
COME ON. DO YOU *REALLY* EXPECT ME TO BELIEVE THAT, CAPTAIN?
MAN, YOU SHOULD'VE SEEN IT! THERE WAS A SODA MACHINE, AND A GAME SYSTEM, AND A STEERING WHEEL THAT—
-:HRMM:-
HE GETS IT, EPPS.
LOOK, SIMMONS, I DON'T KNOW WHERE THEY WENT. BUT MY TEAM CAN HELP YOU LOAD THOSE THINGS UP AND TELL YOU WHAT WE KNOW.
I THINK WE'VE GOT IT UNDER CONTROL. MAYBE YOUR TEAM CAN GO HELP CONTROL TRAFFIC SOMEWHERE, BUT YOU AND "THE MOUTH" THERE NEED TO COME WITH ME.

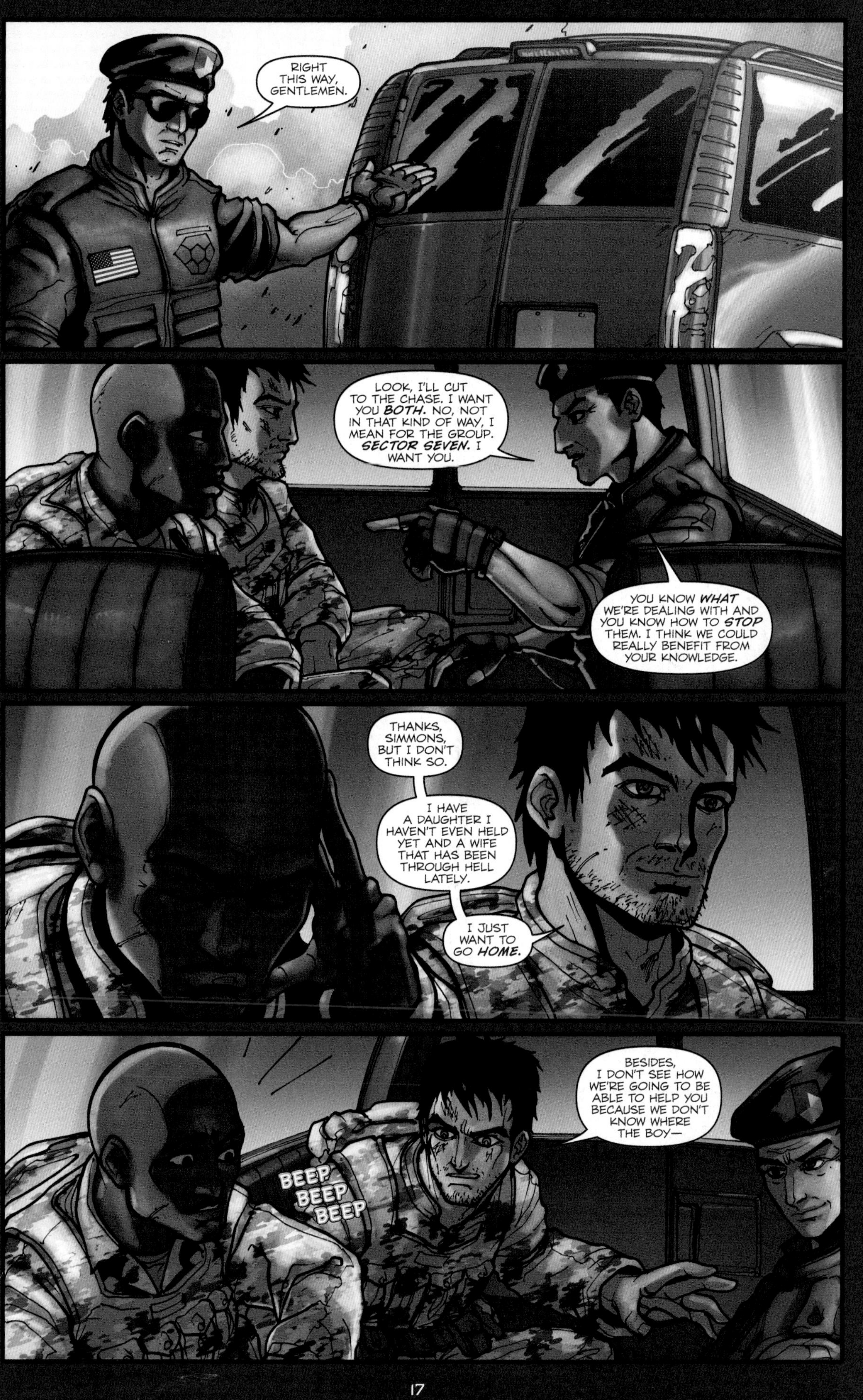
RIGHT THIS WAY, GENTLEMEN.
LOOK, I'LL CUT TO THE CHASE. I WANT YOU BOTH. NO, NOT IN THAT KIND OF WAY, I MEAN FOR THE GROUP. SECTOR SEVEN. I WANT YOU.
YOU KNOW WHAT WE'RE DEALING WITH AND YOU KNOW HOW TO STOP THEM. I THINK WE COULD REALLY BENEFIT FROM YOUR KNOWLEDGE.
THANKS, SIMMONS, BUT I DON'T THINK SO.
I HAVE A DAUGHTER I HAVEN'T EVEN HELD YET AND A WIFE THAT HAS BEEN THROUGH HELL LATELY.
I JUST WANT TO GO HOME.
BESIDES, I DON'T SEE HOW WE'RE GOING TO BE ABLE TO HELP YOU BECAUSE WE DON'T KNOW WHERE THE BOY—
BEEP BEEP BEEP

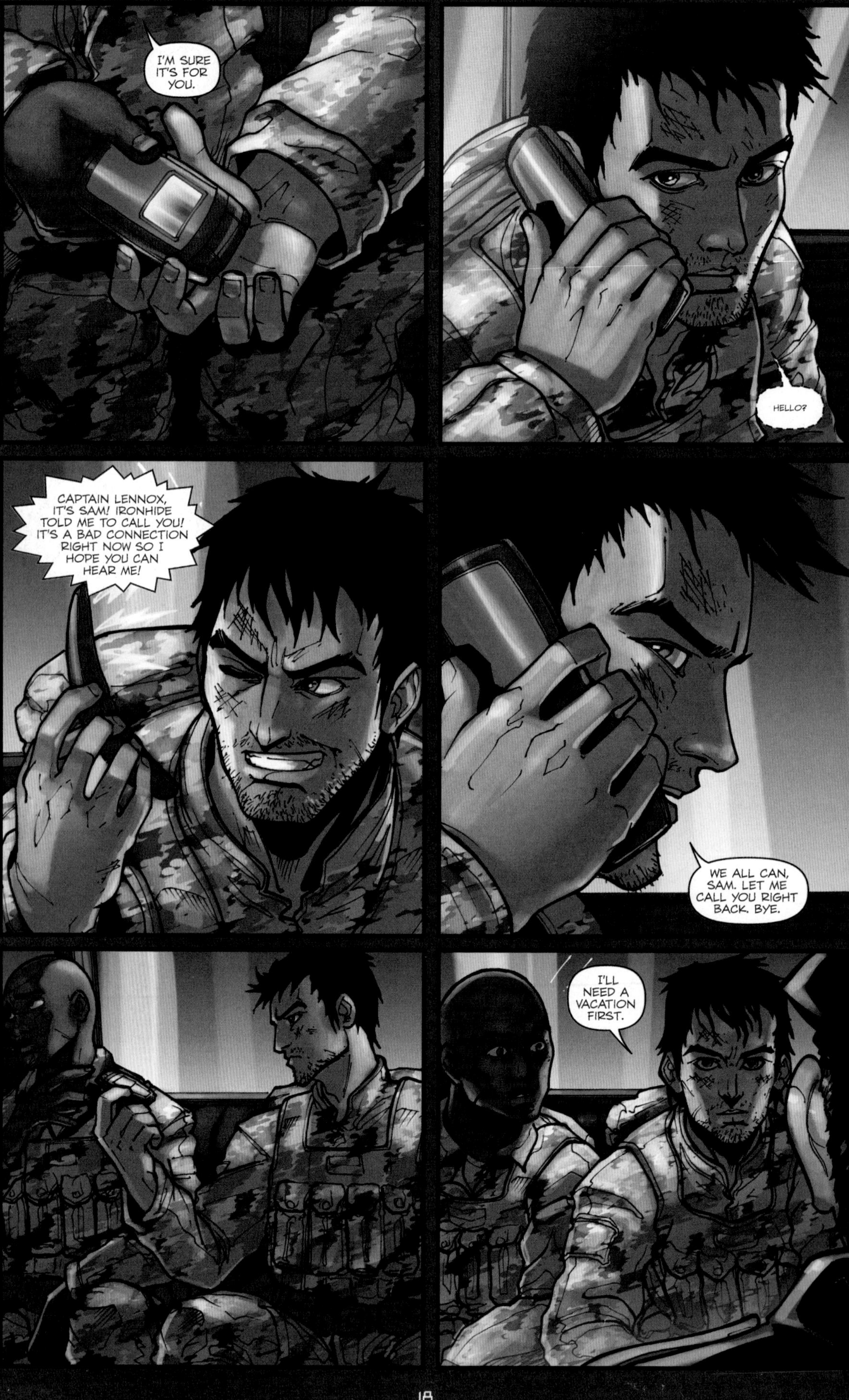
I'M SURE IT'S FOR YOU.
HELLO?
CAPTAIN LENNOX, IT'S SAM! IRONHIDE TOLD ME TO CALL YOU! IT'S A BAD CONNECTION RIGHT NOW SO I HOPE YOU CAN HEAR ME!
WE ALL CAN, SAM. LET ME CALL YOU RIGHT BACK. BYE.
I'LL NEED A VACATION FIRST.

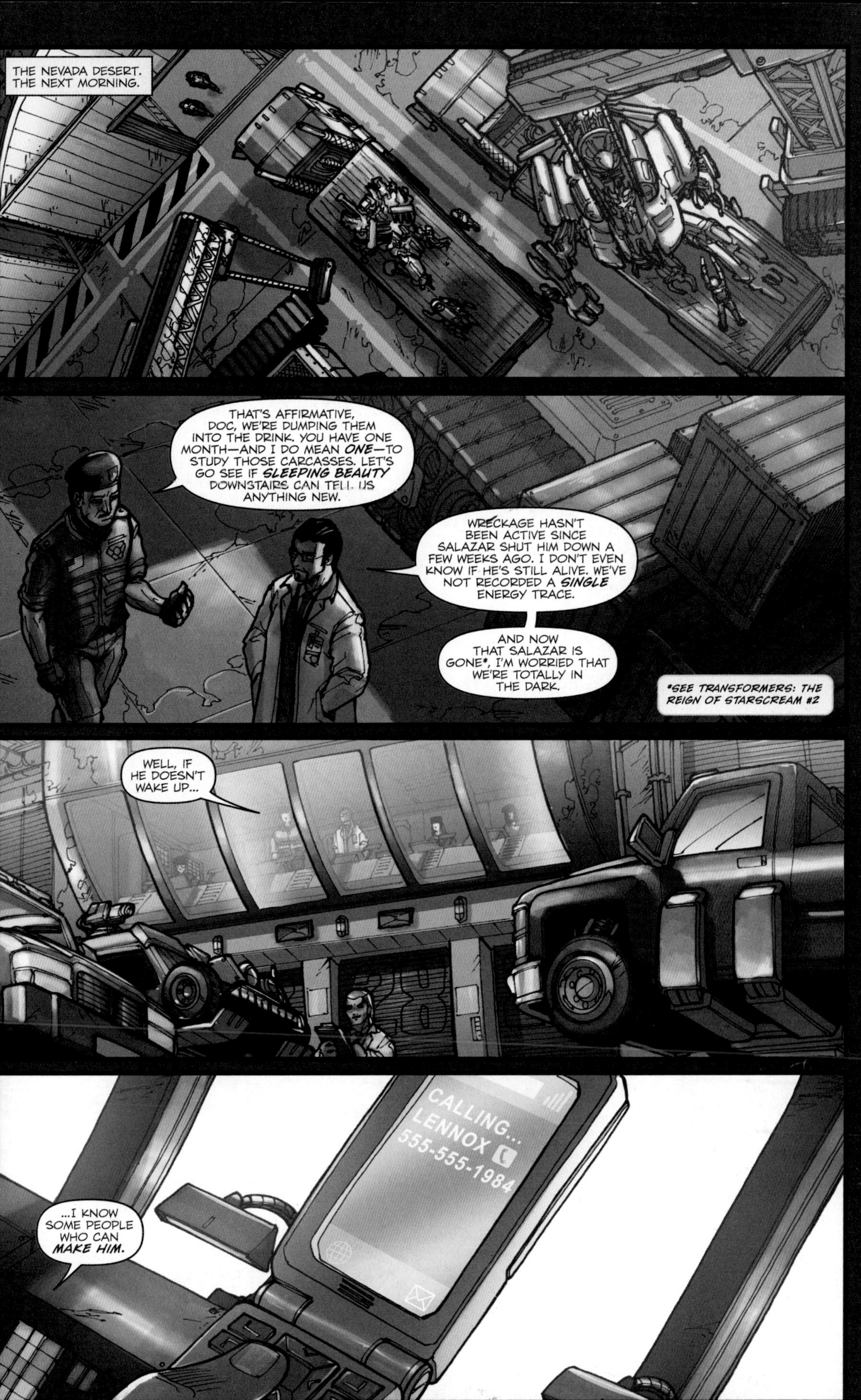
THE NEVADA DESERT. THE NEXT MORNING.
THAT'S AFFIRMATIVE, DOC, WE'RE DUMPING THEM INTO THE DRINK. YOU HAVE ONE MONTH—AND I DO MEAN ONE—TO STUDY THOSE CARCASSES. LET'S GO SEE IF SLEEPING BEAUTY DOWNSTAIRS CAN TELL US ANYTHING NEW.
WRECKAGE HASN'T BEEN ACTIVE SINCE SALAZAR SHUT HIM DOWN A FEW WEEKS AGO. I DON'T EVEN KNOW IF HE'S STILL ALIVE. WE'VE NOT RECORDED A SINGLE ENERGY TRACE.
AND NOW THAT SALAZAR IS GONE*, I'M WORRIED THAT WE'RE TOTALLY IN THE DARK.
*SEE TRANSFORMERS: THE REIGN OF STARSCREAM #2
WELL, IF HE DOESN'T WAKE UP...
CALLING... LENNOX 555-555-1984
...I KNOW SOME PEOPLE WHO CAN MAKE HIM.

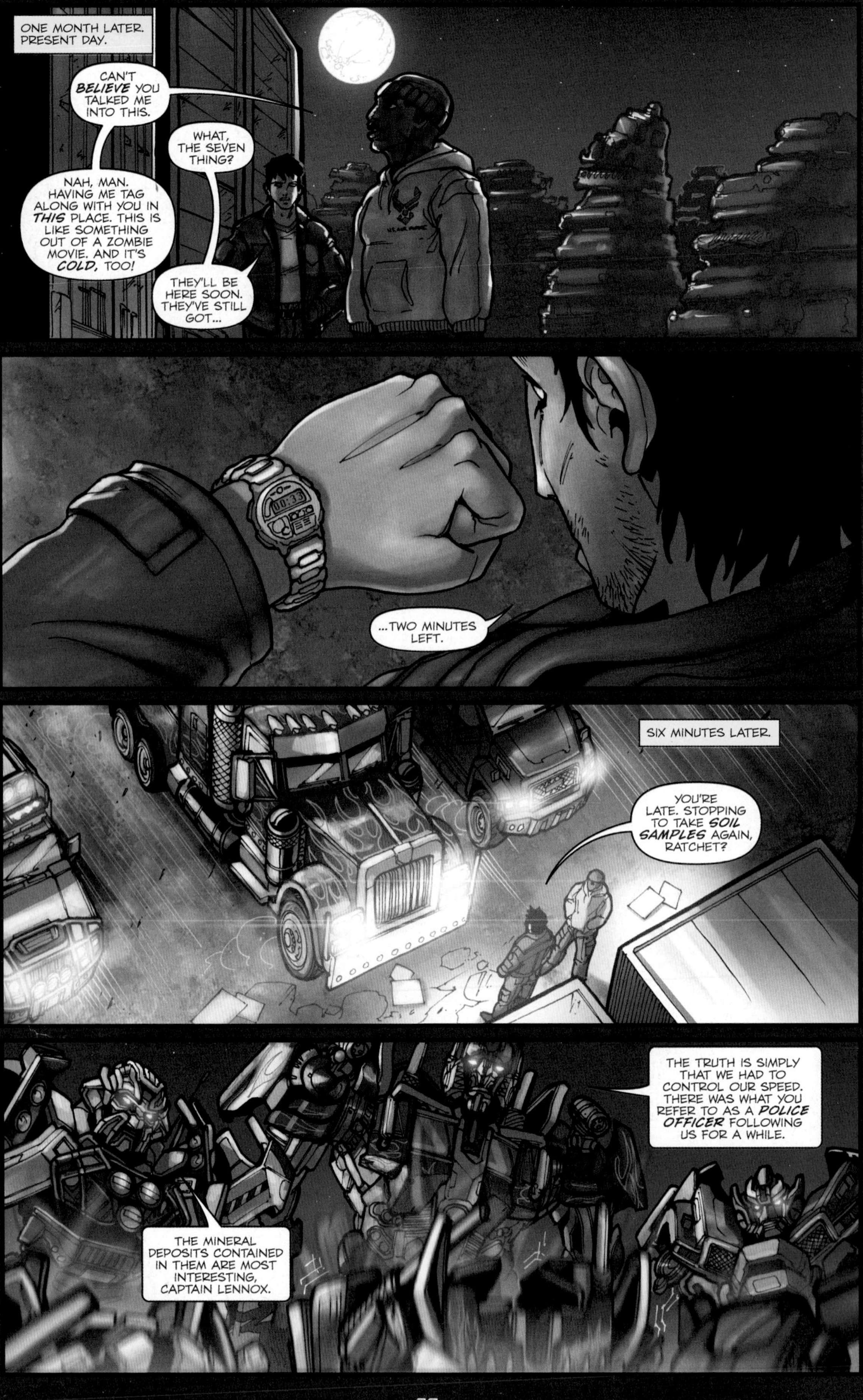
ONE MONTH LATER. PRESENT DAY.
CAN'T BELIEVE YOU TALKED ME INTO THIS.
WHAT, THE SEVEN THING?
NAH, MAN. HAVING ME TAG ALONG WITH YOU IN THIS PLACE. THIS IS LIKE SOMETHING OUT OF A ZOMBIE MOVIE. AND IT'S COLD, TOO!
THEY'LL BE HERE SOON. THEY'VE STILL GOT...
...TWO MINUTES LEFT.
SIX MINUTES LATER.
YOU'RE LATE. STOPPING TO TAKE SOIL SAMPLES AGAIN, RATCHET?
THE TRUTH IS SIMPLY THAT WE HAD TO CONTROL OUR SPEED. THERE WAS WHAT YOU REFER TO AS A POLICE OFFICER FOLLOWING US FOR A WHILE.
THE MINERAL DEPOSITS CONTAINED IN THEM ARE MOST INTERESTING, CAPTAIN LENNOX.

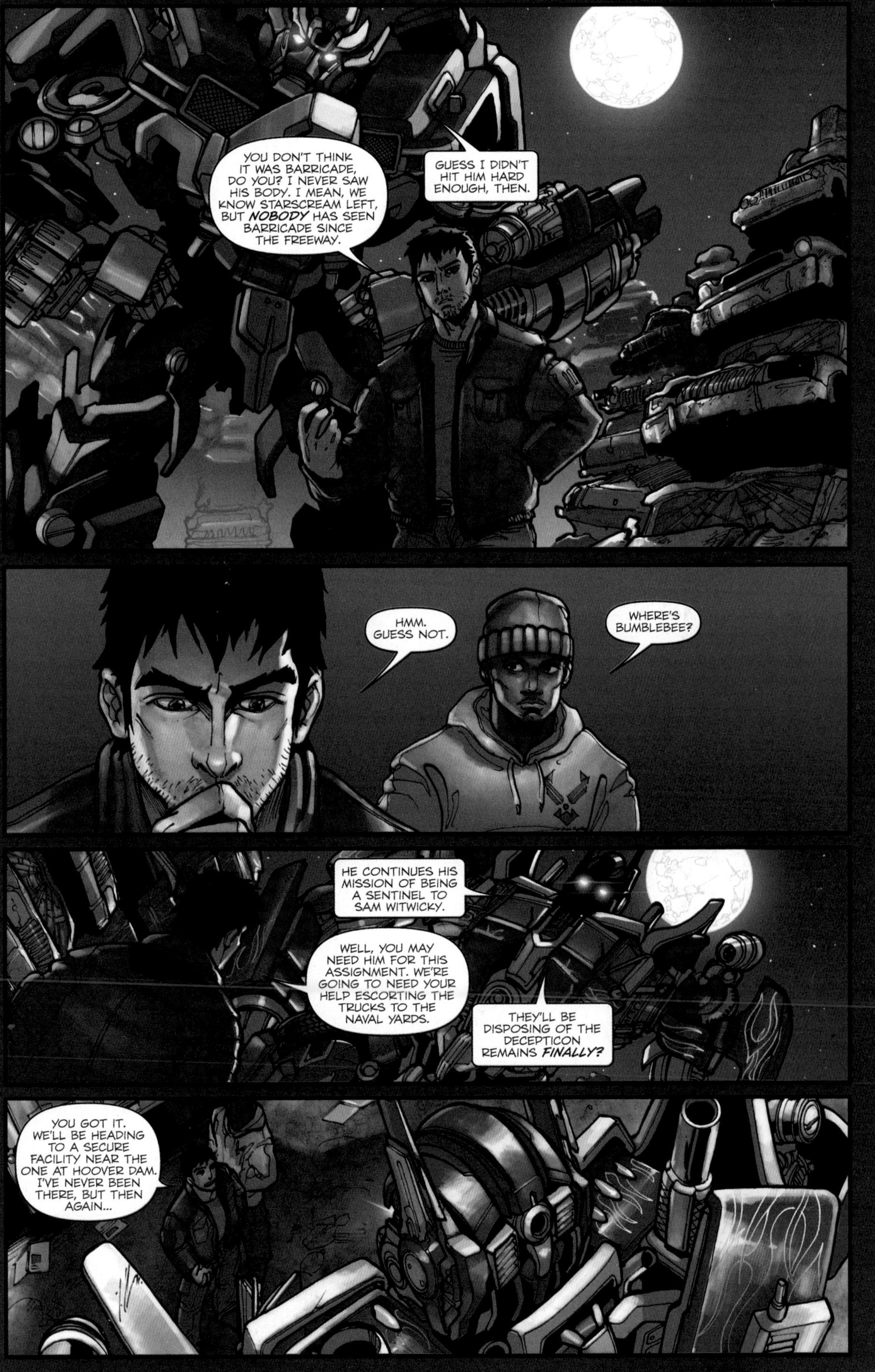
YOU DON'T THINK IT WAS BARRICADE, DO YOU? I NEVER SAW HIS BODY. I MEAN, WE KNOW STARSCREAM LEFT, BUT NOBODY HAS SEEN BARRICADE SINCE THE FREEWAY.
GUESS I DIDN'T HIT HIM HARD ENOUGH, THEN.
HMM. GUESS NOT.
WHERE'S BUMBLEBEE?
HE CONTINUES HIS MISSION OF BEING A SENTINEL TO SAM WITWICKY.
WELL, YOU MAY NEED HIM FOR THIS ASSIGNMENT. WE'RE GOING TO NEED YOUR HELP ESCORTING THE TRUCKS TO THE NAVAL YARDS.
THEY'LL BE DISPOSING OF THE DECEPTICON REMAINS FINALLY?
YOU GOT IT. WE'LL BE HEADING TO A SECURE FACILITY NEAR THE ONE AT HOOVER DAM. I'VE NEVER BEEN THERE, BUT THEN AGAIN...

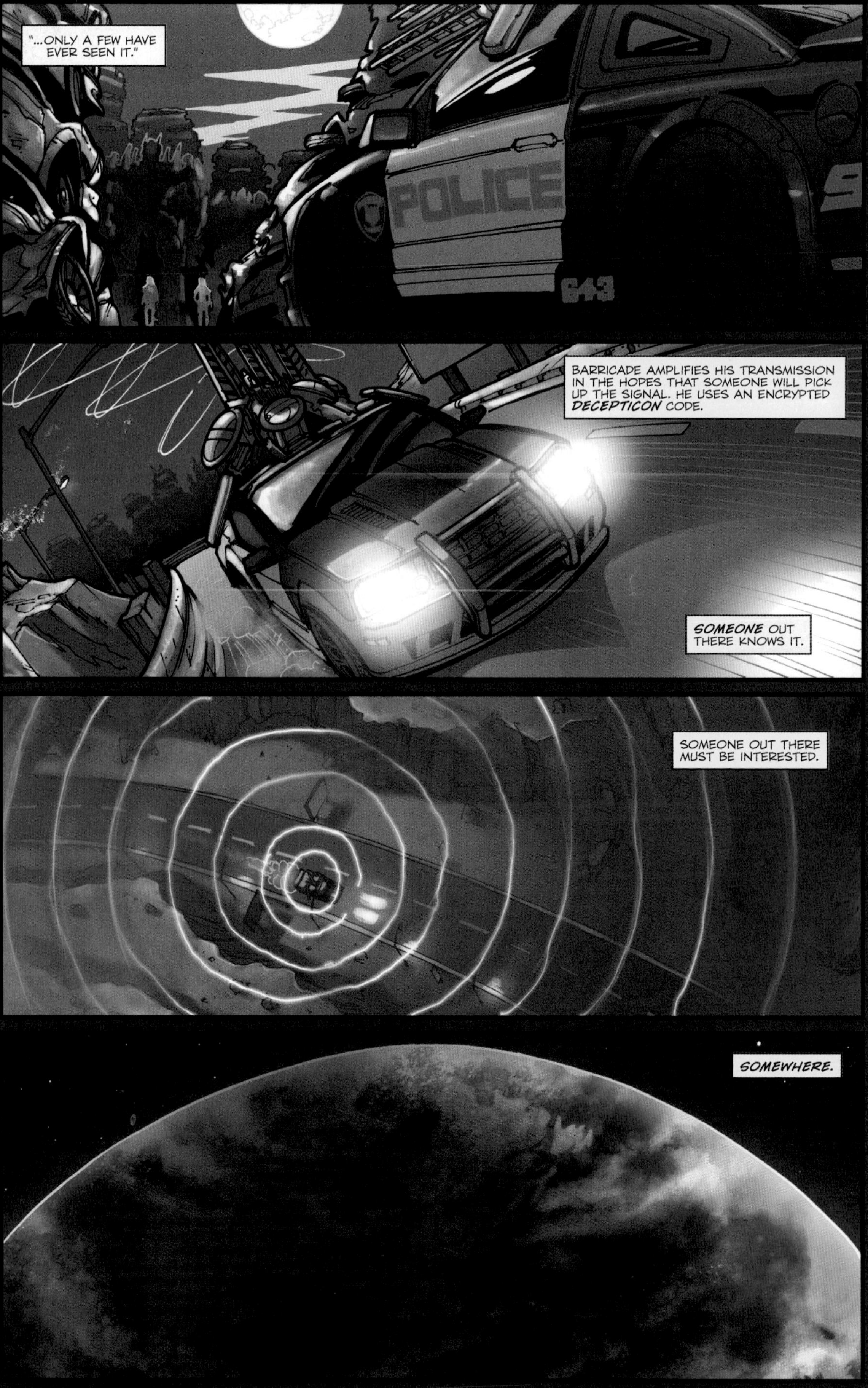
"...ONLY A FEW HAVE EVER SEEN IT."
POLICE
643
BARRICADE AMPLIFIES HIS TRANSMISSION IN THE HOPES THAT SOMEONE WILL PICK UP THE SIGNAL. HE USES AN ENCRYPTED ***DECEPTICON*** CODE.
SOMEONE OUT THERE KNOWS IT.
SOMEONE OUT THERE MUST BE INTERESTED.
SOMEWHERE.

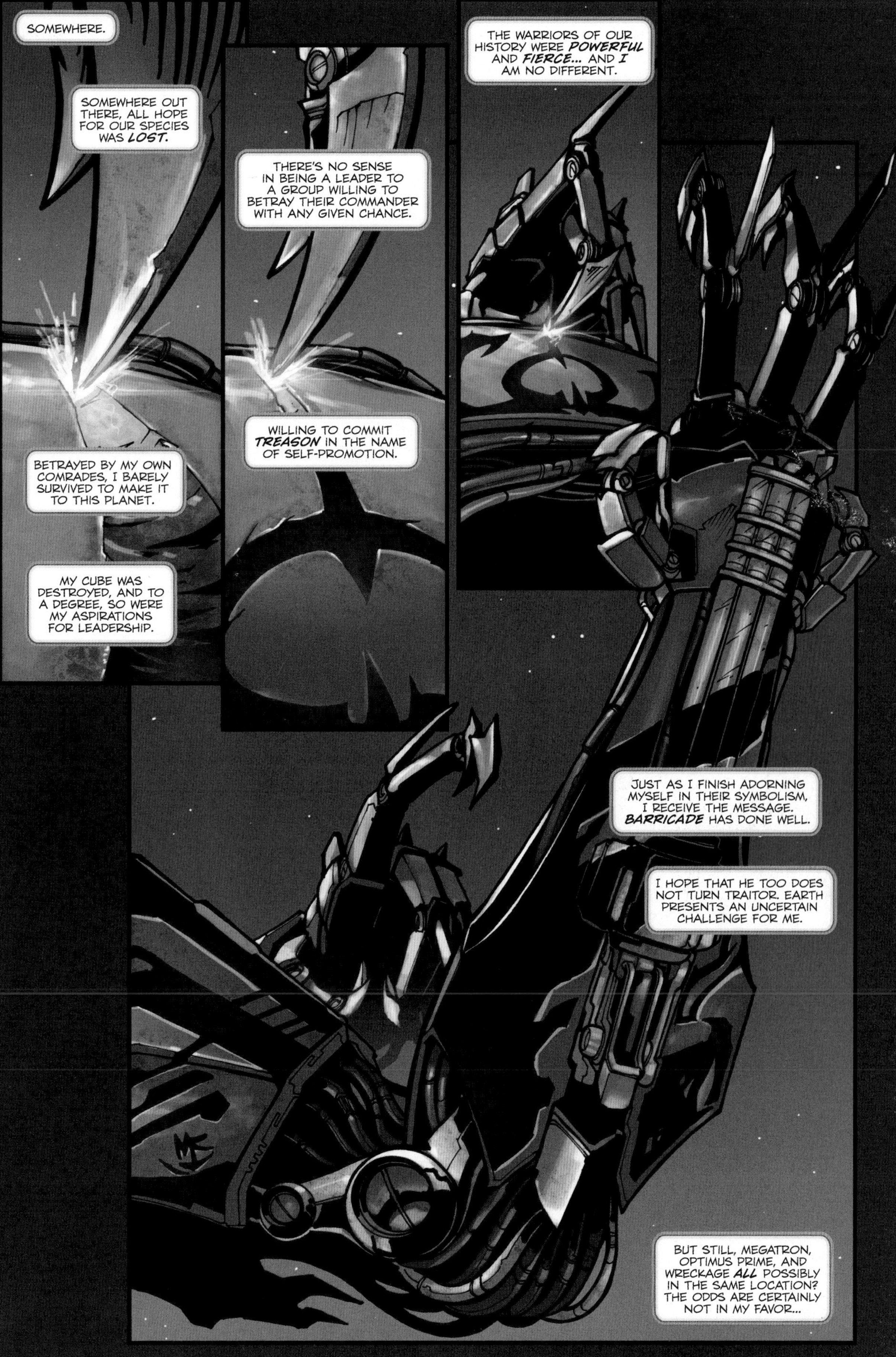
SOMEWHERE.
SOMEWHERE OUT THERE, ALL HOPE FOR OUR SPECIES WAS **LOST.**
BETRAYED BY MY OWN COMRADES, I BARELY SURVIVED TO MAKE IT TO THIS PLANET.
MY CUBE WAS DESTROYED, AND TO A DEGREE, SO WERE MY ASPIRATIONS FOR LEADERSHIP.
THERE'S NO SENSE IN BEING A LEADER TO A GROUP WILLING TO BETRAY THEIR COMMANDER WITH ANY GIVEN CHANCE.
WILLING TO COMMIT **TREASON** IN THE NAME OF SELF-PROMOTION.
THE WARRIORS OF OUR HISTORY WERE **POWERFUL** AND **FIERCE...** AND **I** AM NO DIFFERENT.
JUST AS I FINISH ADORNING MYSELF IN THEIR SYMBOLISM, I RECEIVE THE MESSAGE. **BARRICADE** HAS DONE WELL.
I HOPE THAT HE TOO DOES NOT TURN TRAITOR. EARTH PRESENTS AN UNCERTAIN CHALLENGE FOR ME.
BUT STILL, MEGATRON, OPTIMUS PRIME, AND WRECKAGE **ALL** POSSIBLY IN THE SAME LOCATION? THE ODDS ARE CERTAINLY NOT IN MY FAVOR...

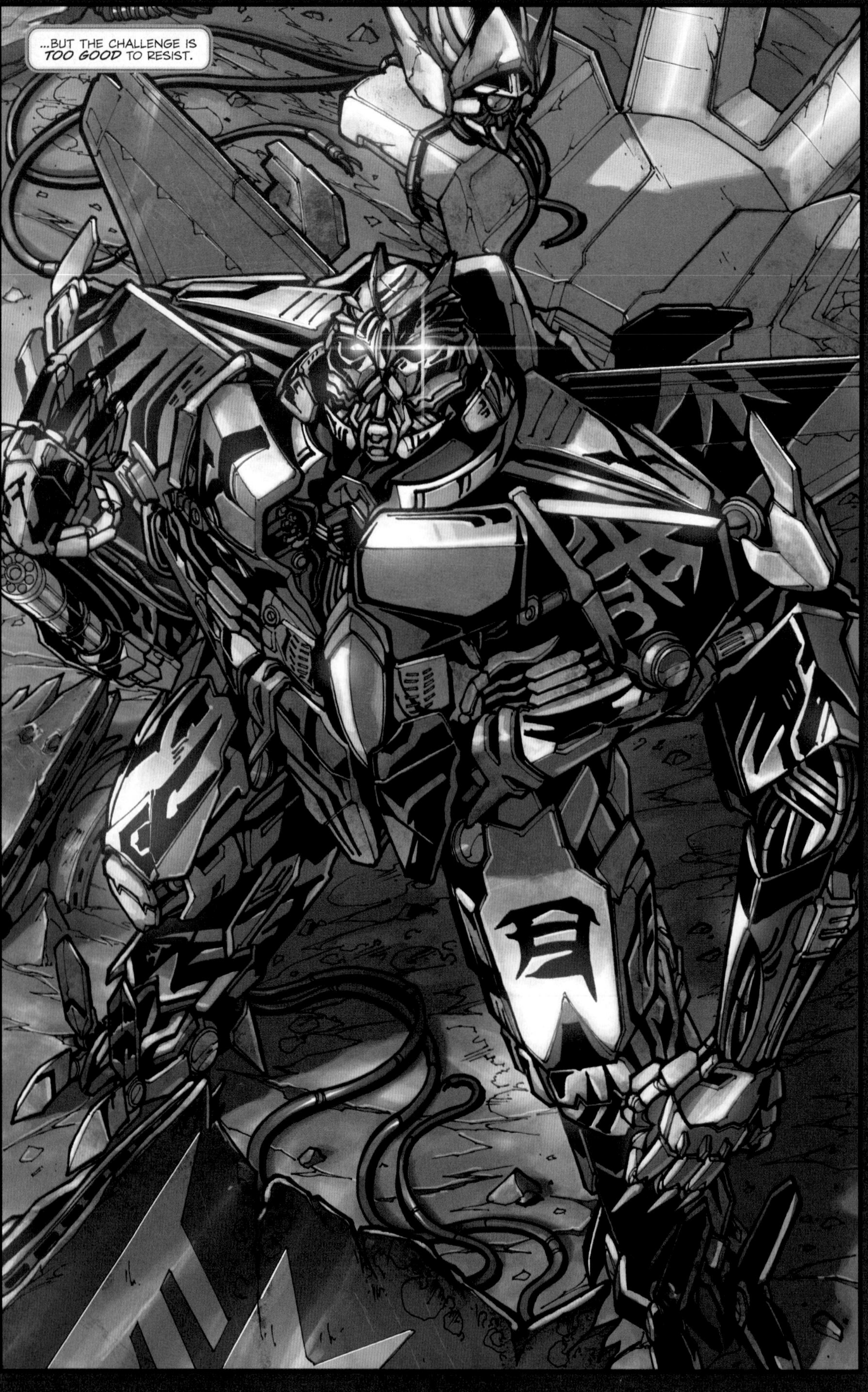
...BUT THE CHALLENGE IS *TOO GOOD* TO RESIST.

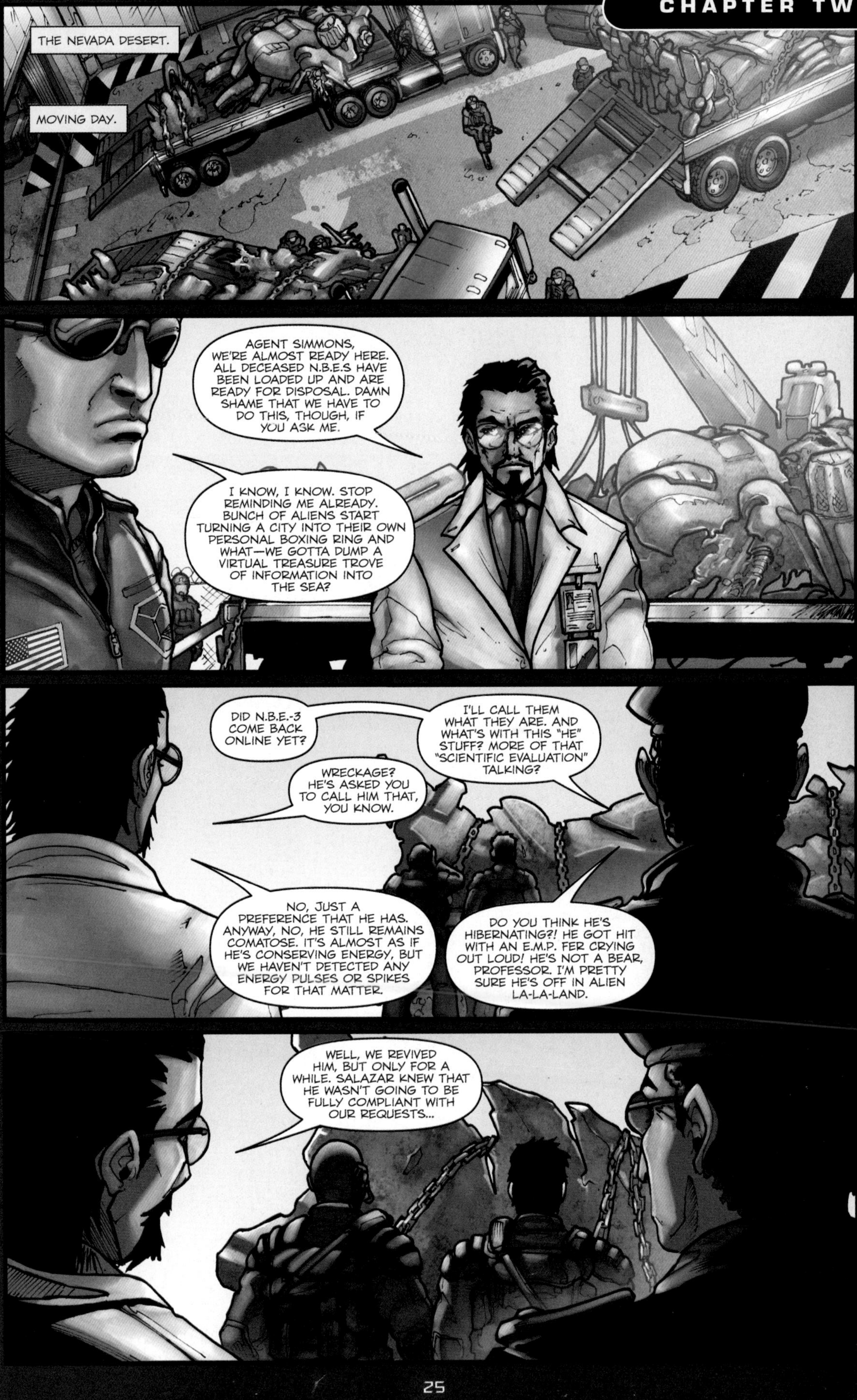
THE NEVADA DESERT.
MOVING DAY.
AGENT SIMMONS, WE'RE ALMOST READY HERE. ALL DECEASED N.B.E.S HAVE BEEN LOADED UP AND ARE READY FOR DISPOSAL. DAMN SHAME THAT WE HAVE TO DO THIS, THOUGH, IF YOU ASK ME.
I KNOW, I KNOW. STOP REMINDING ME ALREADY. BUNCH OF ALIENS START TURNING A CITY INTO THEIR OWN PERSONAL BOXING RING AND WHAT—WE GOTTA DUMP A VIRTUAL TREASURE TROVE OF INFORMATION INTO THE SEA?
DID N.B.E.-3 COME BACK ONLINE YET?
WRECKAGE? HE'S ASKED YOU TO CALL HIM THAT, YOU KNOW.
I'LL CALL THEM WHAT THEY ARE. AND WHAT'S WITH THIS "HE" STUFF? MORE OF THAT "SCIENTIFIC EVALUATION" TALKING?
NO, JUST A PREFERENCE THAT HE HAS. ANYWAY, NO, HE STILL REMAINS COMATOSE. IT'S ALMOST AS IF HE'S CONSERVING ENERGY, BUT WE HAVEN'T DETECTED ANY ENERGY PULSES OR SPIKES FOR THAT MATTER.
DO YOU THINK HE'S HIBERNATING?! HE GOT HIT WITH AN E.M.P. FER CRYING OUT LOUD! HE'S NOT A BEAR, PROFESSOR. I'M PRETTY SURE HE'S OFF IN ALIEN LA-LA-LAND.
WELL, WE REVIVED HIM, BUT ONLY FOR A WHILE. SALAZAR KNEW THAT HE WASN'T GOING TO BE FULLY COMPLIANT WITH OUR REQUESTS...

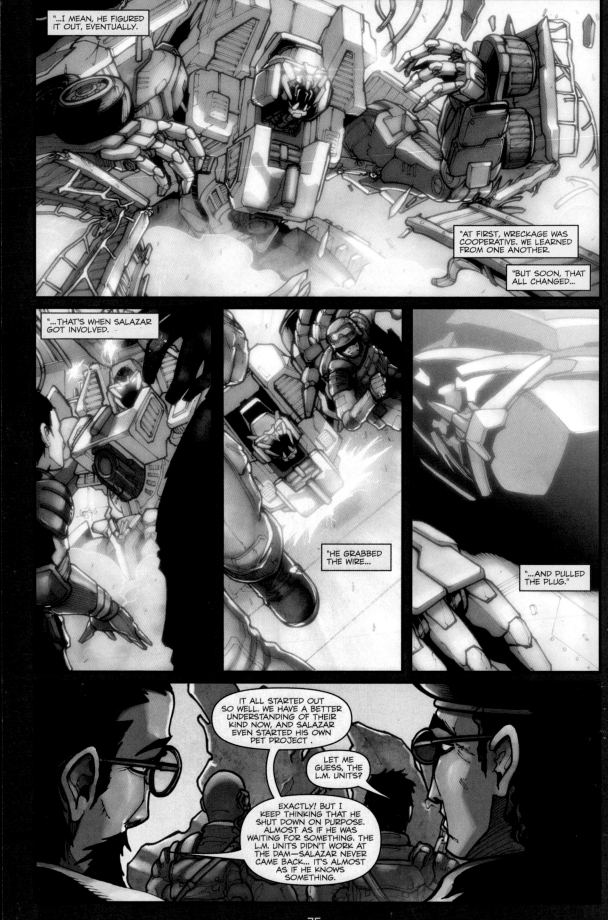

"...I MEAN, HE FIGURED IT OUT, EVENTUALLY.

"AT FIRST, WRECKAGE WAS COOPERATIVE. WE LEARNED FROM ONE ANOTHER.

"BUT SOON, THAT ALL CHANGED...

"...THAT'S WHEN SALAZAR GOT INVOLVED.

"HE GRABBED THE WIRE...

"...AND PULLED THE PLUG."

IT ALL STARTED OUT SO WELL. WE HAVE A BETTER UNDERSTANDING OF THEIR KIND NOW, AND SALAZAR EVEN STARTED HIS OWN PET PROJECT.

LET ME GUESS, THE L.M. UNITS?

EXACTLY! BUT I KEEP THINKING THAT HE SHUT DOWN ON PURPOSE. ALMOST AS IF HE WAS WAITING FOR SOMETHING. THE L.M. UNITS DIDN'T WORK AT THE DAM—SALAZAR NEVER CAME BACK... IT'S ALMOST AS IF HE KNOWS SOMETHING.

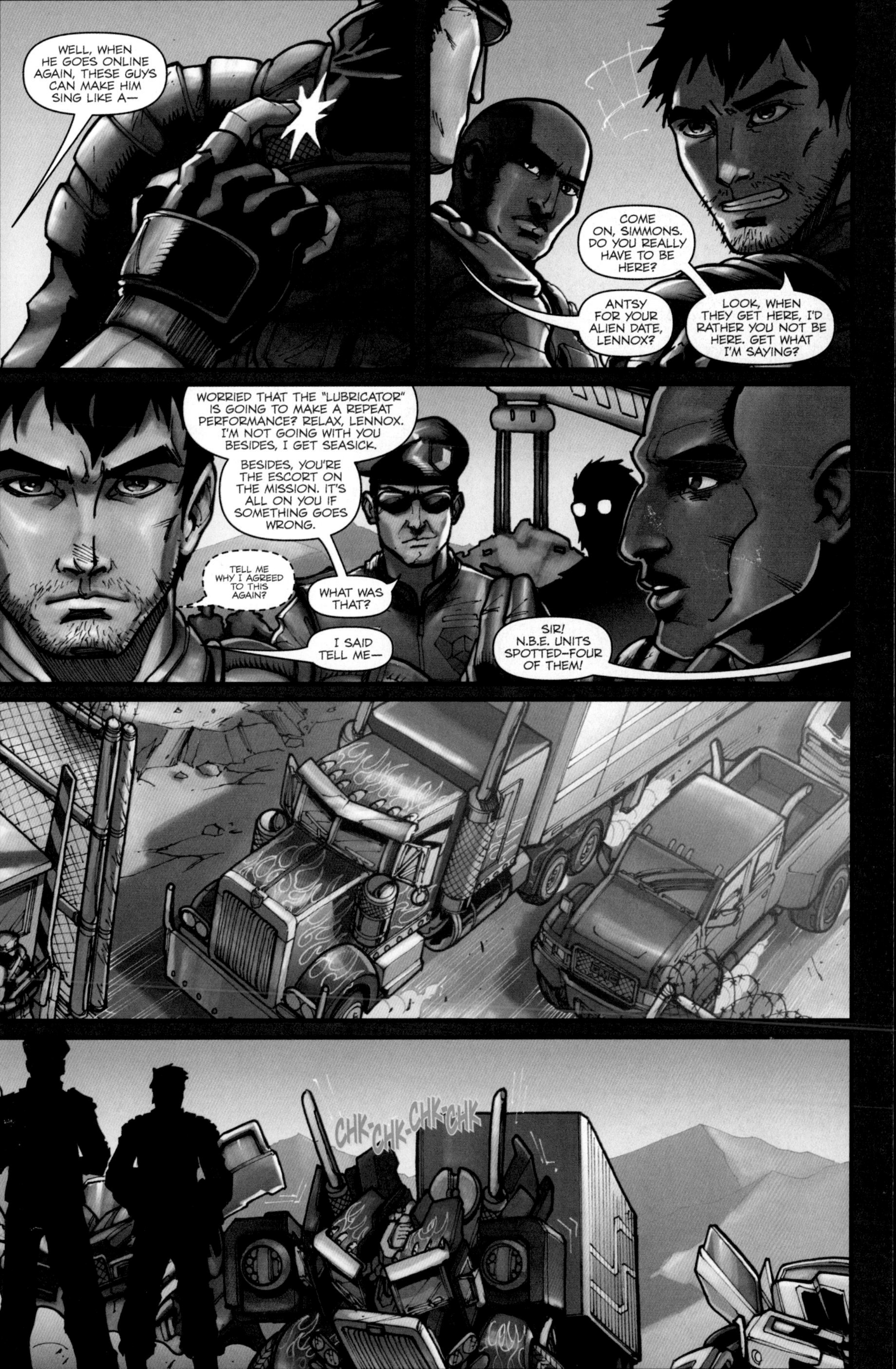
WELL, WHEN HE GOES ONLINE AGAIN, THESE GUYS CAN MAKE HIM SING LIKE A—
COME ON, SIMMONS. DO YOU REALLY HAVE TO BE HERE?
ANTSY FOR YOUR ALIEN DATE, LENNOX?
LOOK, WHEN THEY GET HERE, I'D RATHER YOU NOT BE HERE. GET WHAT I'M SAYING?
WORRIED THAT THE "LUBRICATOR" IS GOING TO MAKE A REPEAT PERFORMANCE? RELAX, LENNOX. I'M NOT GOING WITH YOU BESIDES, I GET SEASICK.
BESIDES, YOU'RE THE ESCORT ON THE MISSION. IT'S ALL ON YOU IF SOMETHING GOES WRONG.
TELL ME WHY I AGREED TO THIS AGAIN?
WHAT WAS THAT?
I SAID TELL ME—
SIR! N.B.E. UNITS SPOTTED—FOUR OF THEM!
CHK-CHK-CHK-CHK

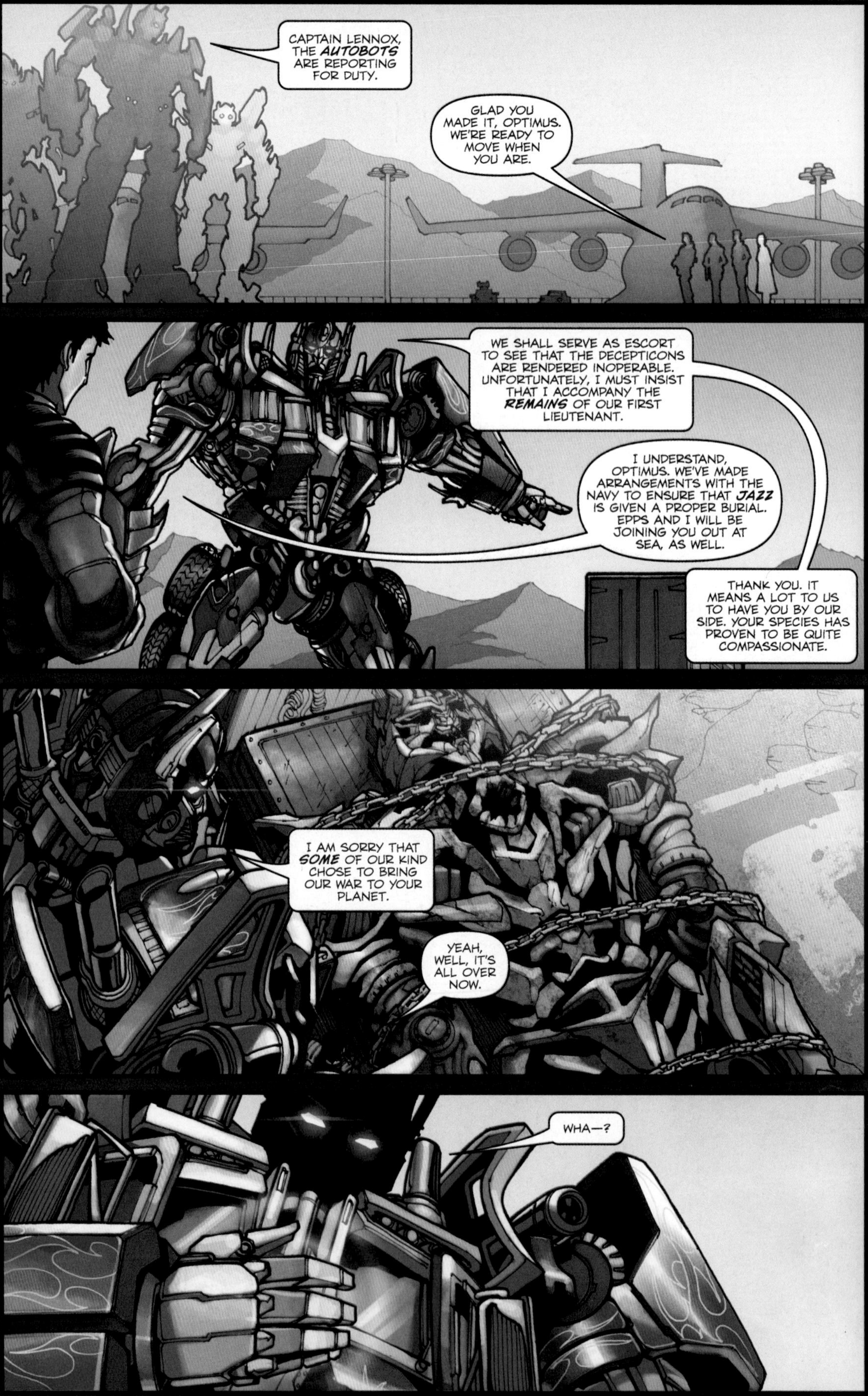

CAPTAIN LENNOX, THE AUTOBOTS ARE REPORTING FOR DUTY.
GLAD YOU MADE IT, OPTIMUS. WE'RE READY TO MOVE WHEN YOU ARE.
WE SHALL SERVE AS ESCORT TO SEE THAT THE DECEPTICONS ARE RENDERED INOPERABLE. UNFORTUNATELY, I MUST INSIST THAT I ACCOMPANY THE REMAINS OF OUR FIRST LIEUTENANT.
I UNDERSTAND, OPTIMUS. WE'VE MADE ARRANGEMENTS WITH THE NAVY TO ENSURE THAT JAZZ IS GIVEN A PROPER BURIAL. EPPS AND I WILL BE JOINING YOU OUT AT SEA, AS WELL.
THANK YOU. IT MEANS A LOT TO US TO HAVE YOU BY OUR SIDE. YOUR SPECIES HAS PROVEN TO BE QUITE COMPASSIONATE.
I AM SORRY THAT SOME OF OUR KIND CHOSE TO BRING OUR WAR TO YOUR PLANET.
YEAH, WELL, IT'S ALL OVER NOW.
WHA—?

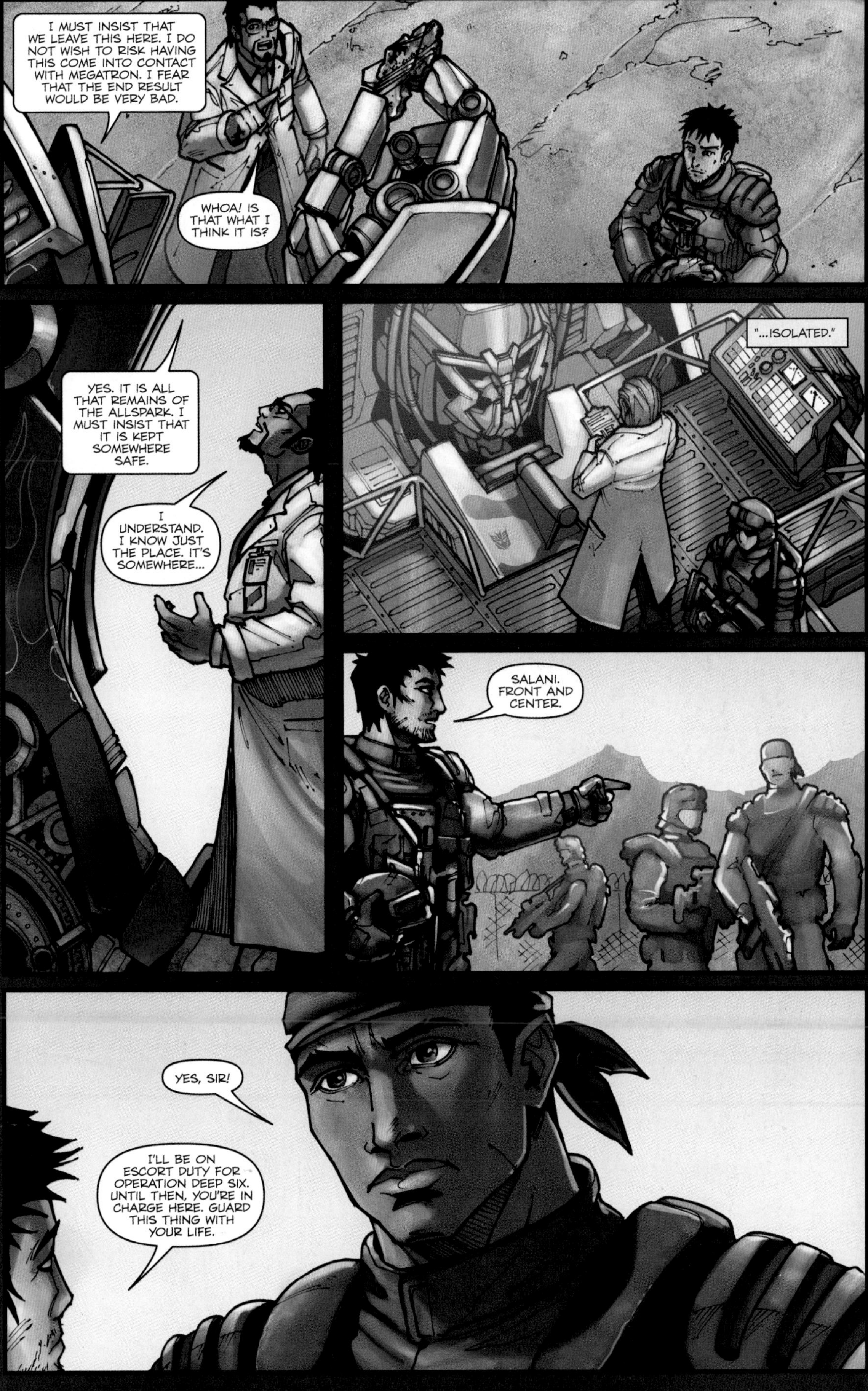
I MUST INSIST THAT WE LEAVE THIS HERE. I DO NOT WISH TO RISK HAVING THIS COME INTO CONTACT WITH MEGATRON. I FEAR THAT THE END RESULT WOULD BE VERY BAD.
WHOA! IS THAT WHAT I THINK IT IS?
YES. IT IS ALL THAT REMAINS OF THE ALLSPARK. I MUST INSIST THAT IT IS KEPT SOMEWHERE SAFE.
I UNDERSTAND. I KNOW JUST THE PLACE. IT'S SOMEWHERE...
"...ISOLATED."
SALANI. FRONT AND CENTER.
YES, SIR!
I'LL BE ON ESCORT DUTY FOR OPERATION DEEP SIX. UNTIL THEN, YOU'RE IN CHARGE HERE. GUARD THIS THING WITH YOUR LIFE.

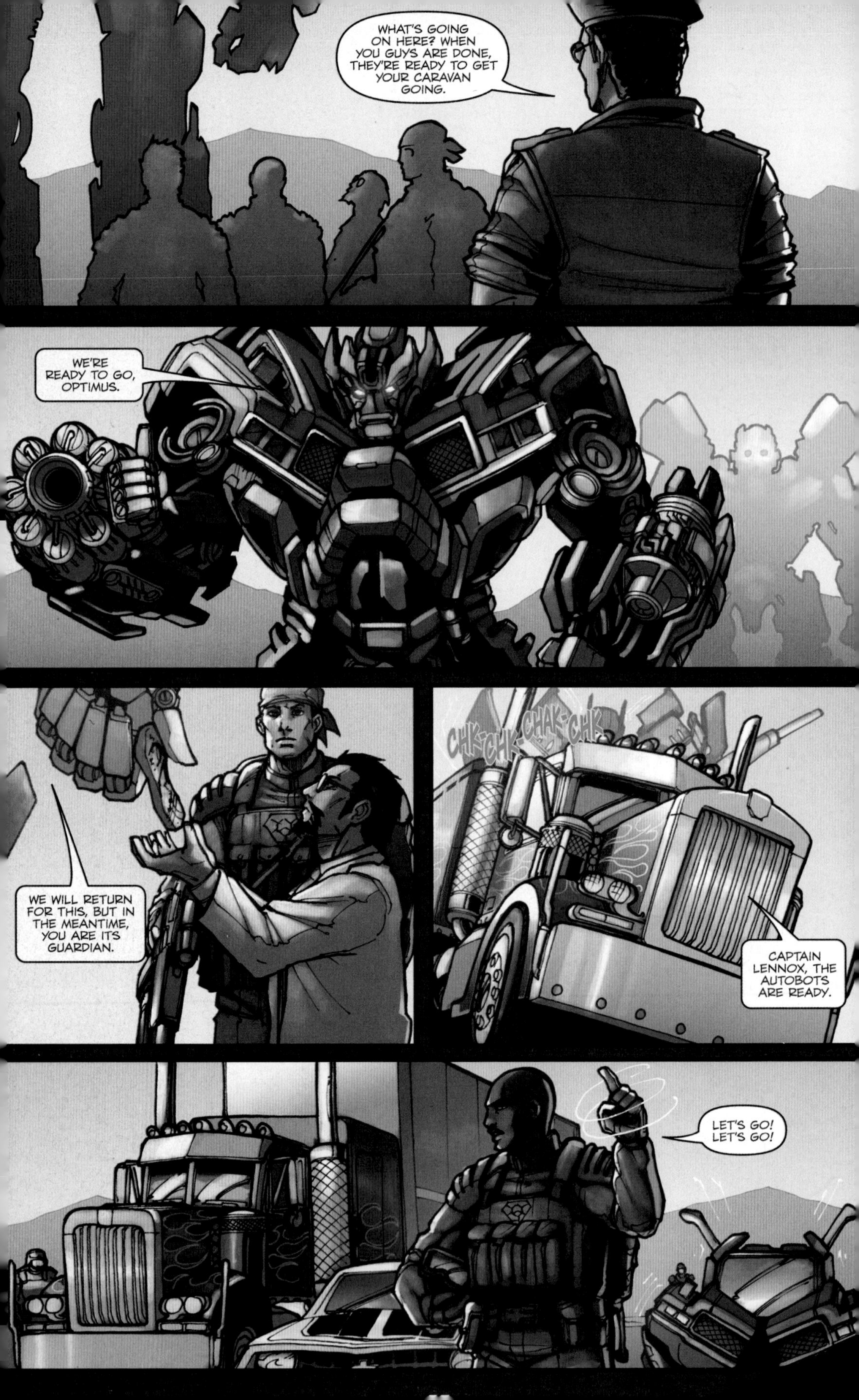
WHAT'S GOING ON HERE? WHEN YOU GUYS ARE DONE, THEY'RE READY TO GET YOUR CARAVAN GOING.
WE'RE READY TO GO, OPTIMUS.
WE WILL RETURN FOR THIS, BUT IN THE MEANTIME, YOU ARE ITS GUARDIAN.
CHK-CHK-CHAK-CHK
CAPTAIN LENNOX, THE AUTOBOTS ARE READY.
LET'S GO! LET'S GO!

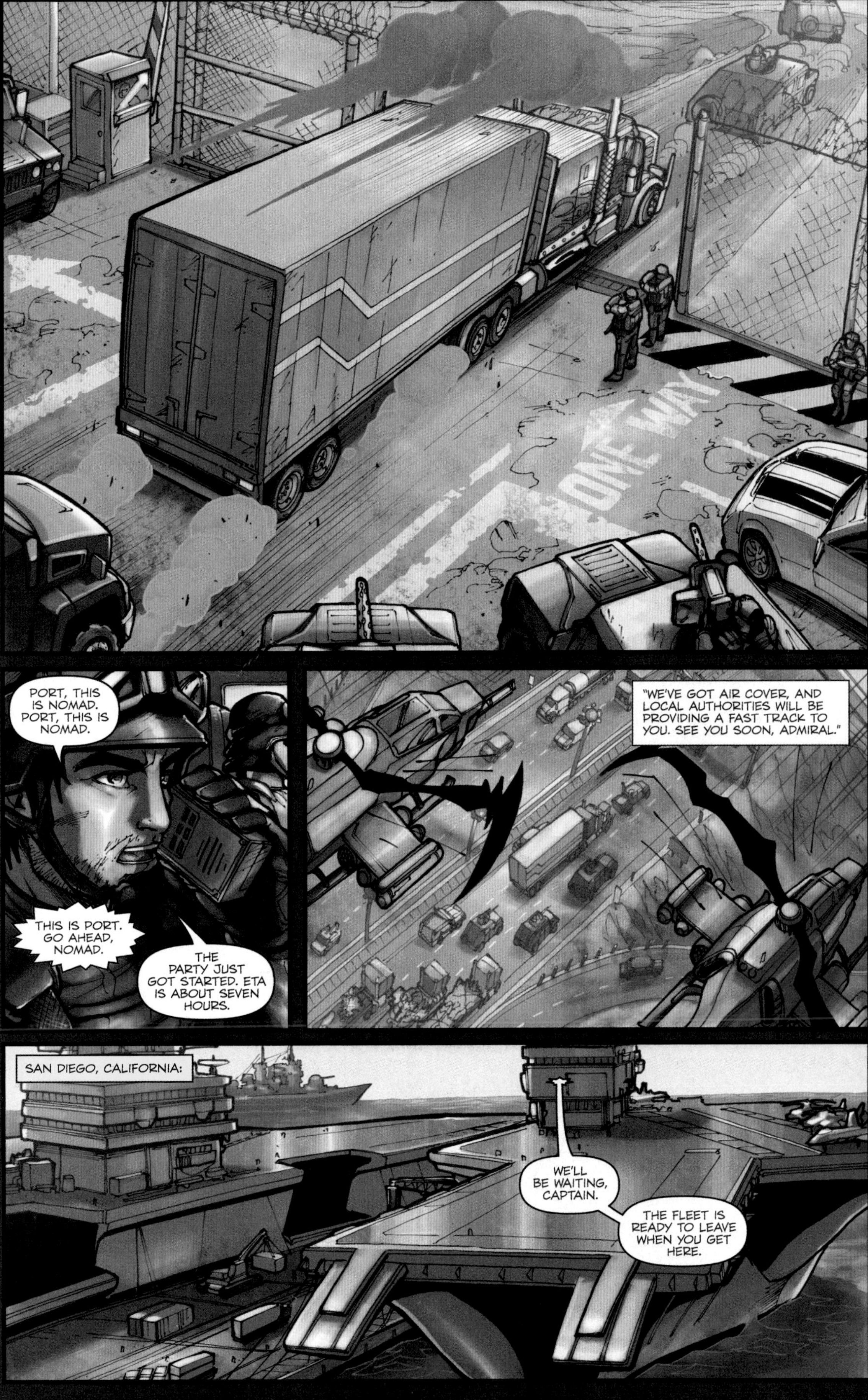
ONE WAY
PORT, THIS IS NOMAD. PORT, THIS IS NOMAD.
THIS IS PORT. GO AHEAD, NOMAD.
THE PARTY JUST GOT STARTED. ETA IS ABOUT SEVEN HOURS.
"WE'VE GOT AIR COVER, AND LOCAL AUTHORITIES WILL BE PROVIDING A FAST TRACK TO YOU. SEE YOU SOON, ADMIRAL."
SAN DIEGO, CALIFORNIA:
WE'LL BE WAITING, CAPTAIN.
THE FLEET IS READY TO LEAVE WHEN YOU GET HERE.

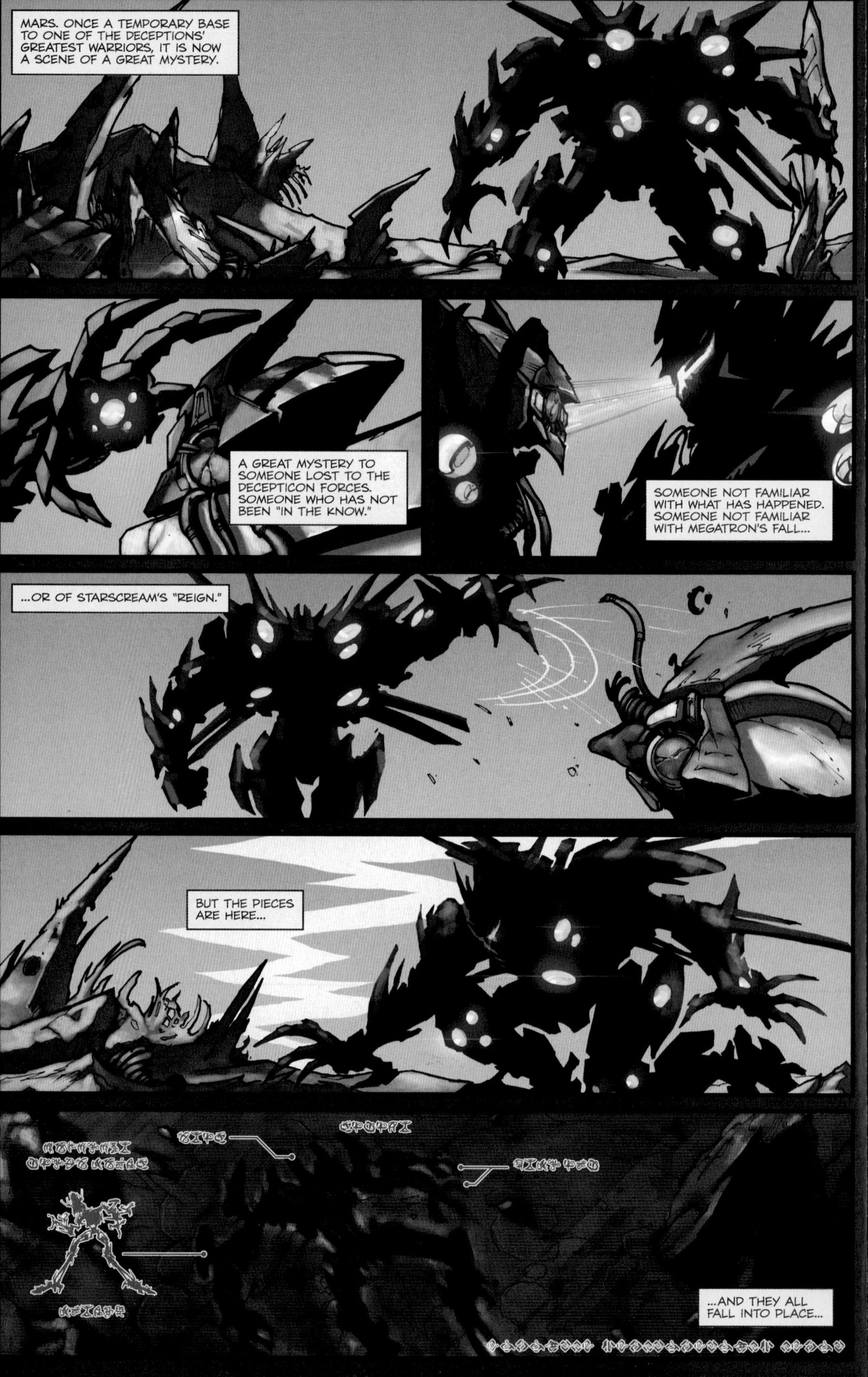
MARS. ONCE A TEMPORARY BASE TO ONE OF THE DECEPTIONS' GREATEST WARRIORS, IT IS NOW A SCENE OF A GREAT MYSTERY.
A GREAT MYSTERY TO SOMEONE LOST TO THE DECEPTICON FORCES. SOMEONE WHO HAS NOT BEEN "IN THE KNOW."
SOMEONE NOT FAMILIAR WITH WHAT HAS HAPPENED. SOMEONE NOT FAMILIAR WITH MEGATRON'S FALL...
...OR OF STARSCREAM'S "REIGN."
BUT THE PIECES ARE HERE...
...AND THEY ALL FALL INTO PLACE...

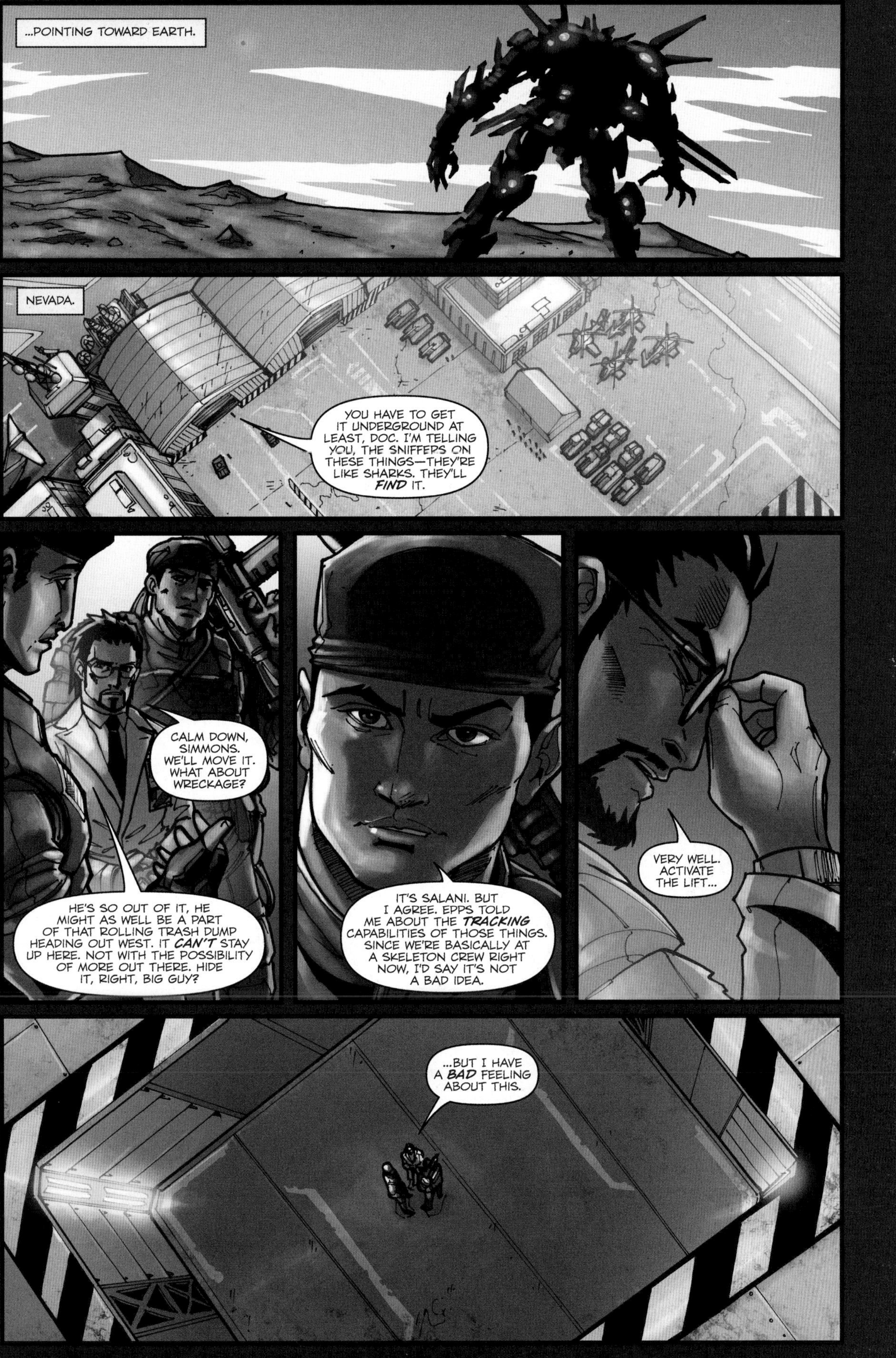
...POINTING TOWARD EARTH.
NEVADA.
YOU HAVE TO GET IT UNDERGROUND AT LEAST, DOC. I'M TELLING YOU, THE SNIFFERS ON THESE THINGS—THEY'RE LIKE SHARKS. THEY'LL *FIND* IT.
CALM DOWN, SIMMONS. WE'LL MOVE IT. WHAT ABOUT WRECKAGE?
HE'S SO OUT OF IT, HE MIGHT AS WELL BE A PART OF THAT ROLLING TRASH DUMP HEADING OUT WEST. IT *CAN'T* STAY UP HERE. NOT WITH THE POSSIBILITY OF MORE OUT THERE. HIDE IT, RIGHT, BIG GUY?
IT'S SALANI. BUT I AGREE. EPPS TOLD ME ABOUT THE *TRACKING* CAPABILITIES OF THOSE THINGS. SINCE WE'RE BASICALLY AT A SKELETON CREW RIGHT NOW, I'D SAY IT'S NOT A BAD IDEA.
VERY WELL. ACTIVATE THE LIFT...
...BUT I HAVE A *BAD* FEELING ABOUT THIS.

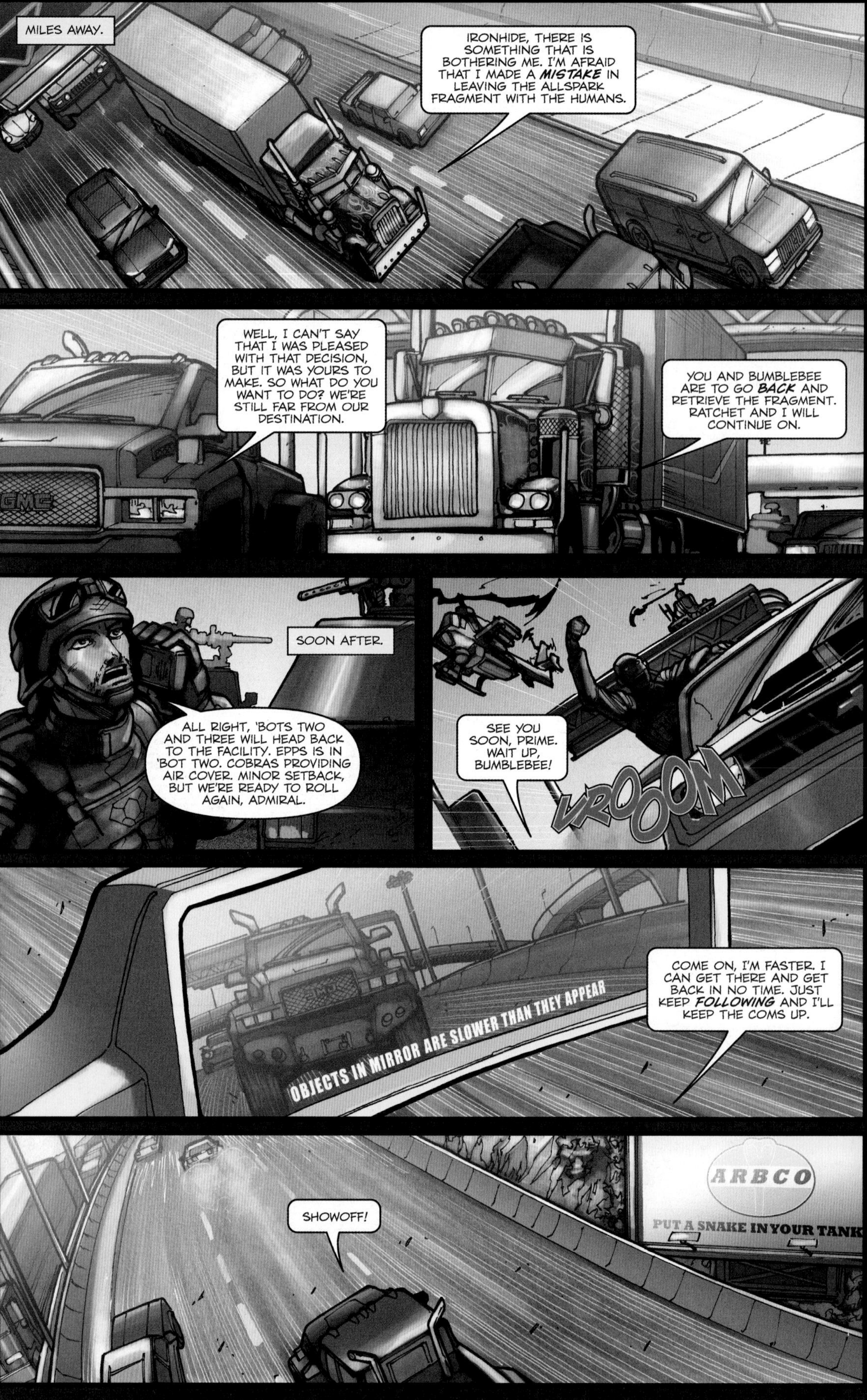
MILES AWAY.
IRONHIDE, THERE IS SOMETHING THAT IS BOTHERING ME. I'M AFRAID THAT I MADE A ***MISTAKE*** IN LEAVING THE ALLSPARK FRAGMENT WITH THE HUMANS.
WELL, I CAN'T SAY THAT I WAS PLEASED WITH THAT DECISION, BUT IT WAS YOURS TO MAKE. SO WHAT DO YOU WANT TO DO? WE'RE STILL FAR FROM OUR DESTINATION.
YOU AND BUMBLEBEE ARE TO GO ***BACK*** AND RETRIEVE THE FRAGMENT. RATCHET AND I WILL CONTINUE ON.
SOON AFTER.
ALL RIGHT, 'BOTS TWO AND THREE WILL HEAD BACK TO THE FACILITY. EPPS IS IN 'BOT TWO. COBRAS PROVIDING AIR COVER. MINOR SETBACK, BUT WE'RE READY TO ROLL AGAIN, ADMIRAL.
SEE YOU SOON, PRIME. WAIT UP, BUMBLEBEE!
VROOOM
OBJECTS IN MIRROR ARE SLOWER THAN THEY APPEAR
COME ON, I'M FASTER. I CAN GET THERE AND GET BACK IN NO TIME. JUST KEEP ***FOLLOWING*** AND I'LL KEEP THE COMS UP.
SHOWOFF!
ARBCO
PUT A SNAKE IN YOUR TANK

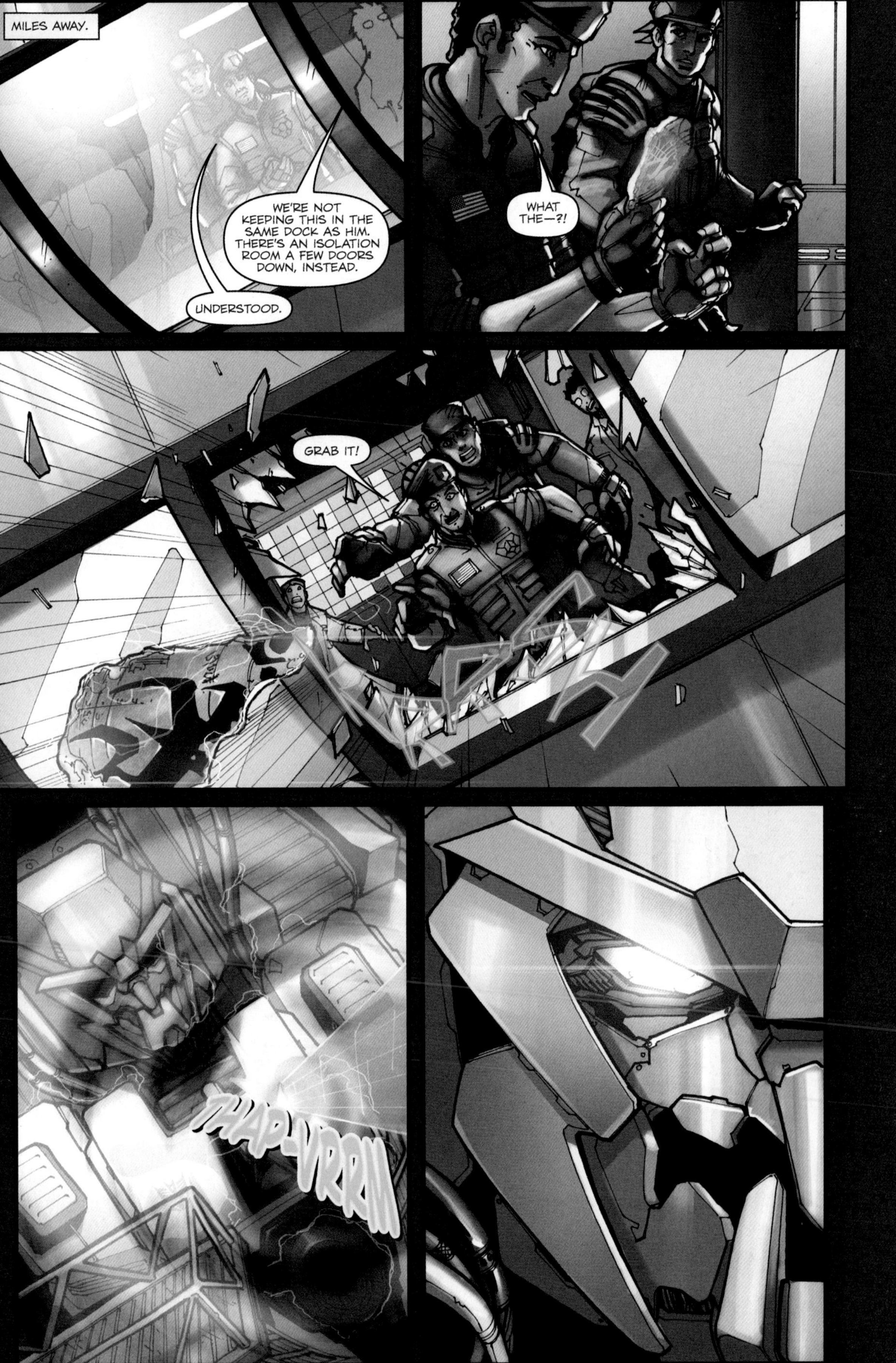
MILES AWAY.
WE'RE NOT KEEPING THIS IN THE SAME DOCK AS HIM. THERE'S AN ISOLATION ROOM A FEW DOORS DOWN, INSTEAD.
UNDERSTOOD.
WHAT THE—?!
GRAB IT!
THAP-VRRM

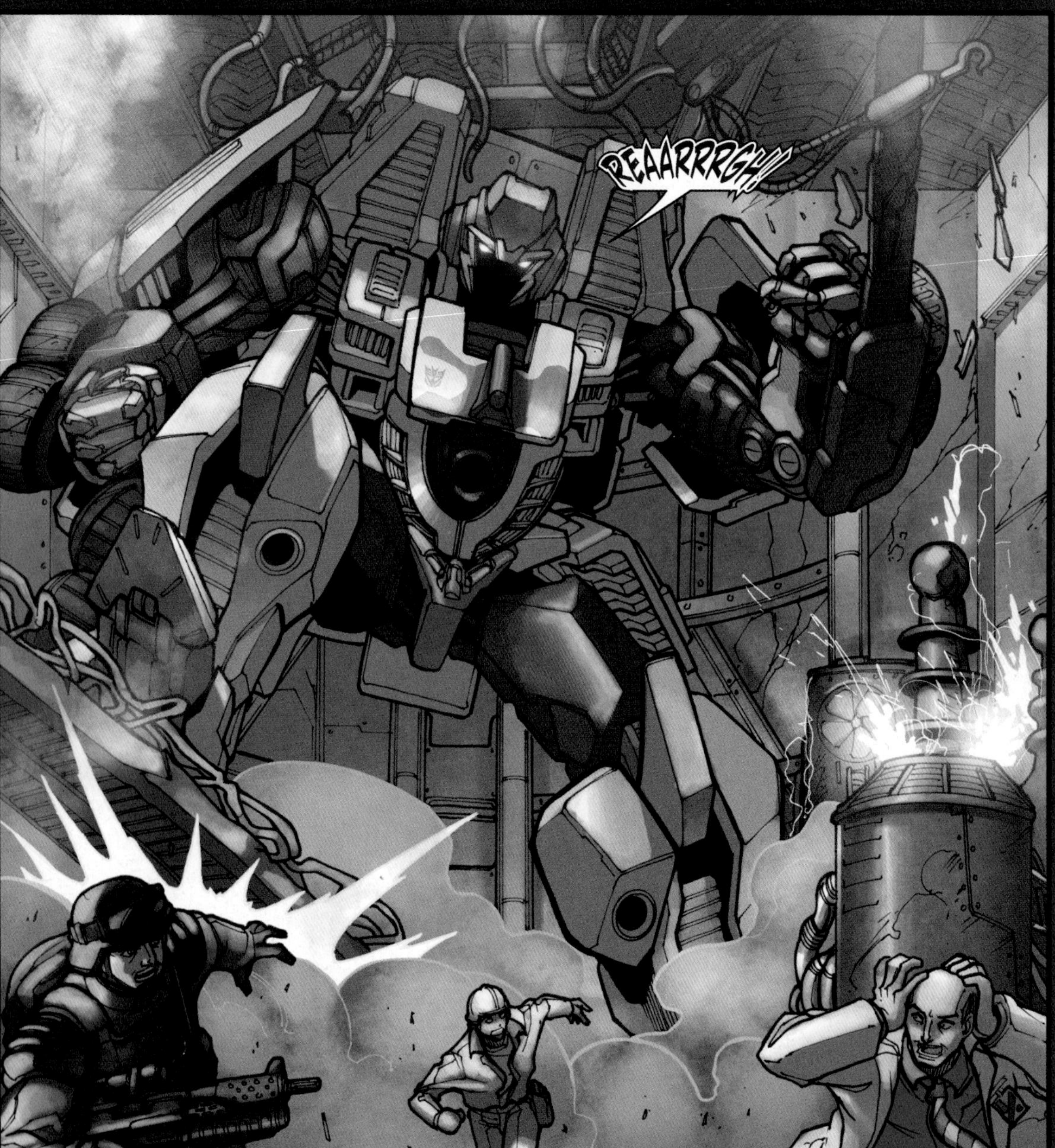
REAARRRGH!!

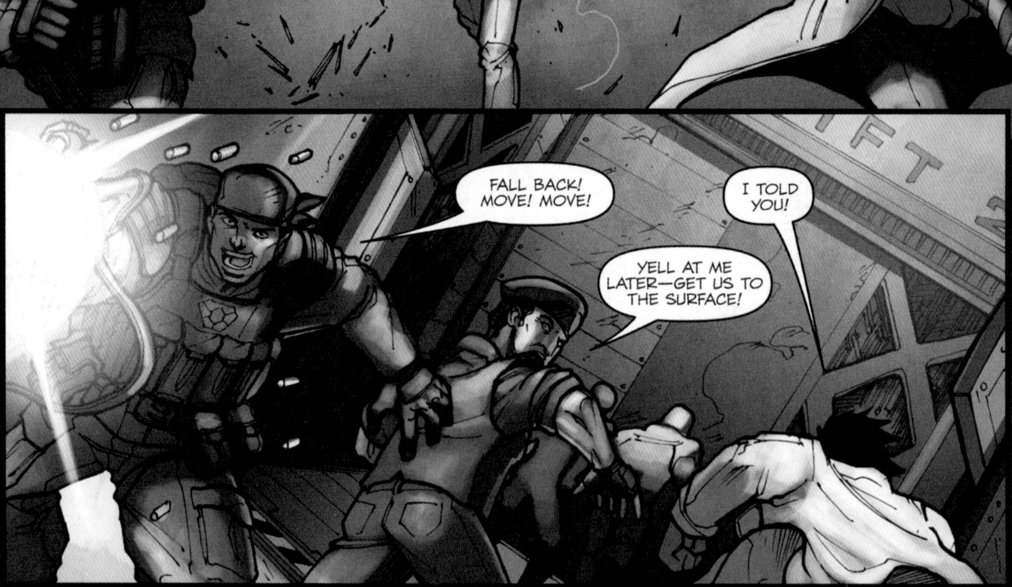
FALL BACK! MOVE! MOVE!
I TOLD YOU!
YELL AT ME LATER—GET US TO THE SURFACE!

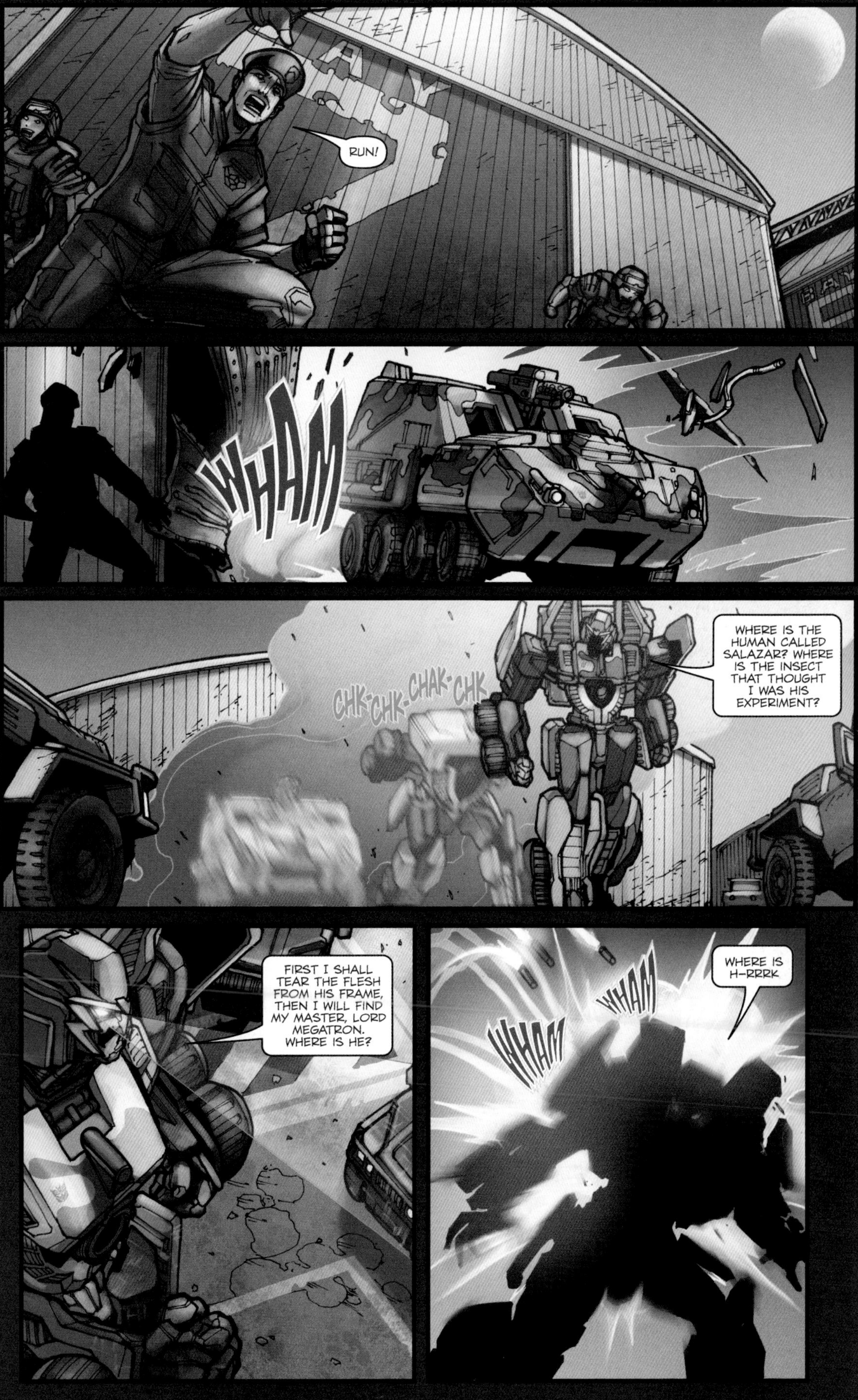
RUN!
WHAM
CHK-CHK-CHAK-CHK
WHERE IS THE HUMAN CALLED SALAZAR? WHERE IS THE INSECT THAT THOUGHT I WAS HIS EXPERIMENT?
FIRST I SHALL TEAR THE FLESH FROM HIS FRAME, THEN I WILL FIND MY MASTER, LORD MEGATRON. WHERE IS HE?
WHERE IS H-RRRK
WHAM
WHAM

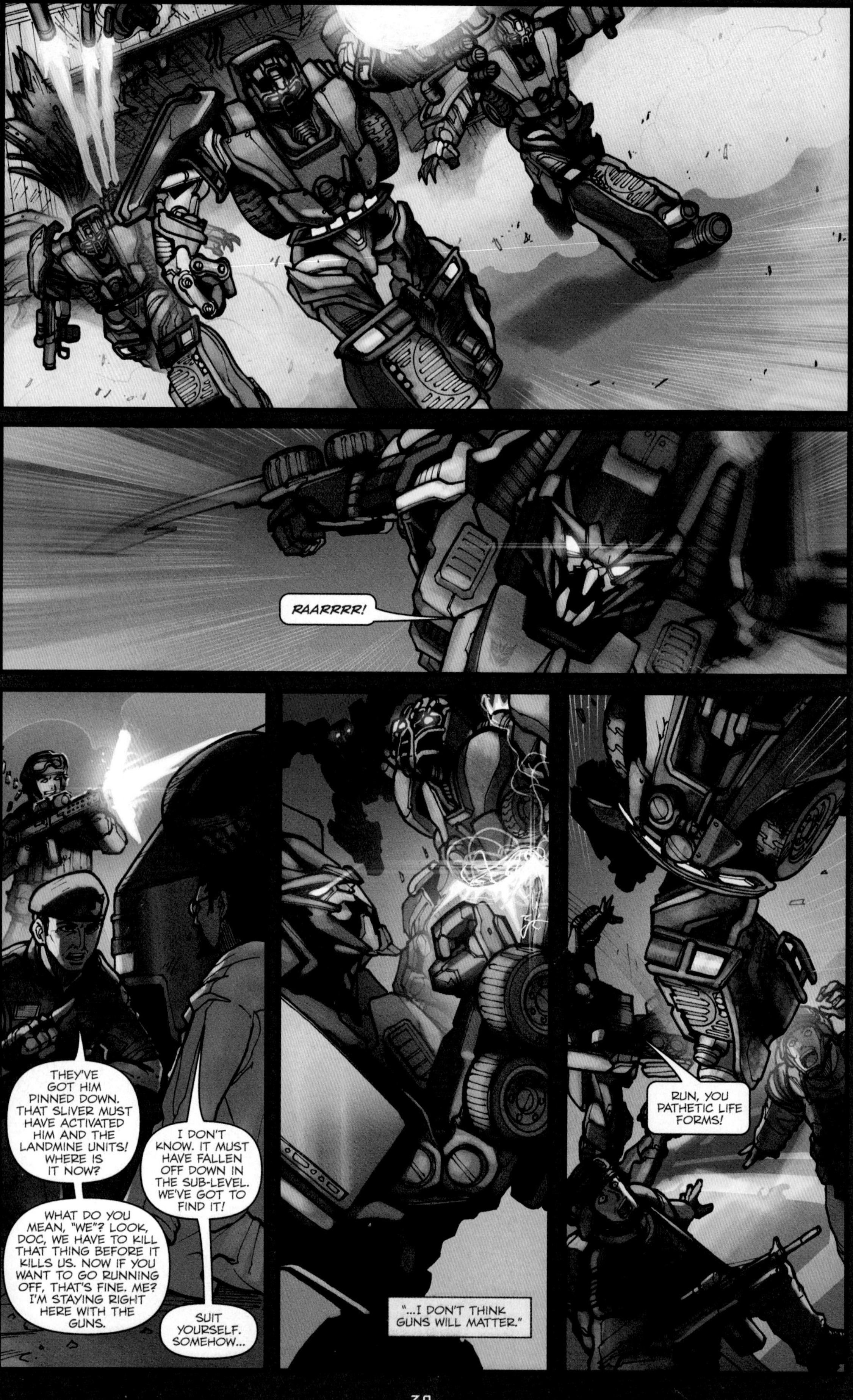
RAARRRR!
THEY'VE GOT HIM PINNED DOWN. THAT SLIVER MUST HAVE ACTIVATED HIM AND THE LANDMINE UNITS! WHERE IS IT NOW?
I DON'T KNOW. IT MUST HAVE FALLEN OFF DOWN IN THE SUB-LEVEL. WE'VE GOT TO FIND IT!
WHAT DO YOU MEAN, "WE"? LOOK, DOC, WE HAVE TO KILL THAT THING BEFORE IT KILLS US. NOW IF YOU WANT TO GO RUNNING OFF, THAT'S FINE. ME? I'M STAYING RIGHT HERE WITH THE GUNS.
SUIT YOURSELF. SOMEHOW...
"...I DON'T THINK GUNS WILL MATTER."
RUN, YOU PATHETIC LIFE FORMS!

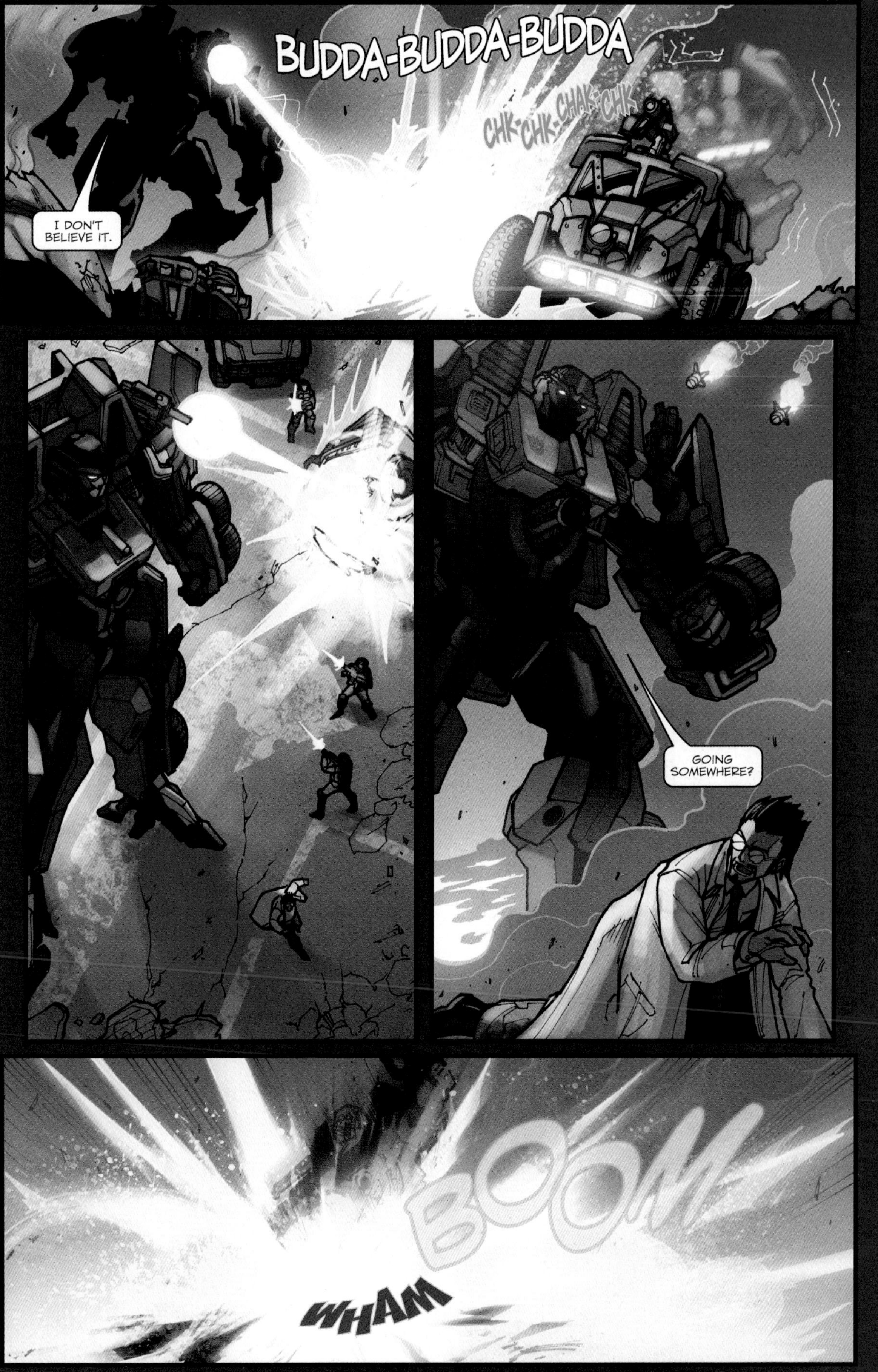
BUDDA-BUDDA-BUDDA
CHK-CHK-CHAK-CHK
I DON'T BELIEVE IT.
GOING SOMEWHERE?
BOOM
WHAM

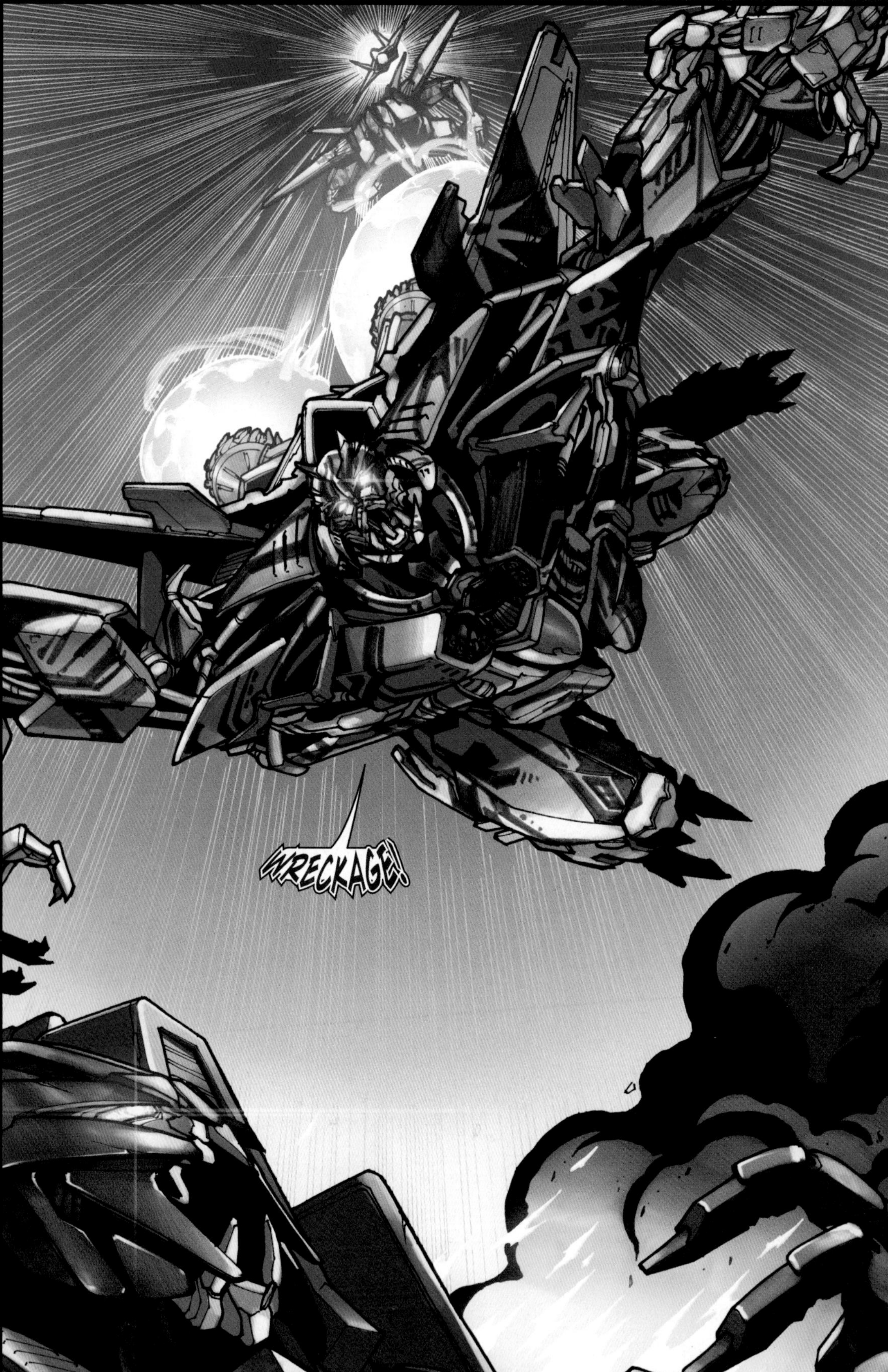
WRECKAGE!

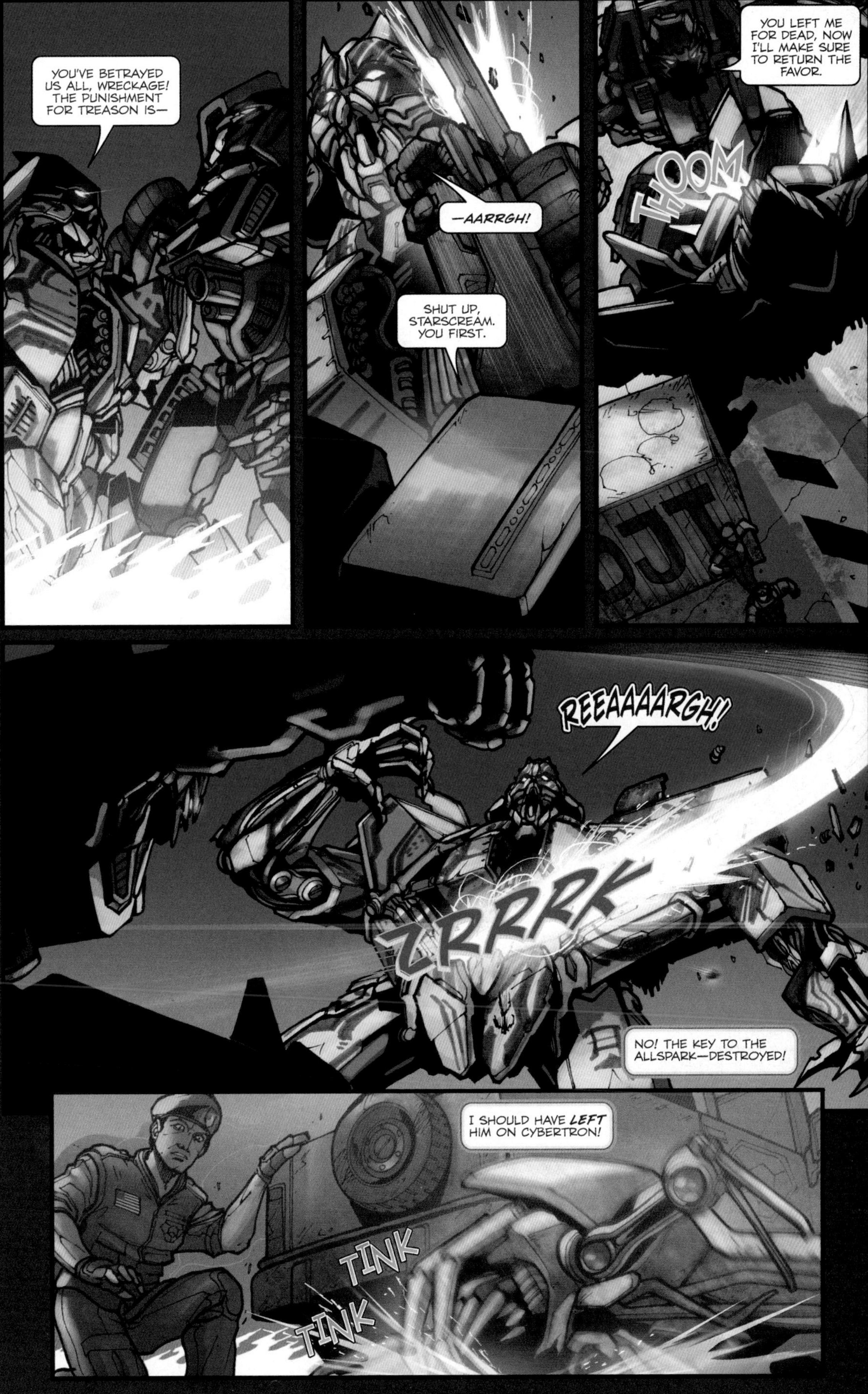

YOU'VE BETRAYED US ALL, WRECKAGE! THE PUNISHMENT FOR TREASON IS—
—AARRGH!
SHUT UP, STARSCREAM. YOU FIRST.
YOU LEFT ME FOR DEAD, NOW I'LL MAKE SURE TO RETURN THE FAVOR.
THOOM
REEAAAAARGH!
ZRRRK
NO! THE KEY TO THE ALLSPARK—DESTROYED!
I SHOULD HAVE LEFT HIM ON CYBERTRON!
TINK
TINK

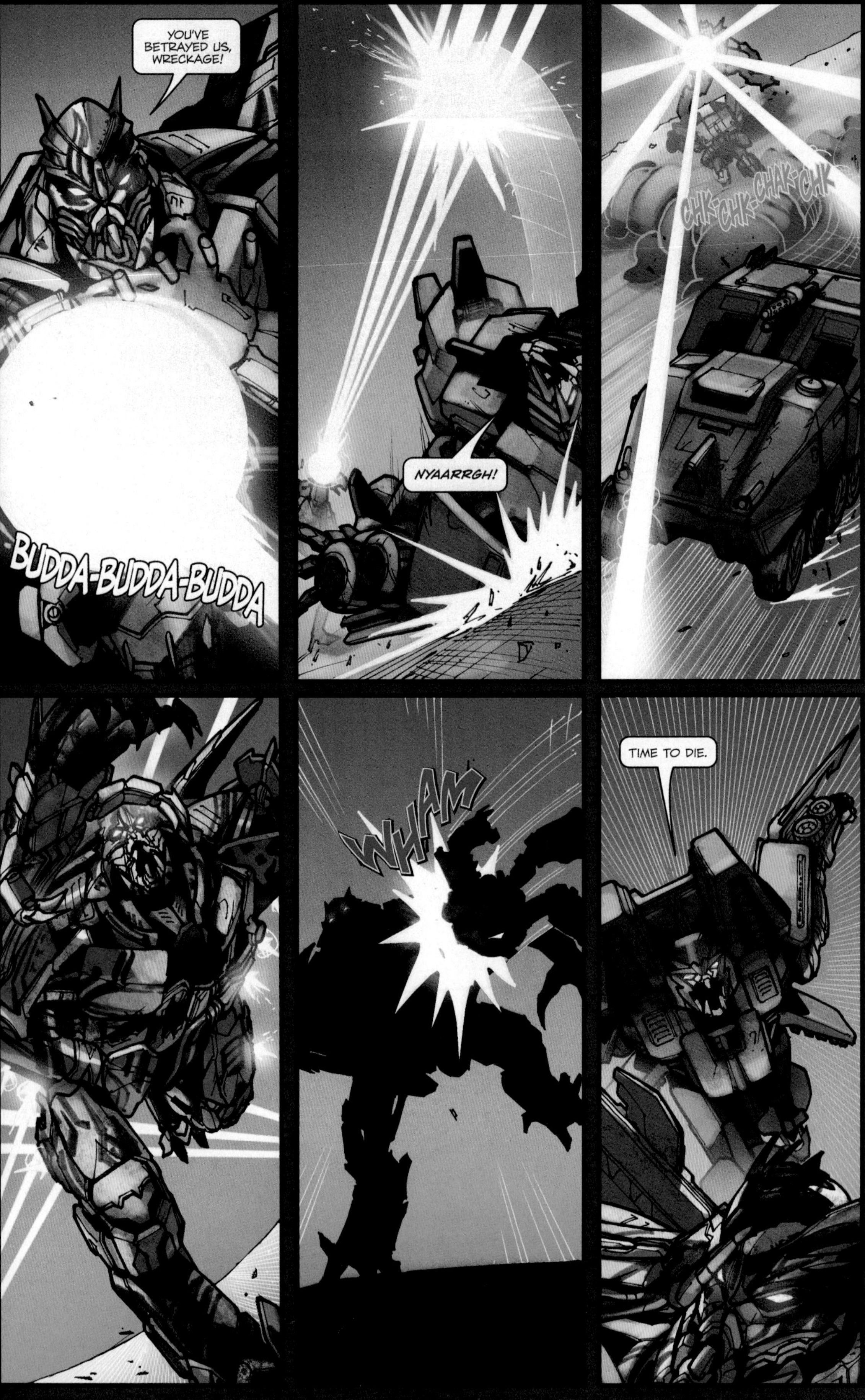
YOU'VE BETRAYED US, WRECKAGE!
BUDDA-BUDDA-BUDDA
NYAARRGH!
CHK-CHK-CHAK-CHK
WHAM
TIME TO DIE.

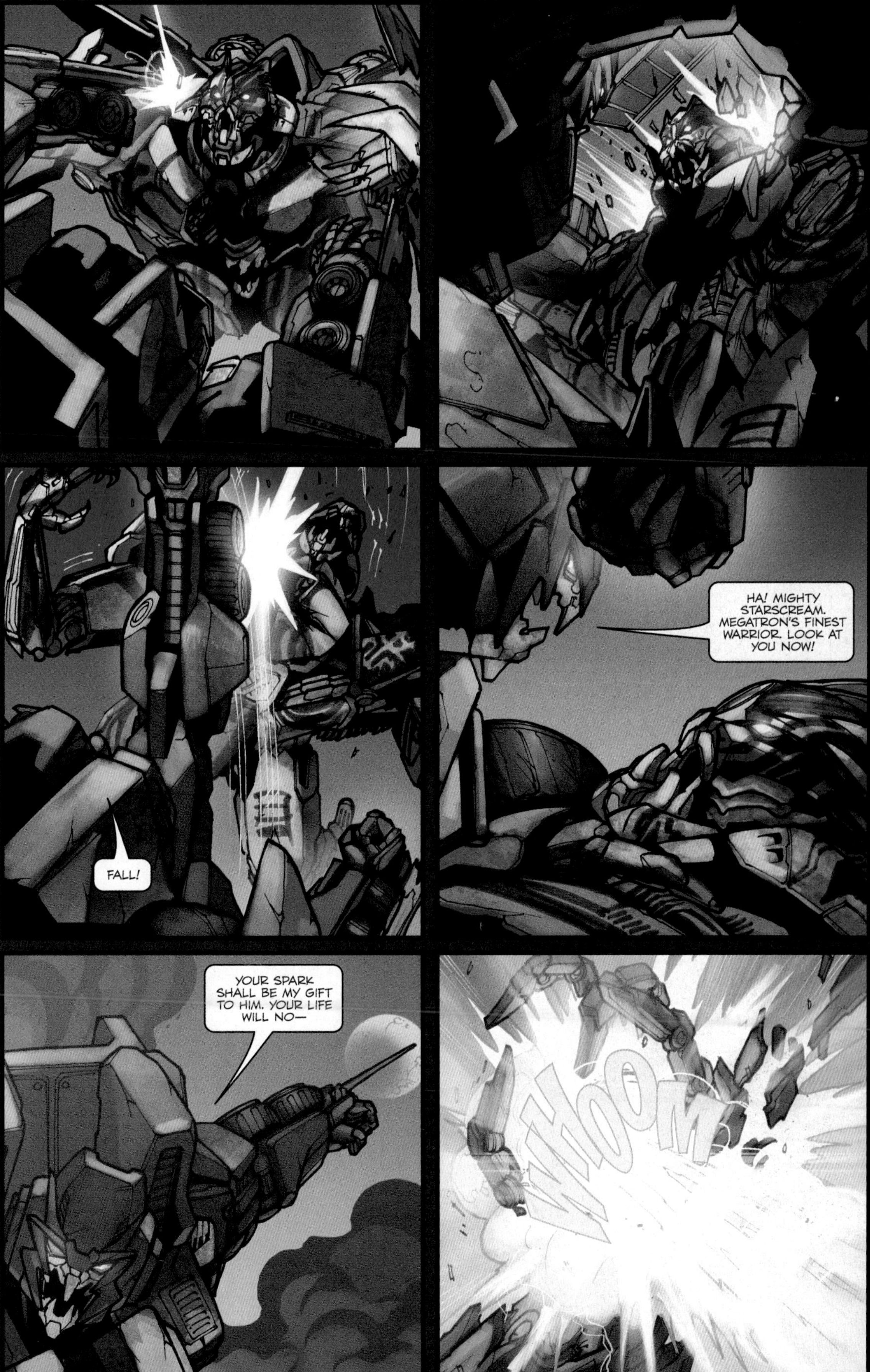
FALL!
HA! MIGHTY STARSCREAM. MEGATRON'S FINEST WARRIOR. LOOK AT YOU NOW!
YOUR SPARK SHALL BE MY GIFT TO HIM. YOUR LIFE WILL NO—
WHOOM

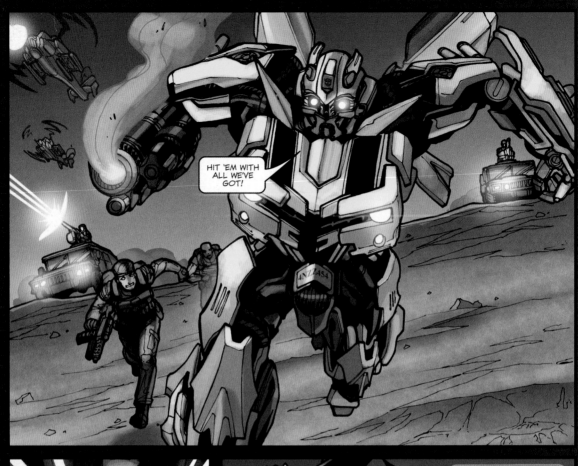

HIT 'EM WITH ALL WE'VE GOT!

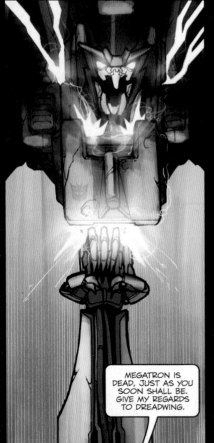

MEGATRON IS DEAD, JUST AS YOU SOON SHALL BE. GIVE MY REGARDS TO DREADWING.

NO SIGN OF MEGATRON OR PRIME. ONE TASK COMPLETED...

...MANY MORE TO GO.

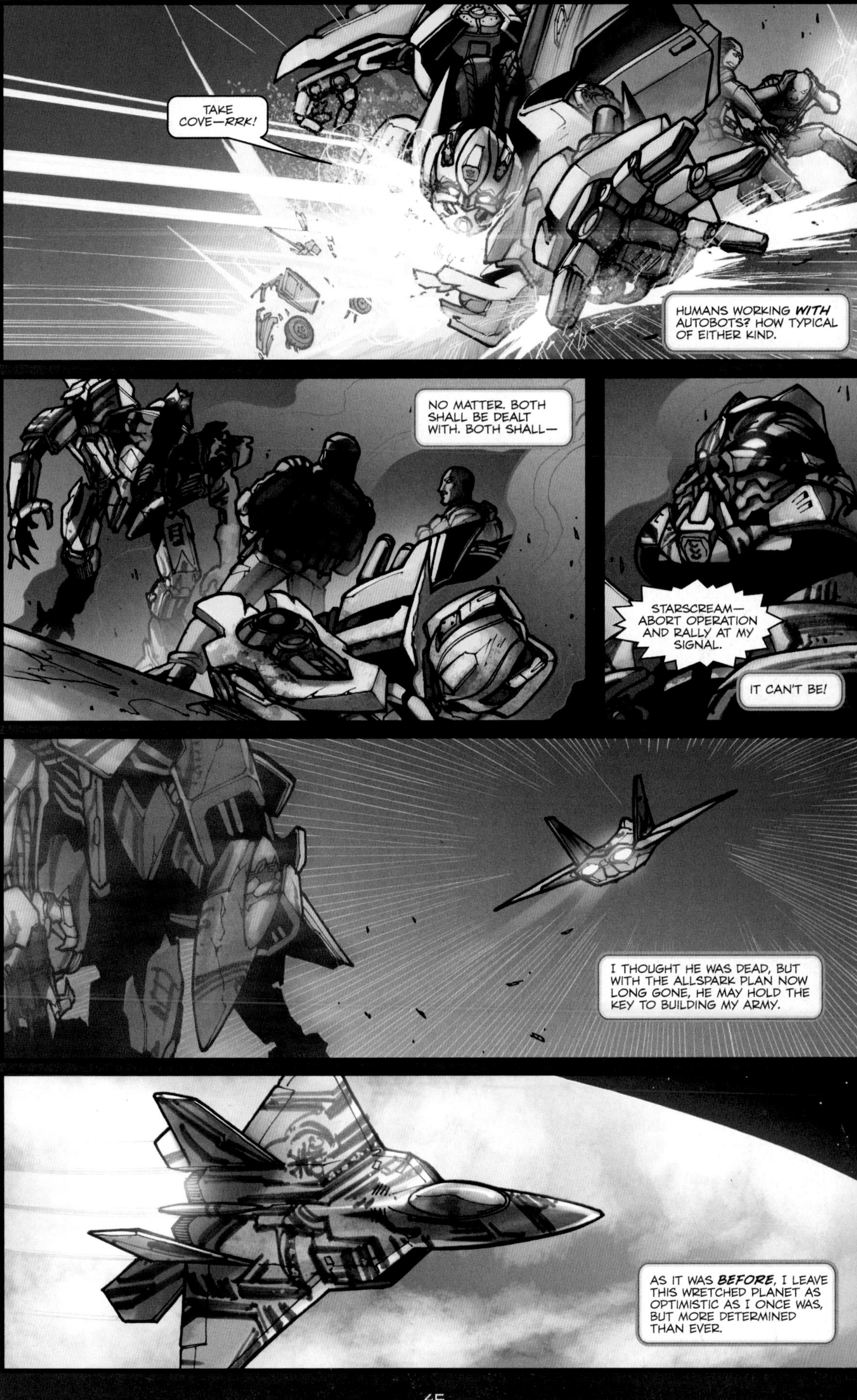
TAKE COVE—RRK!
HUMANS WORKING WITH AUTOBOTS? HOW TYPICAL OF EITHER KIND.
NO MATTER. BOTH SHALL BE DEALT WITH. BOTH SHALL—
STARSCREAM— ABORT OPERATION AND RALLY AT MY SIGNAL.
IT CAN'T BE!
I THOUGHT HE WAS DEAD, BUT WITH THE ALLSPARK PLAN NOW LONG GONE, HE MAY HOLD THE KEY TO BUILDING MY ARMY.
AS IT WAS BEFORE, I LEAVE THIS WRETCHED PLANET AS OPTIMISTIC AS I ONCE WAS, BUT MORE DETERMINED THAN EVER.

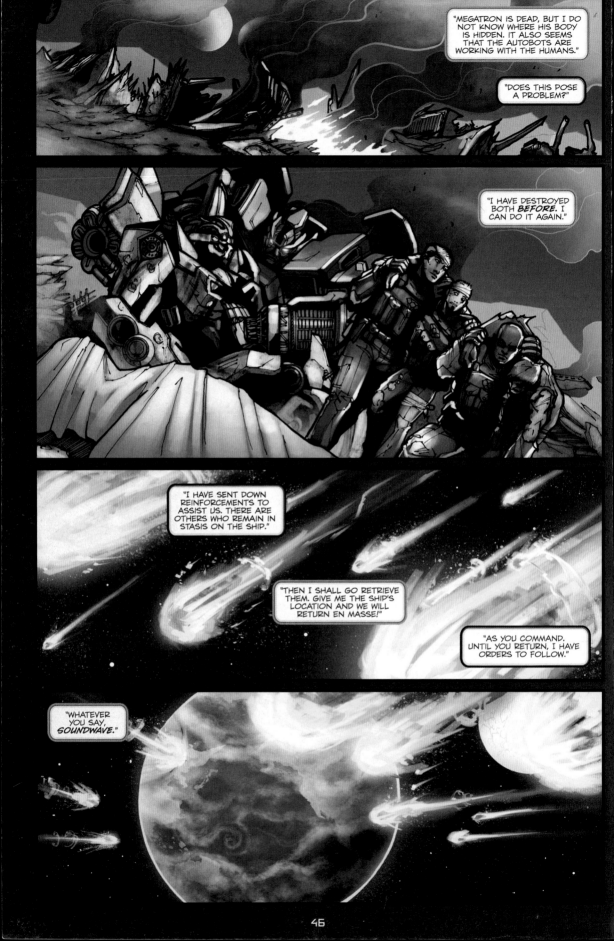

"MEGATRON IS DEAD, BUT I DO NOT KNOW WHERE HIS BODY IS HIDDEN. IT ALSO SEEMS THAT THE AUTOBOTS ARE WORKING WITH THE HUMANS."

"DOES THIS POSE A PROBLEM?"

"I HAVE DESTROYED BOTH *BEFORE.* I CAN DO IT AGAIN."

"I HAVE SENT DOWN REINFORCEMENTS TO ASSIST US. THERE ARE OTHERS WHO REMAIN IN STASIS ON THE SHIP."

"THEN I SHALL GO RETRIEVE THEM. GIVE ME THE SHIP'S LOCATION AND WE WILL RETURN EN MASSE!"

"AS YOU COMMAND. UNTIL YOU RETURN, I HAVE ORDERS TO FOLLOW."

"WHATEVER YOU SAY, *SOUNDWAVE.*"

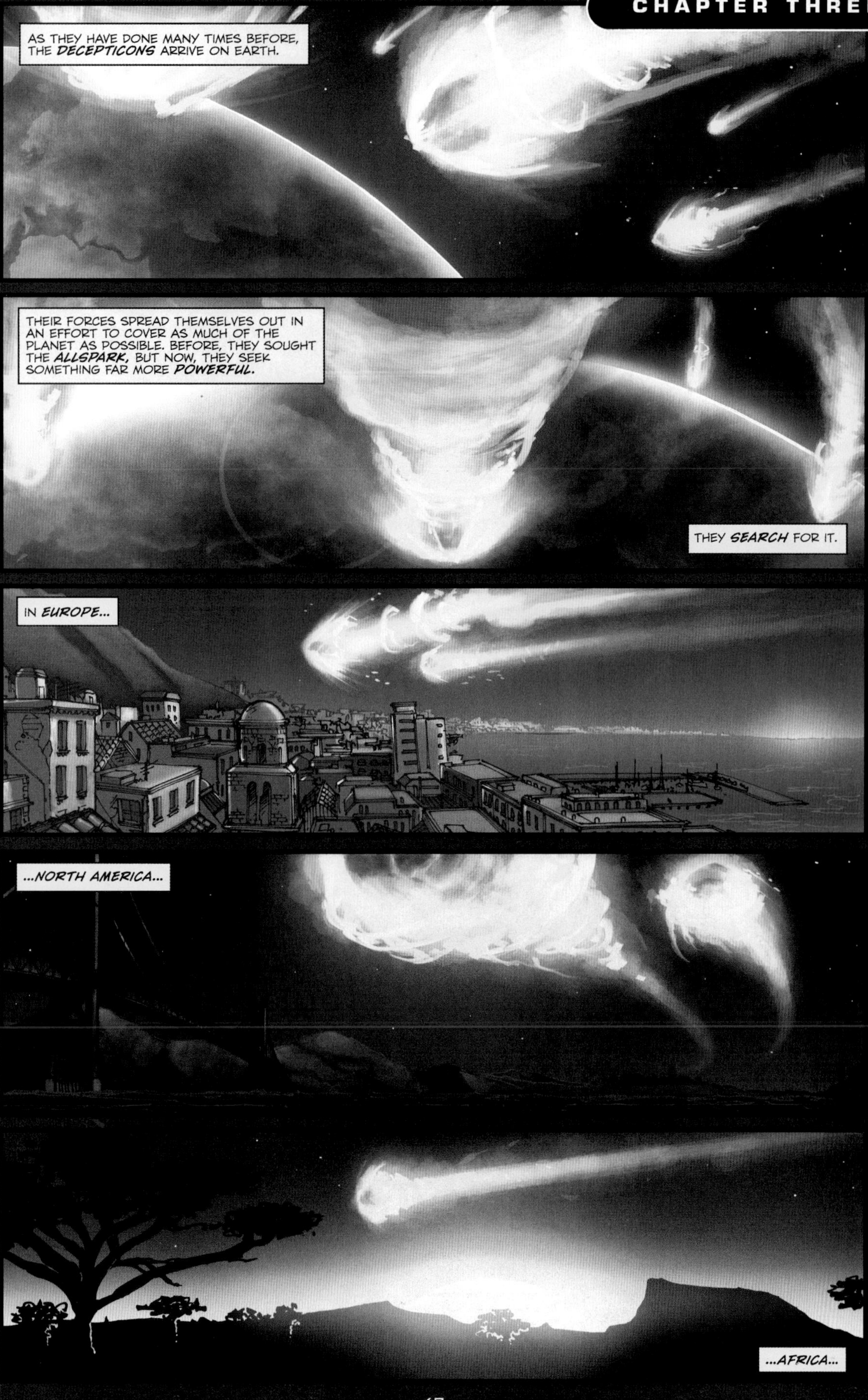
AS THEY HAVE DONE MANY TIMES BEFORE, THE DECEPTICONS ARRIVE ON EARTH.
THEIR FORCES SPREAD THEMSELVES OUT IN AN EFFORT TO COVER AS MUCH OF THE PLANET AS POSSIBLE. BEFORE, THEY SOUGHT THE ALLSPARK, BUT NOW, THEY SEEK SOMETHING FAR MORE POWERFUL.
THEY SEARCH FOR IT.
IN EUROPE...
...NORTH AMERICA...
...AFRICA...

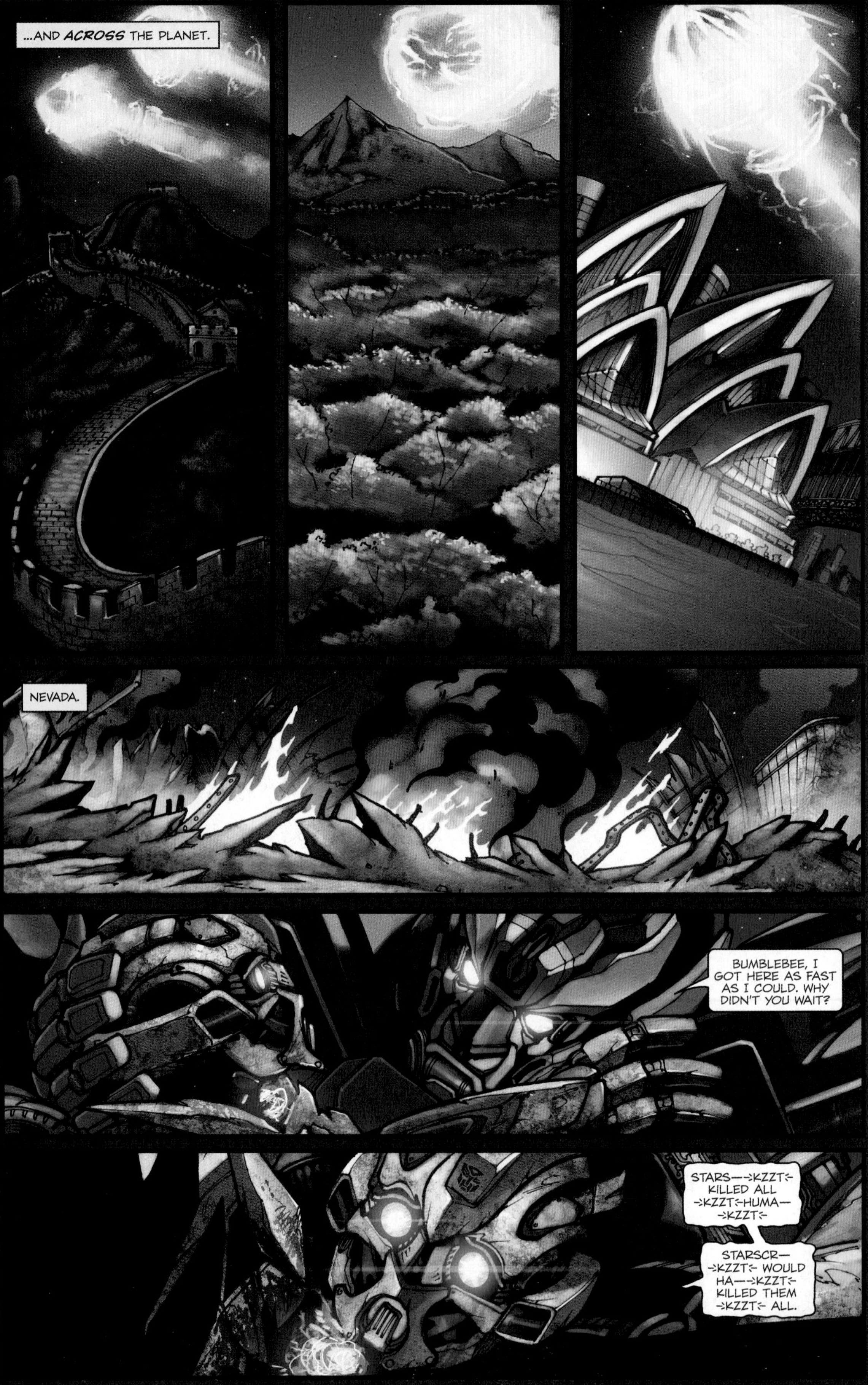
...AND ACROSS THE PLANET.
NEVADA.
BUMBLEBEE, I GOT HERE AS FAST AS I COULD. WHY DIDN'T YOU WAIT?
STARS— -KZZT- KILLED ALL -KZZT- HUMA— -KZZT-
STARSCR— -KZZT- WOULD HA— -KZZT- KILLED THEM -KZZT- ALL.

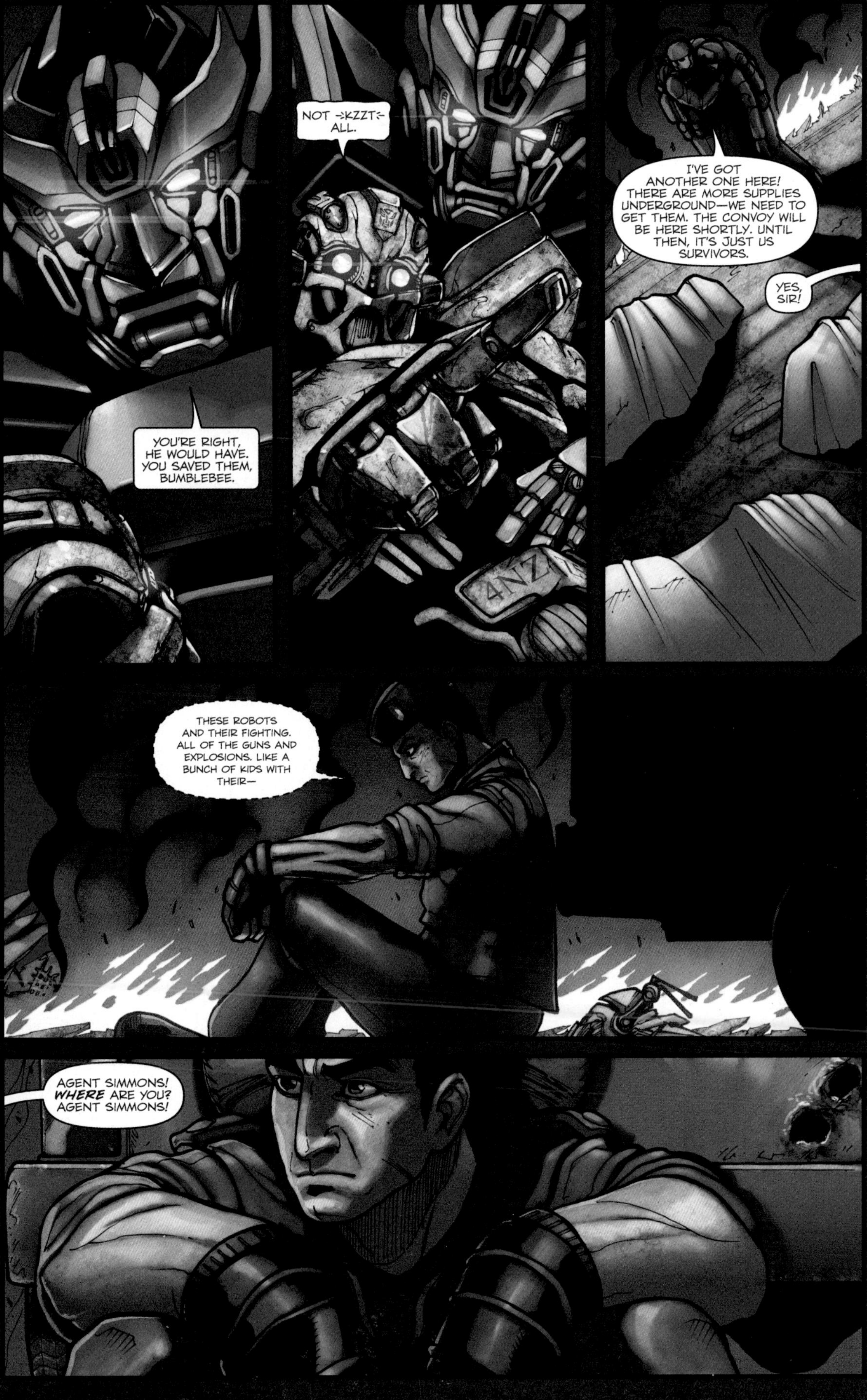
YOU'RE RIGHT, HE WOULD HAVE. YOU SAVED THEM, BUMBLEBEE.
NOT -KZZT- ALL.
4NZ
I'VE GOT ANOTHER ONE HERE! THERE ARE MORE SUPPLIES UNDERGROUND—WE NEED TO GET THEM. THE CONVOY WILL BE HERE SHORTLY. UNTIL THEN, IT'S JUST US SURVIVORS.
YES, SIR!
THESE ROBOTS AND THEIR FIGHTING. ALL OF THE GUNS AND EXPLOSIONS. LIKE A BUNCH OF KIDS WITH THEIR—
AGENT SIMMONS! *WHERE* ARE YOU? AGENT SIMMONS!

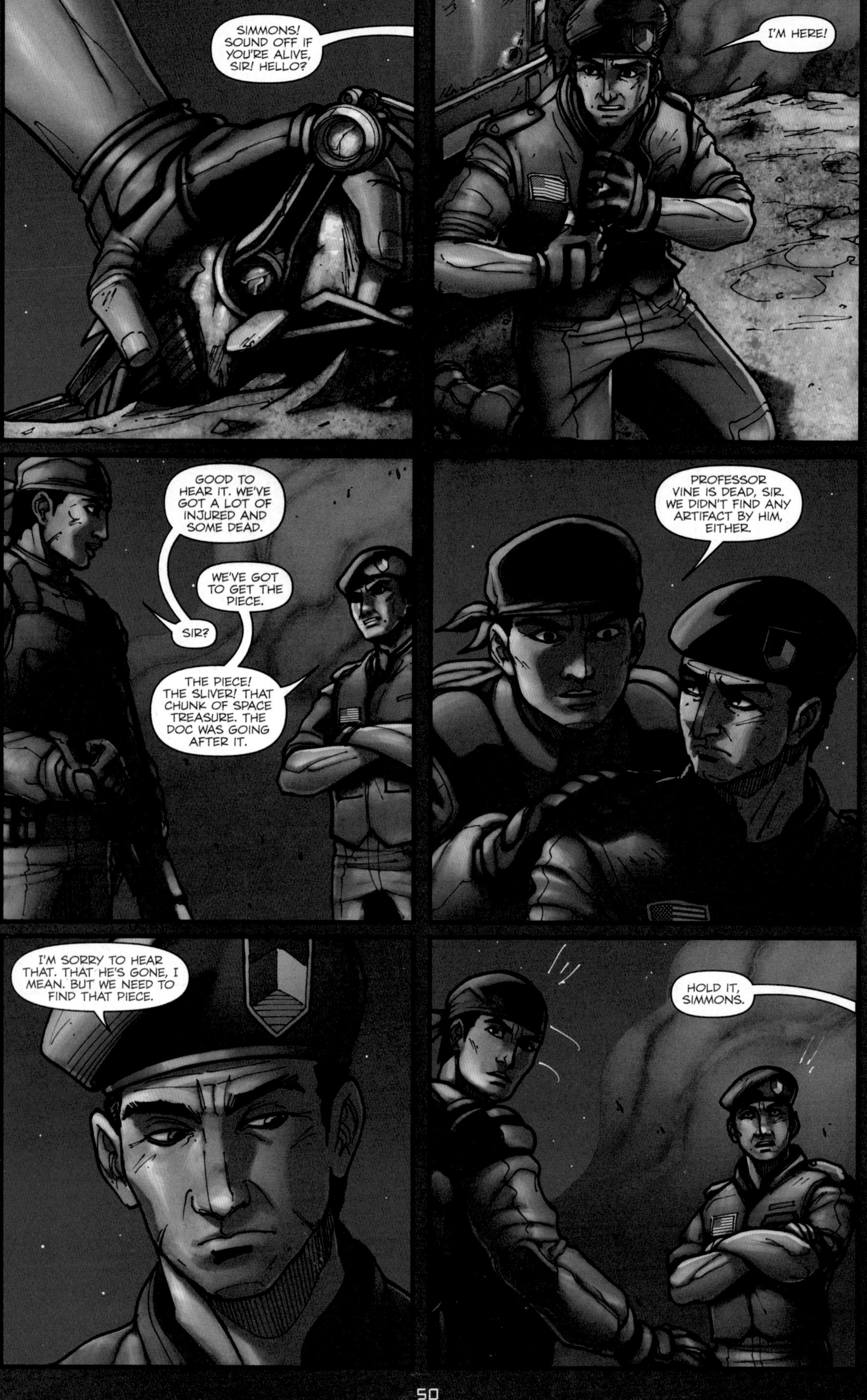
SIMMONS! SOUND OFF IF YOU'RE ALIVE, SIR! HELLO?
I'M HERE!
GOOD TO HEAR IT. WE'VE GOT A LOT OF INJURED AND SOME DEAD.
WE'VE GOT TO GET THE PIECE.
SIR?
THE PIECE! THE SLIVER! THAT CHUNK OF SPACE TREASURE. THE DOC WAS GOING AFTER IT.
PROFESSOR VINE IS DEAD, SIR. WE DIDN'T FIND ANY ARTIFACT BY HIM, EITHER.
I'M SORRY TO HEAR THAT. THAT HE'S GONE, I MEAN. BUT WE NEED TO FIND THAT PIECE.
HOLD IT, SIMMONS.

WE'RE UNDER ORDERS. YOU'RE *NOT* TO GO ANYWHERE.

WHAT DO YOU MEAN, ORDERS?! I GIVE THE ORDERS HERE, NOT YOU, CAPTAIN!

I'M SORRY, SIR. BUT MY ORDERS...

...COME FROM *HIGHER* UP.

THIS IS AGENT SIMMONS. GO AHEAD.

SIMMONS, THIS IS SECRETARY KELLER. YOU ARE TO REPORT TO CAPTAIN LENNOX FOR IMMEDIATE REMOVAL FROM THE SITE. IF YOU DO NOT GO PEACEFULLY, THEY WILL BE AUTHORIZED TO USE FORCE. YOUR SERVICES ARE *NO LONGER* NEEDED.

WE HAVE TEAMS EN ROUTE TO HELP CLEAN UP THE MESS AND DISPOSE OF THE ALIEN REMAINS ONCE AND FOR ALL. THE AGENCY KNOWN AS SECTOR SEVEN IS AT THIS POINT OFFICIALLY *DISBANDED.*

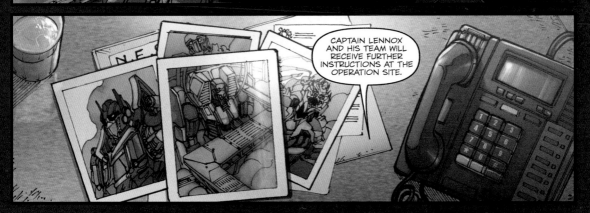

CAPTAIN LENNOX AND HIS TEAM WILL RECEIVE FURTHER INSTRUCTIONS AT THE OPERATION SITE.

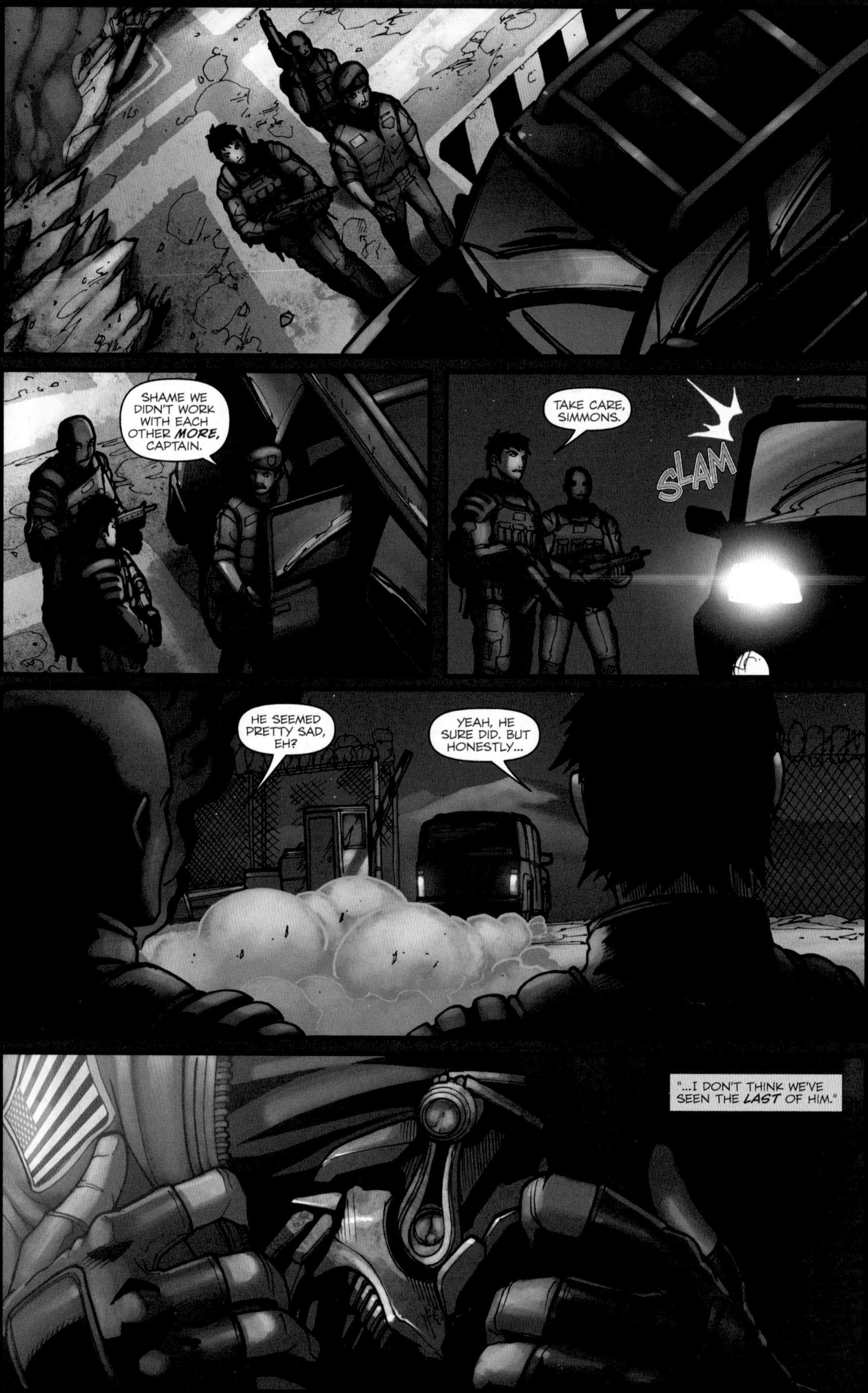
SHAME WE DIDN'T WORK WITH EACH OTHER *MORE,* CAPTAIN.
TAKE CARE, SIMMONS.
SLAM
HE SEEMED PRETTY SAD, EH?
YEAH, HE SURE DID. BUT HONESTLY...
"...I DON'T THINK WE'VE SEEN THE *LAST* OF HIM."

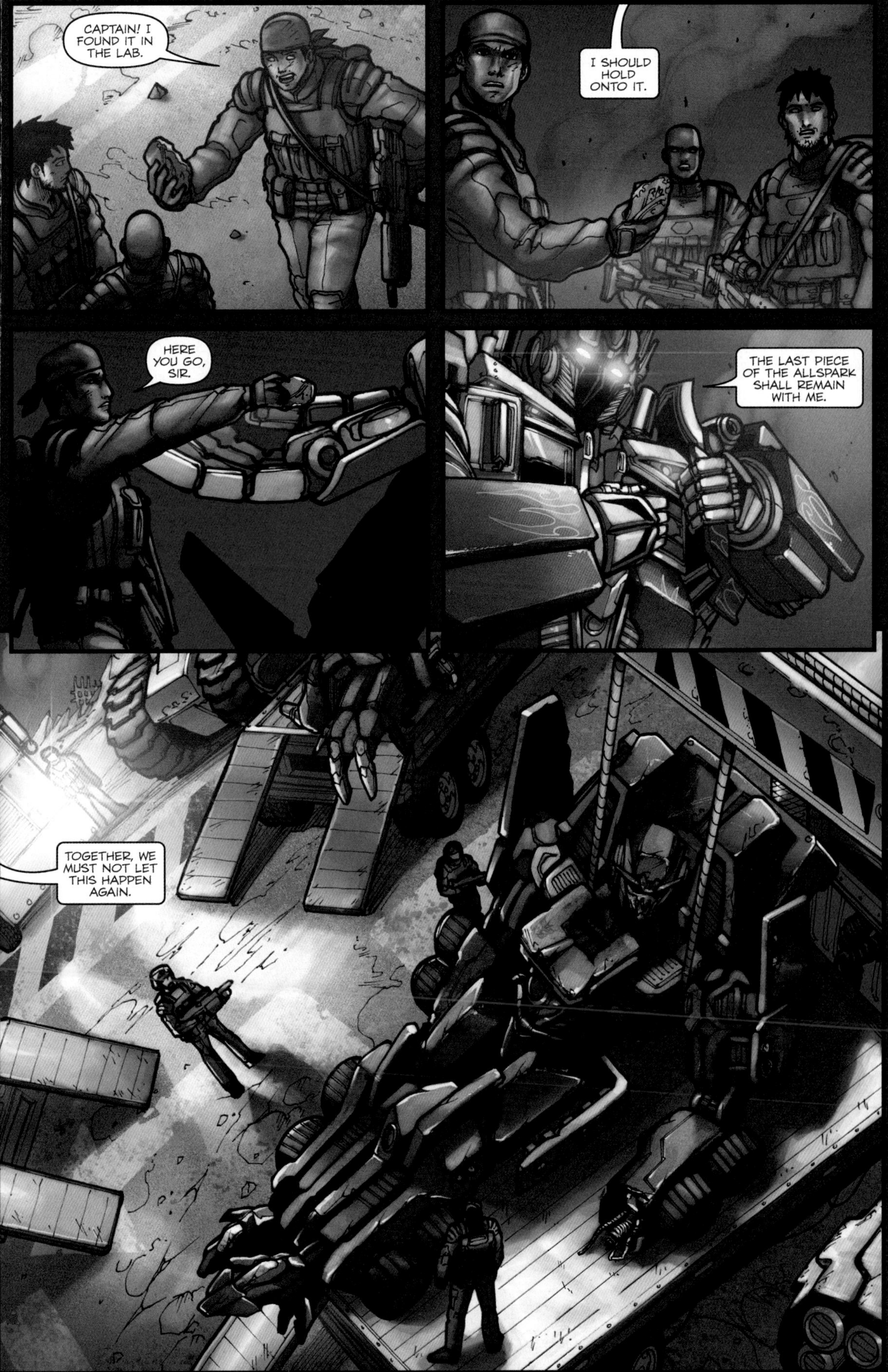
CAPTAIN! I FOUND IT IN THE LAB.
I SHOULD HOLD ONTO IT.
HERE YOU GO, SIR.
THE LAST PIECE OF THE ALLSPARK SHALL REMAIN WITH ME.
TOGETHER, WE MUST NOT LET THIS HAPPEN AGAIN.

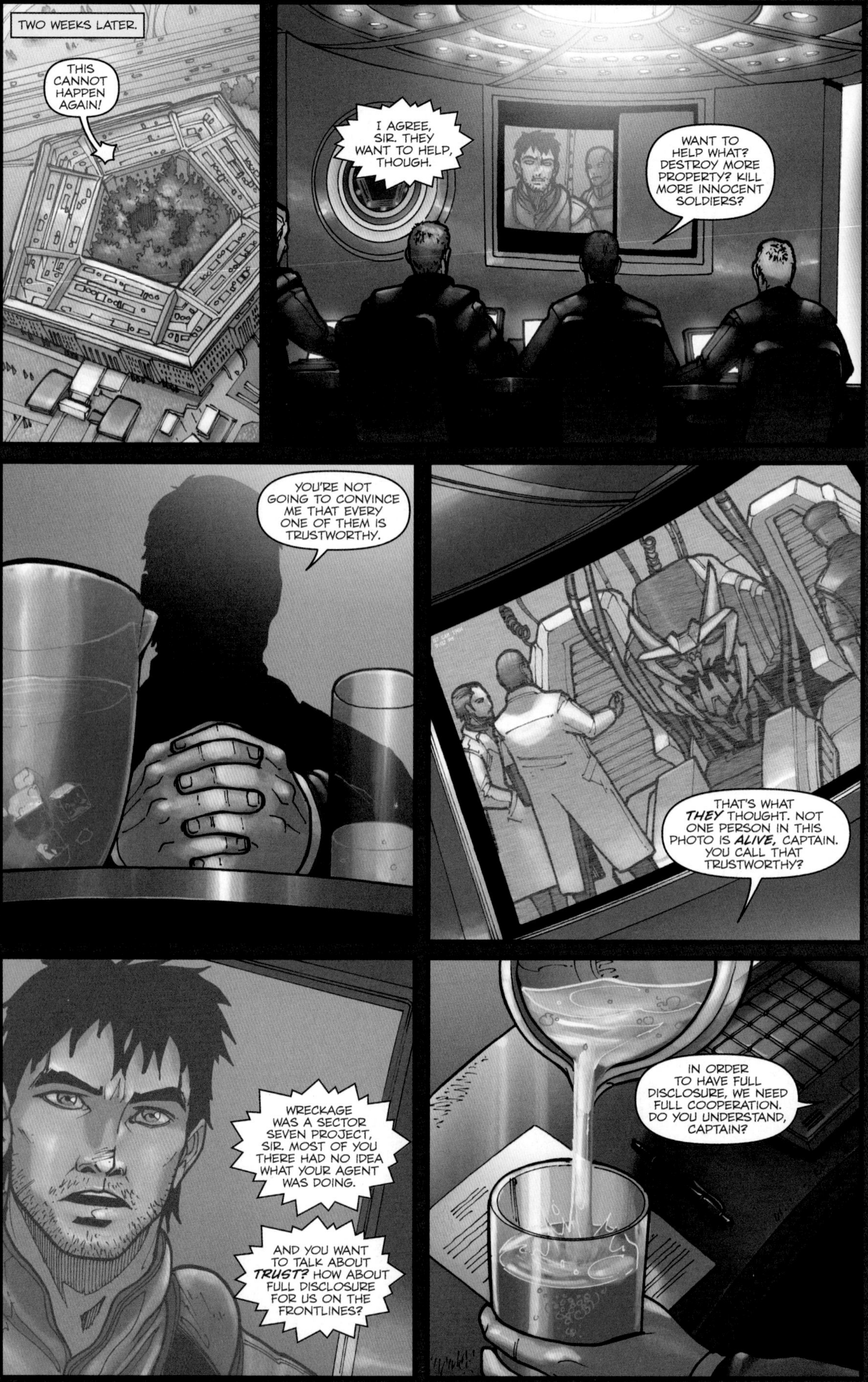
TWO WEEKS LATER.
THIS CANNOT HAPPEN AGAIN!
I AGREE, SIR. THEY WANT TO HELP, THOUGH.
WANT TO HELP WHAT? DESTROY MORE PROPERTY? KILL MORE INNOCENT SOLDIERS?
YOU'RE NOT GOING TO CONVINCE ME THAT EVERY ONE OF THEM IS TRUSTWORTHY.
THAT'S WHAT *THEY* THOUGHT. NOT ONE PERSON IN THIS PHOTO IS *ALIVE,* CAPTAIN. YOU CALL THAT TRUSTWORTHY?
WRECKAGE WAS A SECTOR SEVEN PROJECT, SIR. MOST OF YOU THERE HAD NO IDEA WHAT YOUR AGENT WAS DOING.
AND YOU WANT TO TALK ABOUT *TRUST?* HOW ABOUT FULL DISCLOSURE FOR US ON THE FRONTLINES?
IN ORDER TO HAVE FULL DISCLOSURE, WE NEED FULL COOPERATION. DO YOU UNDERSTAND, CAPTAIN?

~SIGH~ YES, SIR.

VERY GOOD, CAPTAIN. FINISH YOUR CURRENT TASK. YOU'LL RECEIVE YOUR ORDERS ONCE YOU REACH YOUR NEXT DESTINATION. IT'S *YOUR TEAM* NOW, CAPTAIN. YOUR RESPONSIBILITY.

I UNDERSTAND, SIR. HOW—

TSSHH

WHAT A JERK.

LET'S GET TO THE MAIN HANGAR DECK. WE SHOULD BE THERE WITH *THEM*.

RIGHT, LET'S GO.

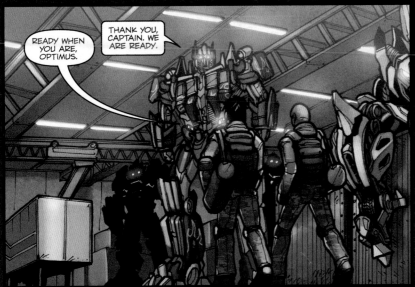

READY WHEN YOU ARE, OPTIMUS.

THANK YOU, CAPTAIN. WE ARE READY.

THIS IS EPPS. WE'RE ALL SET DOWN HERE, ADMIRAL.

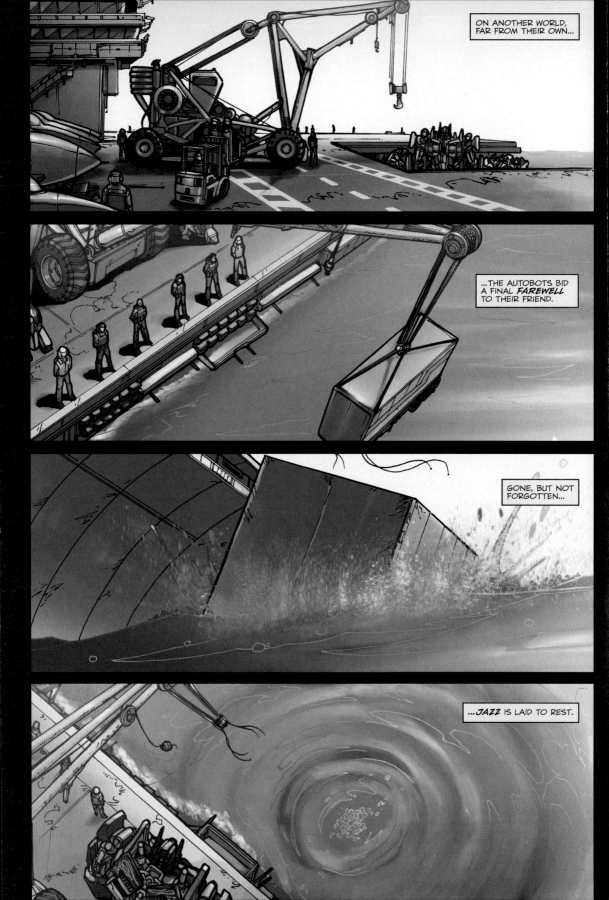

ON ANOTHER WORLD, FAR FROM THEIR OWN...

...THE AUTOBOTS BID A FINAL *FAREWELL* TO THEIR FRIEND.

GONE, BUT NOT FORGOTTEN...

...*JAZZ* IS LAID TO REST.

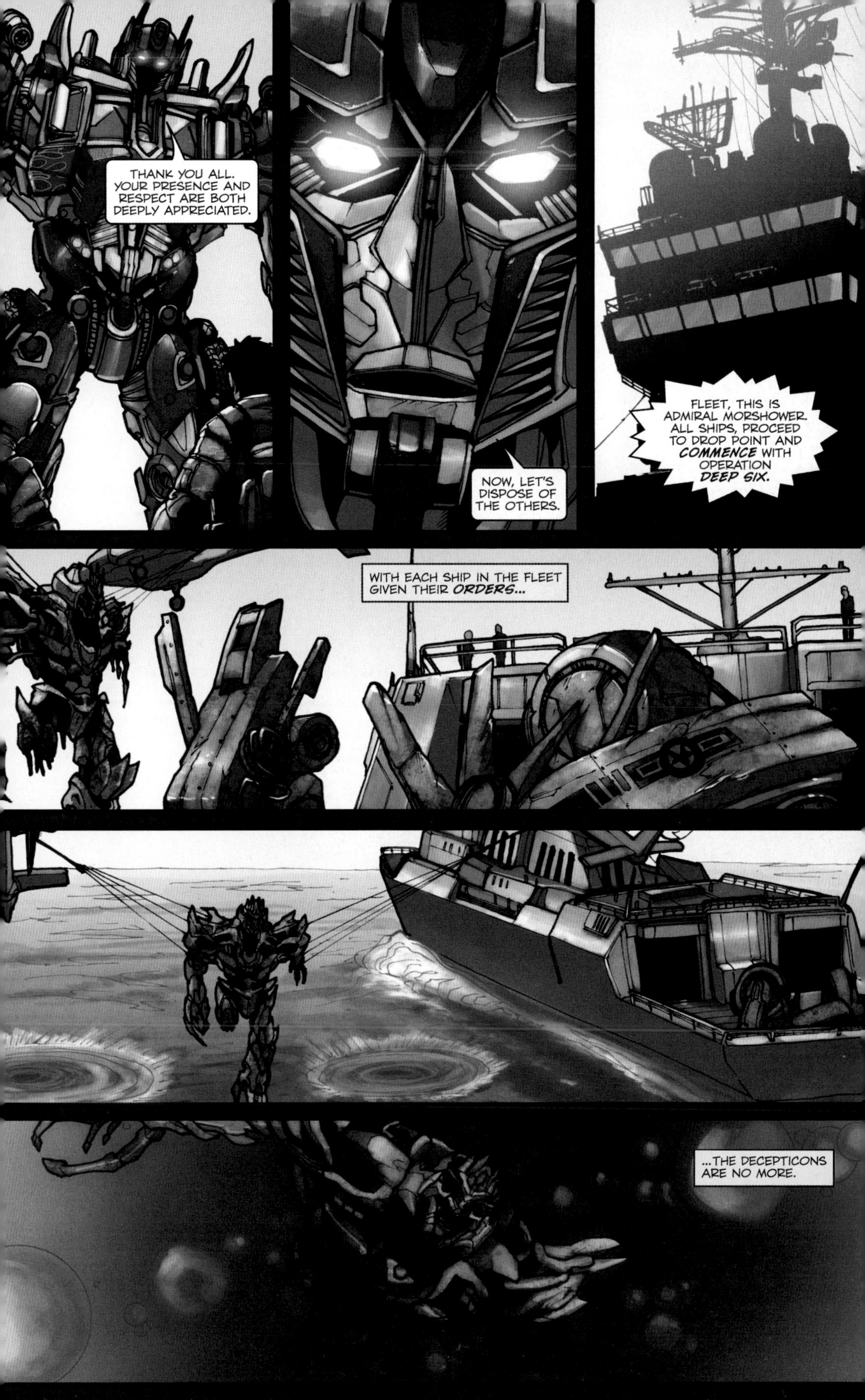
THANK YOU ALL. YOUR PRESENCE AND RESPECT ARE BOTH DEEPLY APPRECIATED.
NOW, LET'S DISPOSE OF THE OTHERS.
FLEET, THIS IS ADMIRAL MORSHOWER. ALL SHIPS, PROCEED TO DROP POINT AND COMMENCE WITH OPERATION DEEP SIX.
WITH EACH SHIP IN THE FLEET GIVEN THEIR ORDERS...
...THE DECEPTICONS ARE NO MORE.

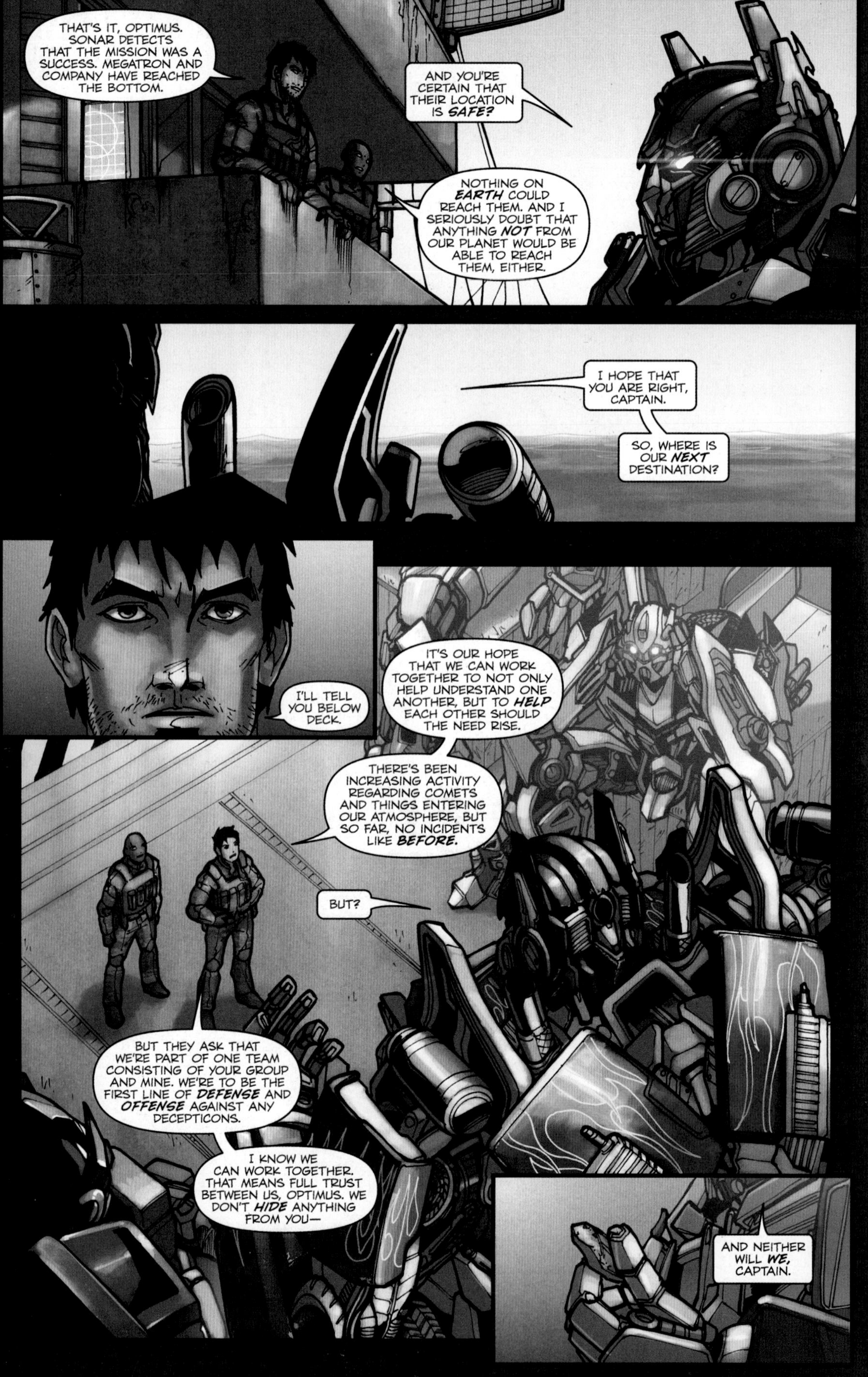
THAT'S IT, OPTIMUS. SONAR DETECTS THAT THE MISSION WAS A SUCCESS. MEGATRON AND COMPANY HAVE REACHED THE BOTTOM.
AND YOU'RE CERTAIN THAT THEIR LOCATION IS SAFE?
NOTHING ON EARTH COULD REACH THEM. AND I SERIOUSLY DOUBT THAT ANYTHING NOT FROM OUR PLANET WOULD BE ABLE TO REACH THEM, EITHER.
I HOPE THAT YOU ARE RIGHT, CAPTAIN.
SO, WHERE IS OUR NEXT DESTINATION?
I'LL TELL YOU BELOW DECK.
IT'S OUR HOPE THAT WE CAN WORK TOGETHER TO NOT ONLY HELP UNDERSTAND ONE ANOTHER, BUT TO HELP EACH OTHER SHOULD THE NEED RISE.
THERE'S BEEN INCREASING ACTIVITY REGARDING COMETS AND THINGS ENTERING OUR ATMOSPHERE, BUT SO FAR, NO INCIDENTS LIKE BEFORE.
BUT?
BUT THEY ASK THAT WE'RE PART OF ONE TEAM CONSISTING OF YOUR GROUP AND MINE. WE'RE TO BE THE FIRST LINE OF DEFENSE AND OFFENSE AGAINST ANY DECEPTICONS.
I KNOW WE CAN WORK TOGETHER. THAT MEANS FULL TRUST BETWEEN US, OPTIMUS. WE DON'T HIDE ANYTHING FROM YOU—
AND NEITHER WILL WE, CAPTAIN.

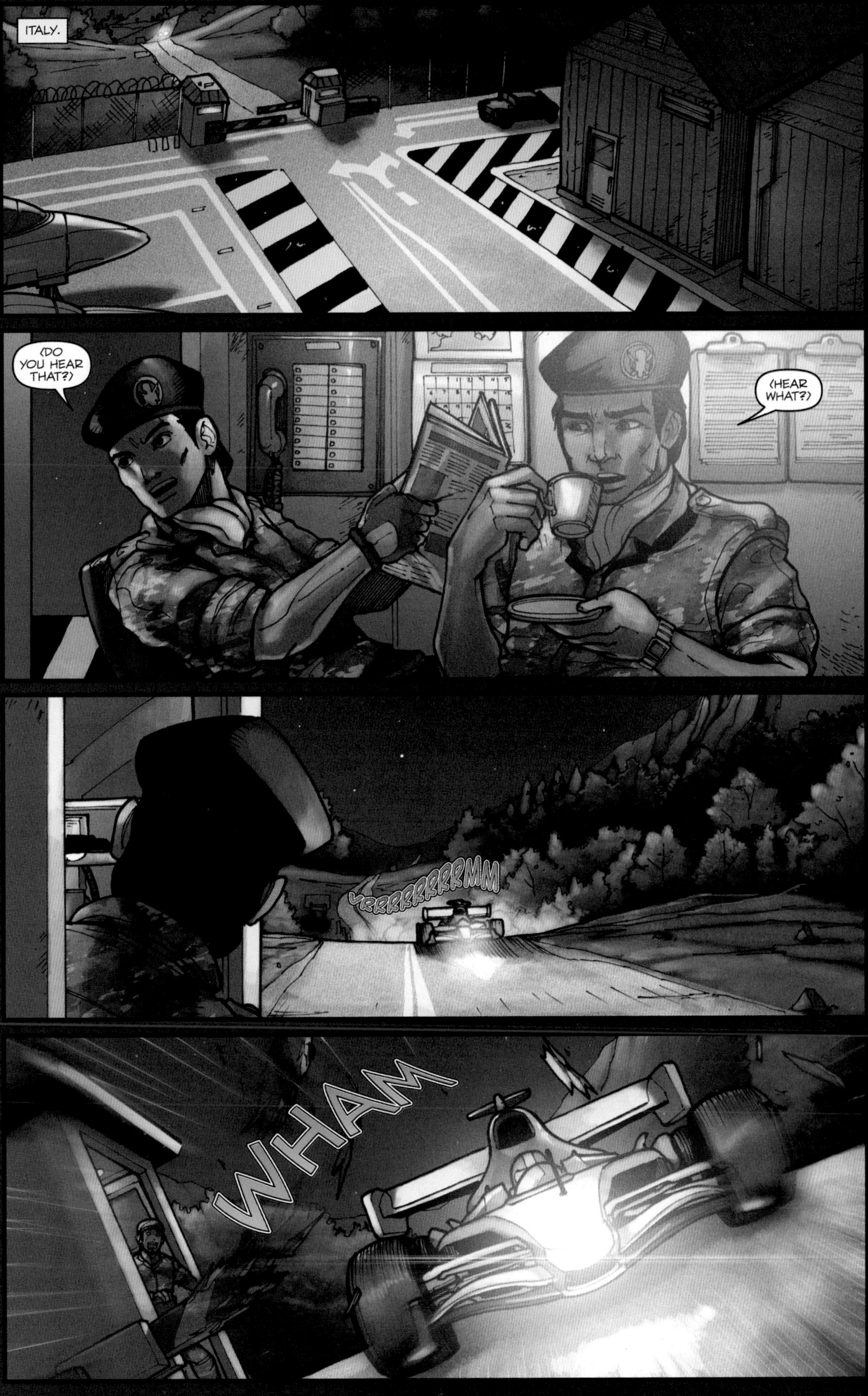
ITALY.
‹DO YOU HEAR THAT?›
‹HEAR WHAT?›
VRRRRRRRRRMM
WHAM

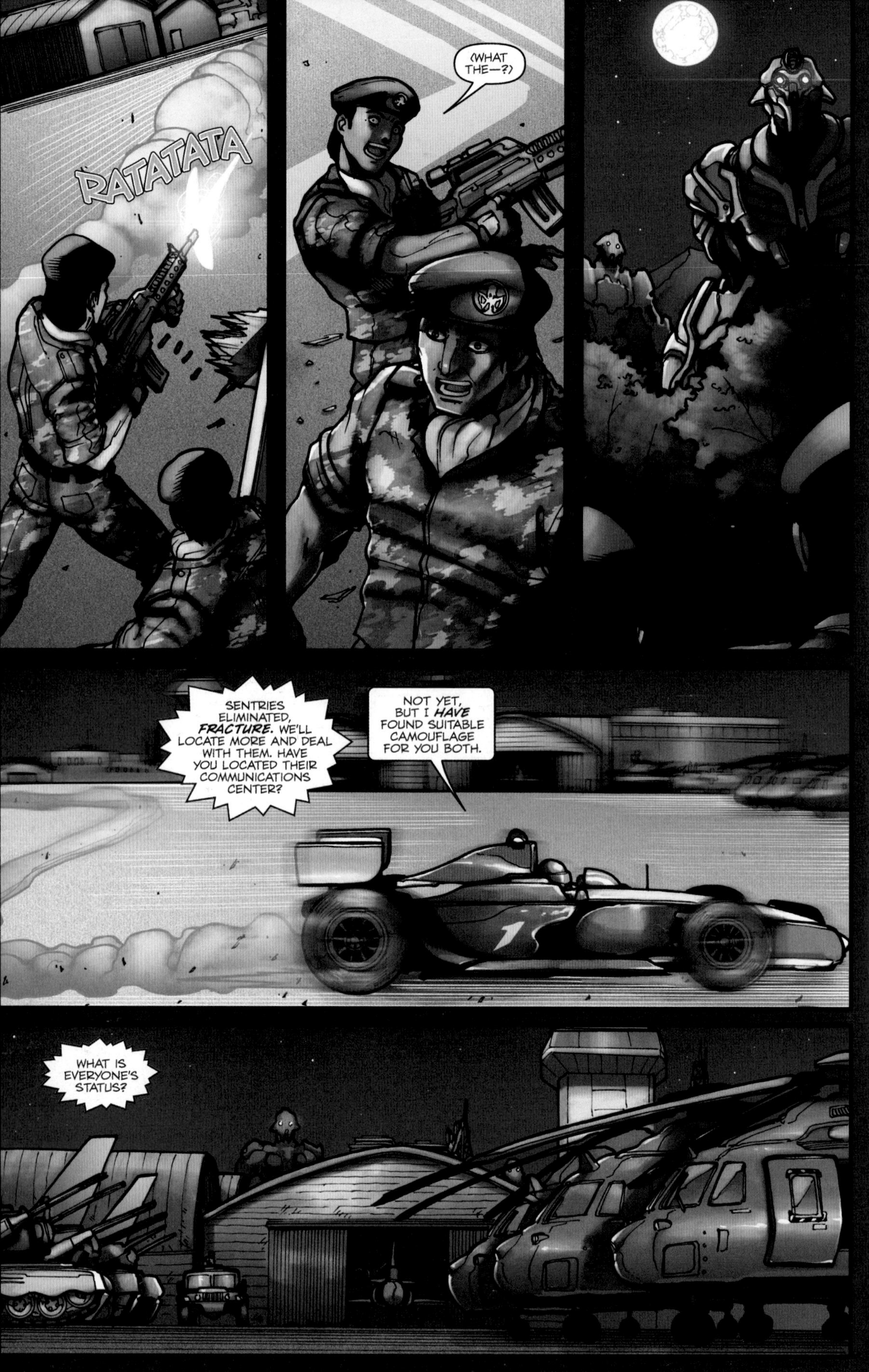
RATATATA
‹WHAT THE—?›
SENTRIES ELIMINATED, FRACTURE. WE'LL LOCATE MORE AND DEAL WITH THEM. HAVE YOU LOCATED THEIR COMMUNICATIONS CENTER?
NOT YET, BUT I HAVE FOUND SUITABLE CAMOUFLAGE FOR YOU BOTH.
WHAT IS EVERYONE'S STATUS?

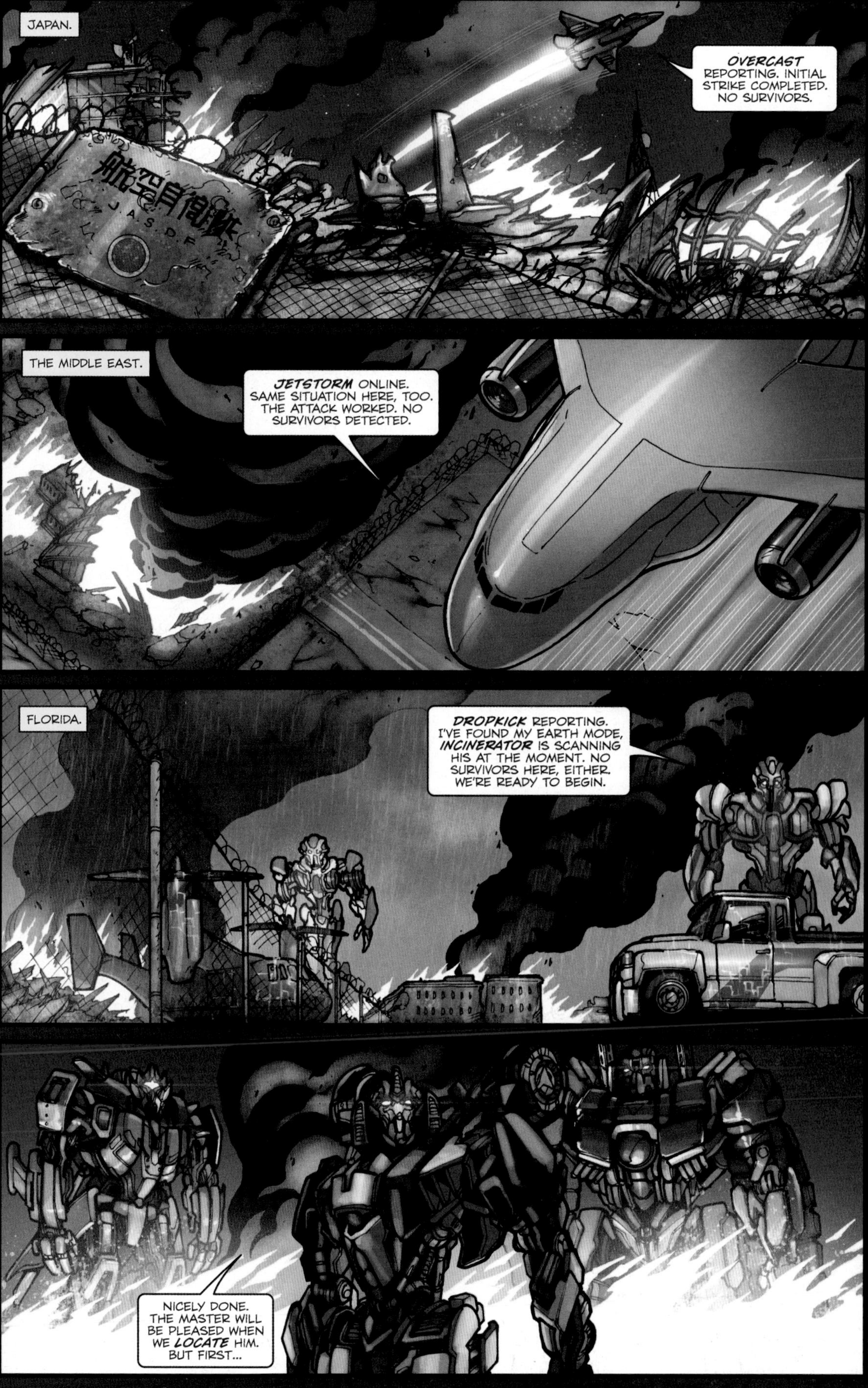
JAPAN.
OVERCAST REPORTING. INITIAL STRIKE COMPLETED. NO SURVIVORS.
航空自衛隊
J.A.S.D.F.
THE MIDDLE EAST.
JETSTORM ONLINE. SAME SITUATION HERE, TOO. THE ATTACK WORKED. NO SURVIVORS DETECTED.
FLORIDA.
DROPKICK REPORTING. I'VE FOUND MY EARTH MODE, INCINERATOR IS SCANNING HIS AT THE MOMENT. NO SURVIVORS HERE, EITHER. WE'RE READY TO BEGIN.
NICELY DONE. THE MASTER WILL BE PLEASED WHEN WE LOCATE HIM. BUT FIRST...

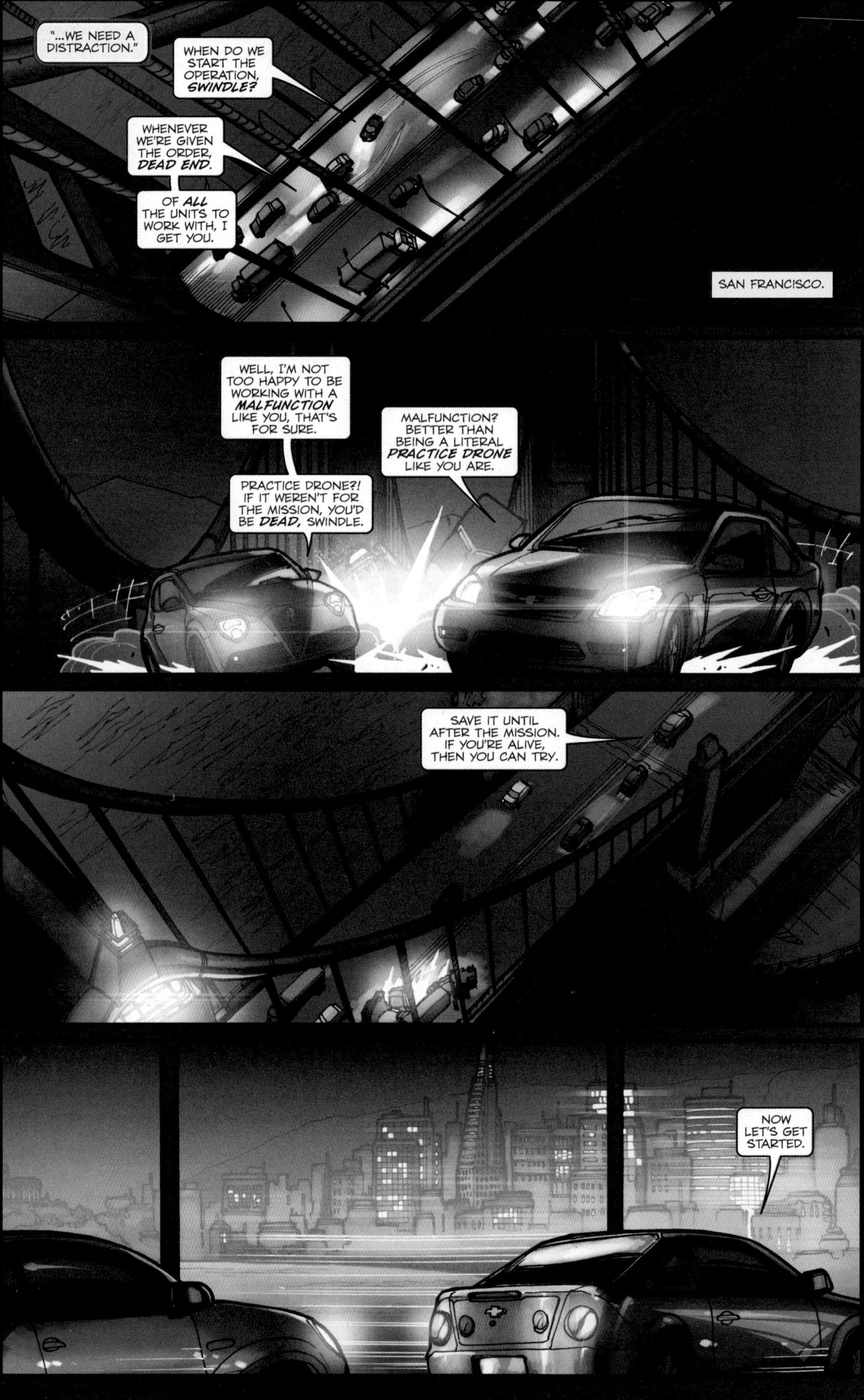
"...WE NEED A DISTRACTION."
WHEN DO WE START THE OPERATION, SWINDLE?
WHENEVER WE'RE GIVEN THE ORDER, DEAD END.
OF ALL THE UNITS TO WORK WITH, I GET YOU.
SAN FRANCISCO.
WELL, I'M NOT TOO HAPPY TO BE WORKING WITH A MALFUNCTION LIKE YOU, THAT'S FOR SURE.
MALFUNCTION? BETTER THAN BEING A LITERAL PRACTICE DRONE LIKE YOU ARE.
PRACTICE DRONE?! IF IT WEREN'T FOR THE MISSION, YOU'D BE DEAD, SWINDLE.
SAVE IT UNTIL AFTER THE MISSION. IF YOU'RE ALIVE, THEN YOU CAN TRY.
NOW LET'S GET STARTED.

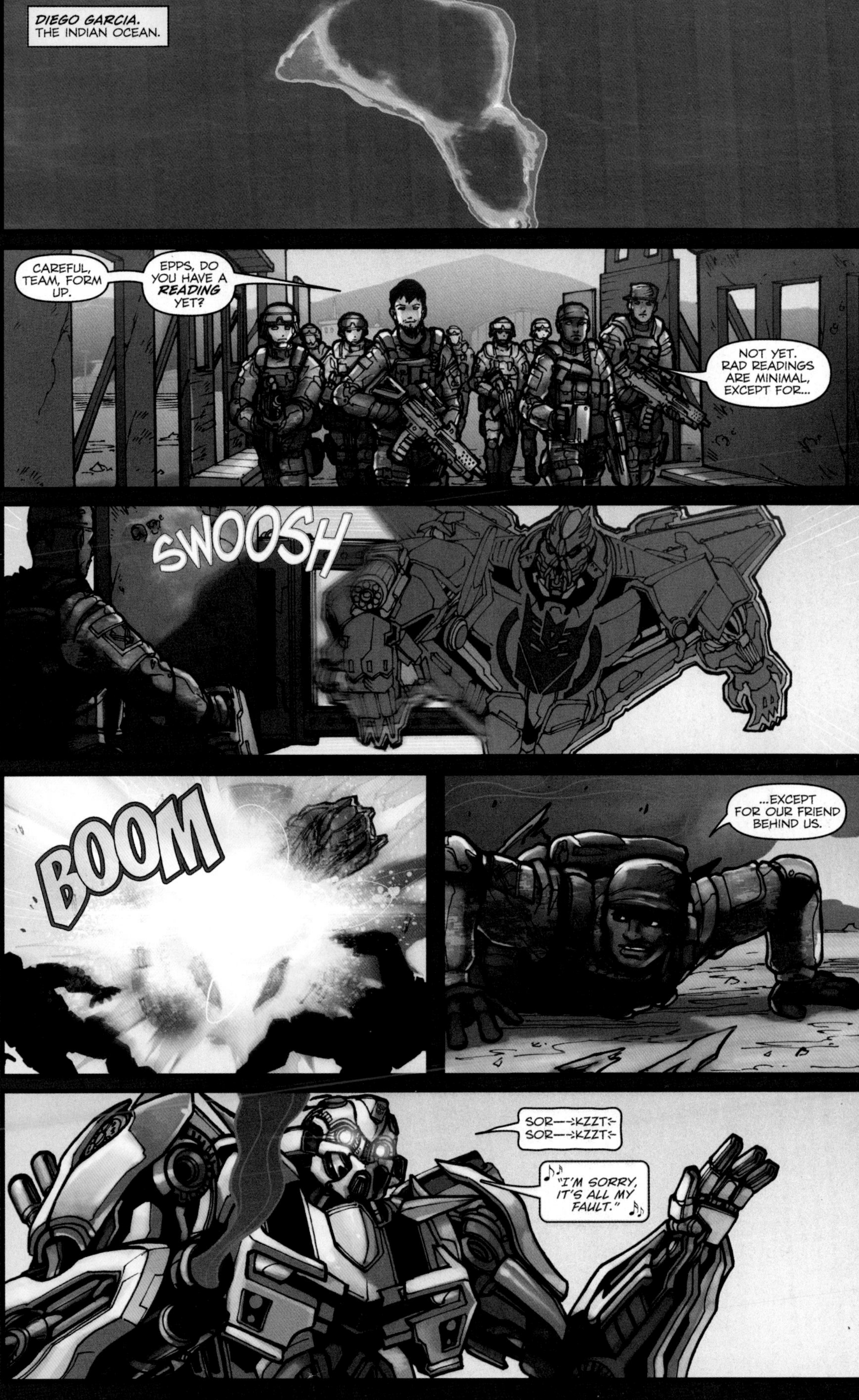
DIEGO GARCIA.
THE INDIAN OCEAN.
CAREFUL, TEAM, FORM UP.
EPPS, DO YOU HAVE A READING YET?
NOT YET. RAD READINGS ARE MINIMAL, EXCEPT FOR...
SWOOSH
BOOM
...EXCEPT FOR OUR FRIEND BEHIND US.
SOR—KZZT— SOR—KZZT—
"I'M SORRY, IT'S ALL MY FAULT."

CHK-CHK-CHK-CHK

AT EASE, EVERYONE, AT EASE. PUT THOSE SAFETIES ON!

NICE SHOT. THAT WAS AWESOME.

ARE YOU TWO FINISHED?

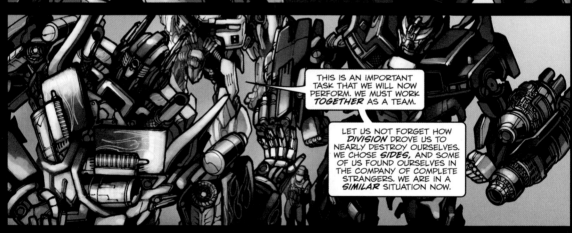

THIS IS AN IMPORTANT TASK THAT WE WILL NOW PERFORM. WE MUST WORK *TOGETHER* AS A TEAM.

LET US NOT FORGET HOW *DIVISION* DROVE US TO NEARLY DESTROY OURSELVES. WE CHOSE *SIDES,* AND SOME OF US FOUND OURSELVES IN THE COMPANY OF COMPLETE STRANGERS. WE ARE IN A *SIMILAR* SITUATION NOW.

HE'S RIGHT. NONE OF US EVER THOUGHT THAT WE'D BE GIVEN THIS OPPORTUNITY. WE'RE NOT PART OF SOME SHADOW GROUP ANYMORE. WE'RE A *TEAM* NOW, AND THEY'RE *PART* OF IT.

THINK OF ALL THAT WE'VE TAUGHT EACH OTHER AND ALL THAT WE WILL *CONTINUE* TO LEARN FROM ONE ANOTHER.

THIS IS THE CHANCE OF A LIFETIME, AND WHILE WE'RE HERE ON THIS ISLAND RUNNING DRILLS, THERE VERY WELL MAY BE THE NEED FOR OUR SERVICES. WHEN THAT DAY COMES, WE HAVE TO BE READY.

HUMAN OR AUTOBOT, WE'RE ALL BROTHERS HERE.

WE'RE DONE. FALL OUT.

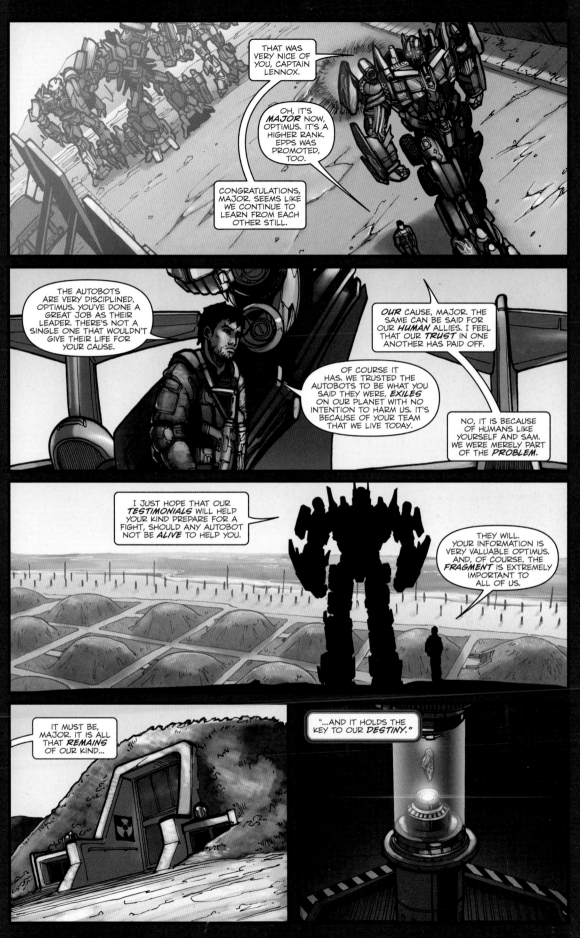

THAT WAS VERY NICE OF YOU, CAPTAIN LENNOX.

OH, IT'S *MAJOR* NOW, OPTIMUS. IT'S A HIGHER RANK. EPPS WAS PROMOTED, TOO.

CONGRATULATIONS, MAJOR. SEEMS LIKE WE CONTINUE TO LEARN FROM EACH OTHER STILL.

THE AUTOBOTS ARE VERY DISCIPLINED, OPTIMUS. YOU'VE DONE A GREAT JOB AS THEIR LEADER. THERE'S NOT A SINGLE ONE THAT WOULDN'T GIVE THEIR LIFE FOR YOUR CAUSE.

OUR CAUSE, MAJOR. THE SAME CAN BE SAID FOR OUR *HUMAN* ALLIES. I FEEL THAT OUR *TRUST* IN ONE ANOTHER HAS PAID OFF.

OF COURSE IT HAS. WE TRUSTED THE AUTOBOTS TO BE WHAT YOU SAID THEY WERE, *EXILES* ON OUR PLANET WITH NO INTENTION TO HARM US. IT'S BECAUSE OF YOUR TEAM THAT WE LIVE TODAY.

NO, IT IS BECAUSE OF HUMANS LIKE YOURSELF AND SAM. WE WERE MERELY PART OF THE *PROBLEM.*

I JUST HOPE THAT OUR *TESTIMONIALS* WILL HELP YOUR KIND PREPARE FOR A FIGHT, SHOULD ANY AUTOBOT NOT BE *ALIVE* TO HELP YOU.

THEY WILL. YOUR INFORMATION IS VERY VALUABLE OPTIMUS. AND, OF COURSE, THE *FRAGMENT* IS EXTREMELY IMPORTANT TO ALL OF US.

IT MUST BE, MAJOR. IT IS ALL THAT *REMAINS* OF OUR KIND...

"...AND IT HOLDS THE KEY TO OUR *DESTINY.*"

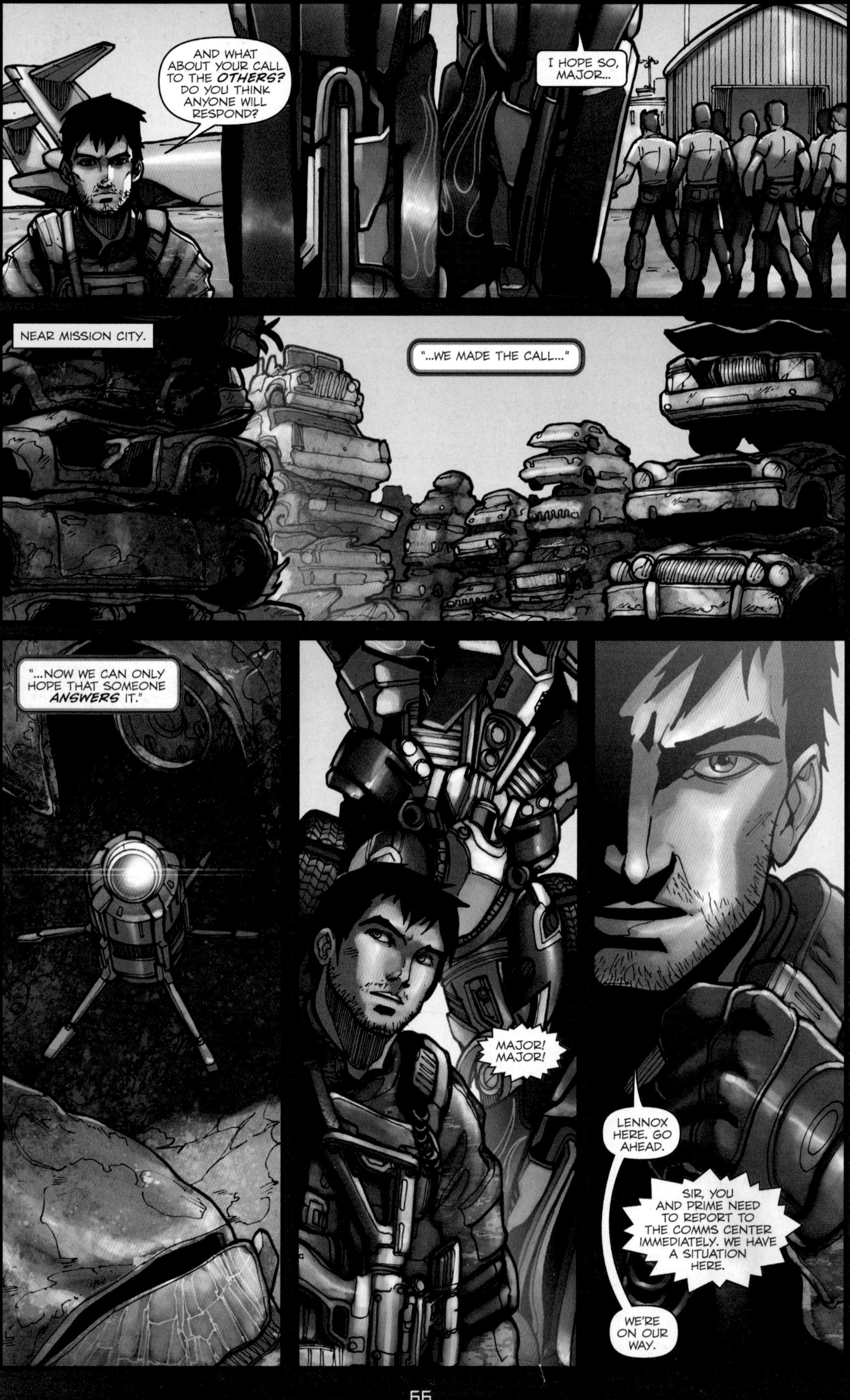
AND WHAT ABOUT YOUR CALL TO THE *OTHERS?* DO YOU THINK ANYONE WILL RESPOND?
I HOPE SO, MAJOR...
NEAR MISSION CITY.
"...WE MADE THE CALL..."
"...NOW WE CAN ONLY HOPE THAT SOMEONE *ANSWERS* IT."
MAJOR! MAJOR!
LENNOX HERE. GO AHEAD.
SIR, YOU AND PRIME NEED TO REPORT TO THE COMMS CENTER IMMEDIATELY. WE HAVE A SITUATION HERE.
WE'RE ON OUR WAY.

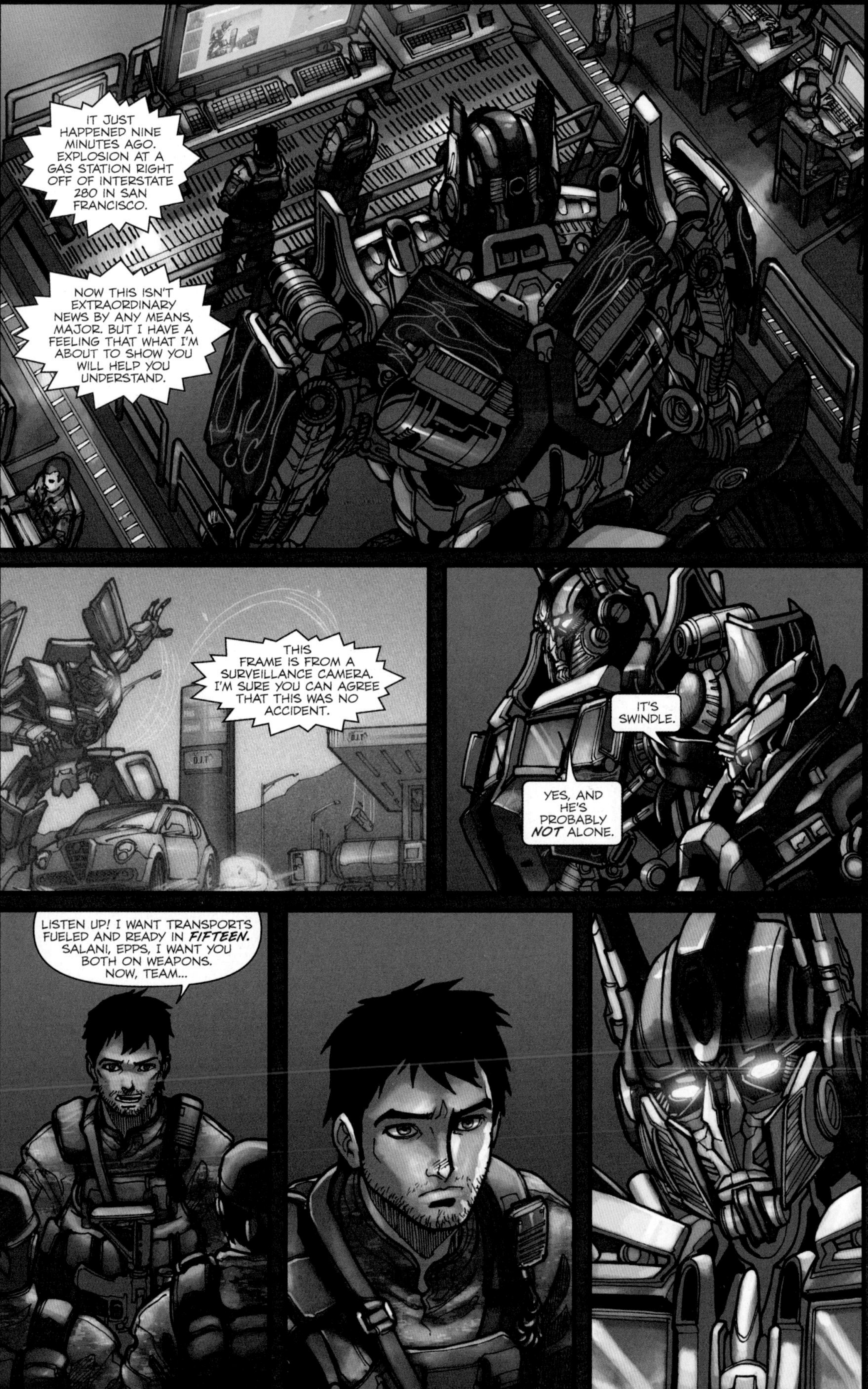
IT JUST HAPPENED NINE MINUTES AGO. EXPLOSION AT A GAS STATION RIGHT OFF OF INTERSTATE 280 IN SAN FRANCISCO.
NOW THIS ISN'T EXTRAORDINARY NEWS BY ANY MEANS, MAJOR. BUT I HAVE A FEELING THAT WHAT I'M ABOUT TO SHOW YOU WILL HELP YOU UNDERSTAND.
THIS FRAME IS FROM A SURVEILLANCE CAMERA. I'M SURE YOU CAN AGREE THAT THIS WAS NO ACCIDENT.
IT'S SWINDLE.
YES, AND HE'S PROBABLY NOT ALONE.
LISTEN UP! I WANT TRANSPORTS FUELED AND READY IN FIFTEEN. SALANI, EPPS, I WANT YOU BOTH ON WEAPONS. NOW, TEAM...

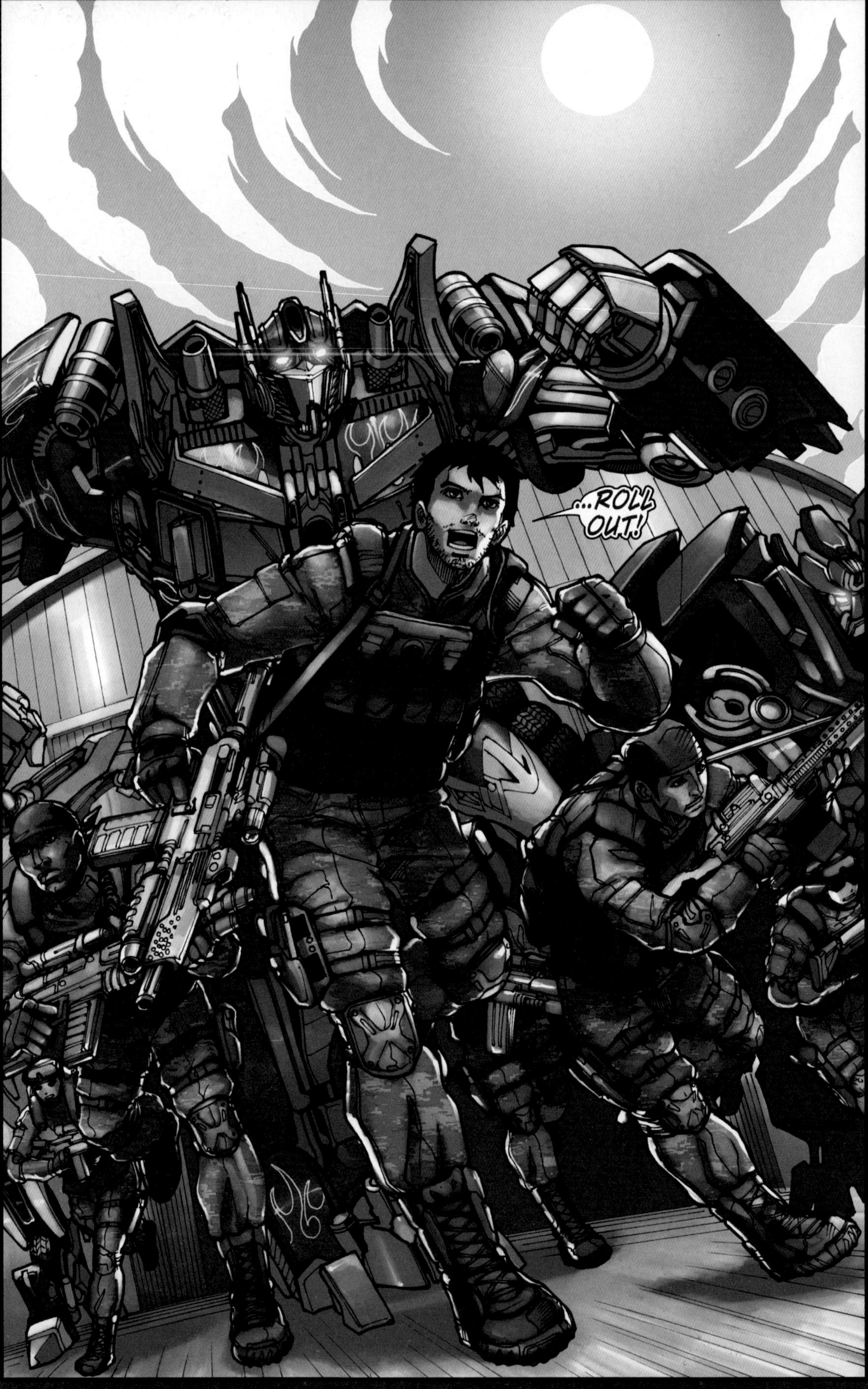
...ROLL OUT!

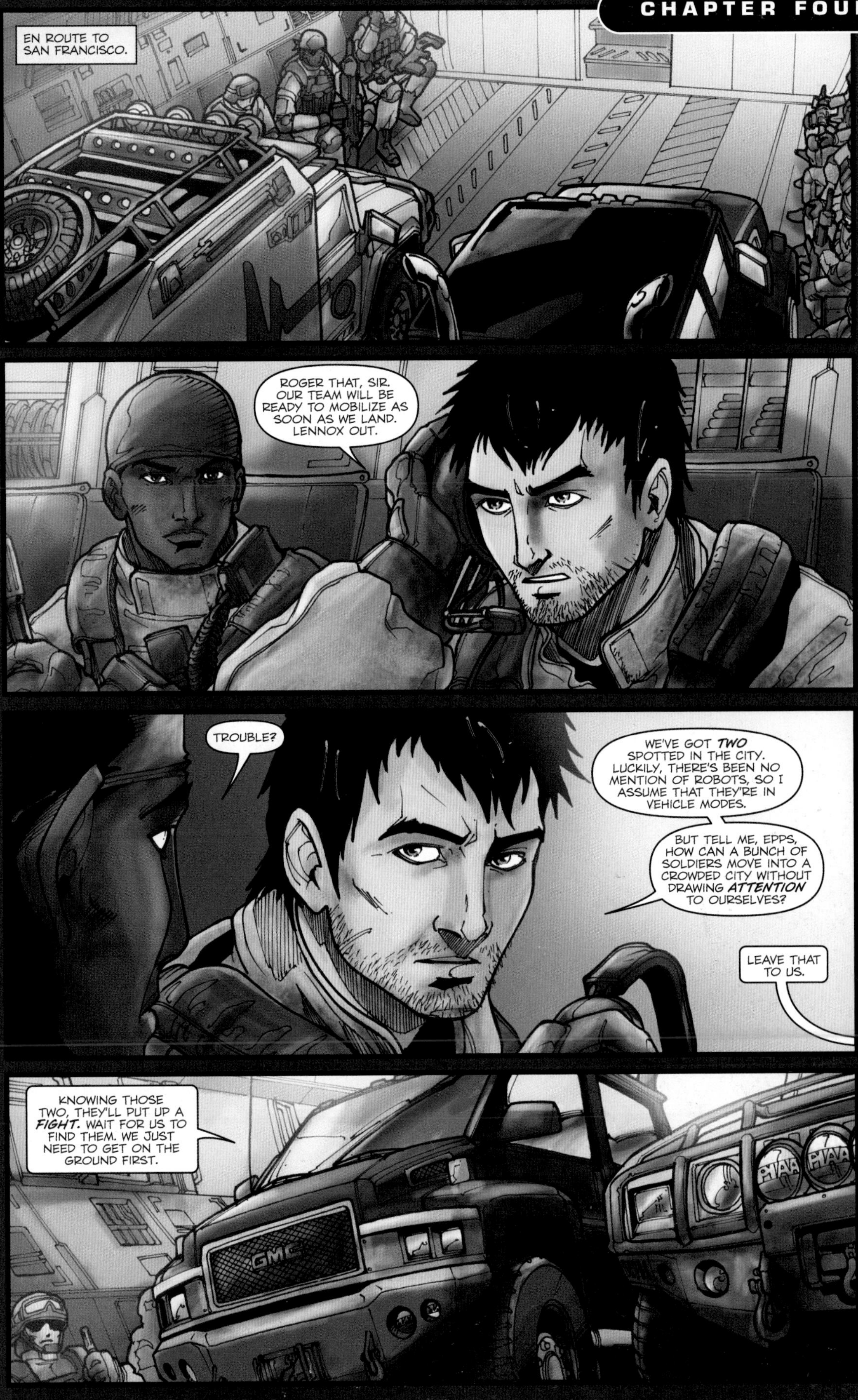
EN ROUTE TO SAN FRANCISCO.
ROGER THAT, SIR. OUR TEAM WILL BE READY TO MOBILIZE AS SOON AS WE LAND. LENNOX OUT.
TROUBLE?
WE'VE GOT ***TWO*** SPOTTED IN THE CITY. LUCKILY, THERE'S BEEN NO MENTION OF ROBOTS, SO I ASSUME THAT THEY'RE IN VEHICLE MODES.
BUT TELL ME, EPPS, HOW CAN A BUNCH OF SOLDIERS MOVE INTO A CROWDED CITY WITHOUT DRAWING ***ATTENTION*** TO OURSELVES?
LEAVE THAT TO US.
KNOWING THOSE TWO, THEY'LL PUT UP A ***FIGHT.*** WAIT FOR US TO FIND THEM. WE JUST NEED TO GET ON THE GROUND FIRST.
GMC

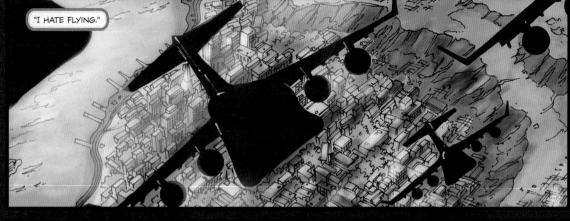

"I HATE FLYING."

OKAY, MEN. THIS IS THE *REAL* THING. NO MORE PRACTICES. TEAM THREE, YOU SERVE AS PERIMETER DEFENSE.

TEAM TWO, WE SET THE *TRAP*.

AND TEAM ONE HERE WILL FLUSH THEM OUT.

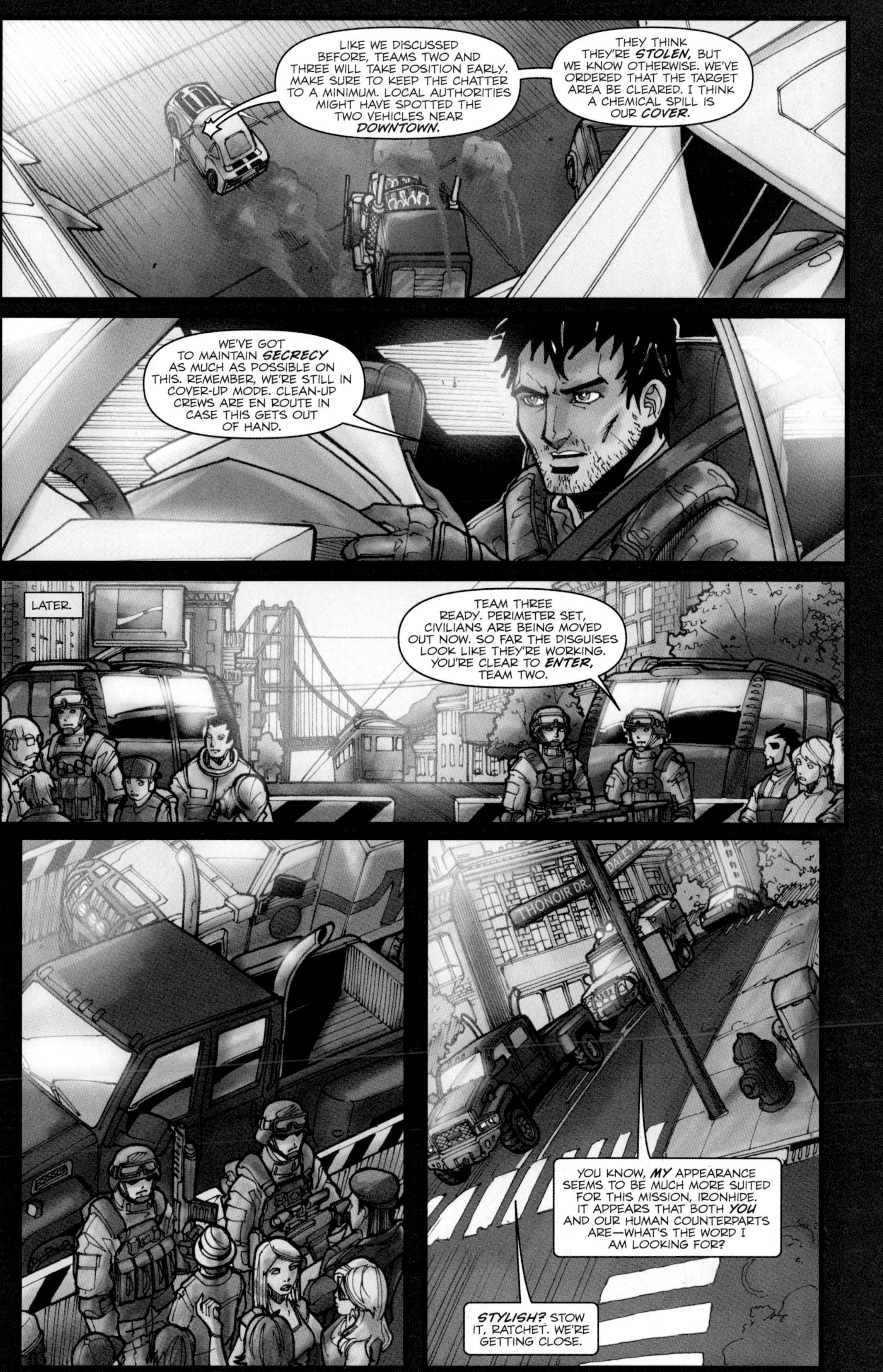
LIKE WE DISCUSSED BEFORE, TEAMS TWO AND THREE WILL TAKE POSITION EARLY. MAKE SURE TO KEEP THE CHATTER TO A MINIMUM. LOCAL AUTHORITIES MIGHT HAVE SPOTTED THE TWO VEHICLES NEAR DOWNTOWN.
THEY THINK THEY'RE STOLEN, BUT WE KNOW OTHERWISE. WE'VE ORDERED THAT THE TARGET AREA BE CLEARED. I THINK A CHEMICAL SPILL IS OUR COVER.
WE'VE GOT TO MAINTAIN SECRECY AS MUCH AS POSSIBLE ON THIS. REMEMBER, WE'RE STILL IN COVER-UP MODE. CLEAN-UP CREWS ARE EN ROUTE IN CASE THIS GETS OUT OF HAND.
LATER.
TEAM THREE READY. PERIMETER SET, CIVILIANS ARE BEING MOVED OUT NOW. SO FAR THE DISGUISES LOOK LIKE THEY'RE WORKING. YOU'RE CLEAR TO ENTER, TEAM TWO.
THONOIR DR.
YOU KNOW, MY APPEARANCE SEEMS TO BE MUCH MORE SUITED FOR THIS MISSION, IRONHIDE. IT APPEARS THAT BOTH YOU AND OUR HUMAN COUNTERPARTS ARE—WHAT'S THE WORD I AM LOOKING FOR?
STYLISH? STOW IT, RATCHET. WE'RE GETTING CLOSE.

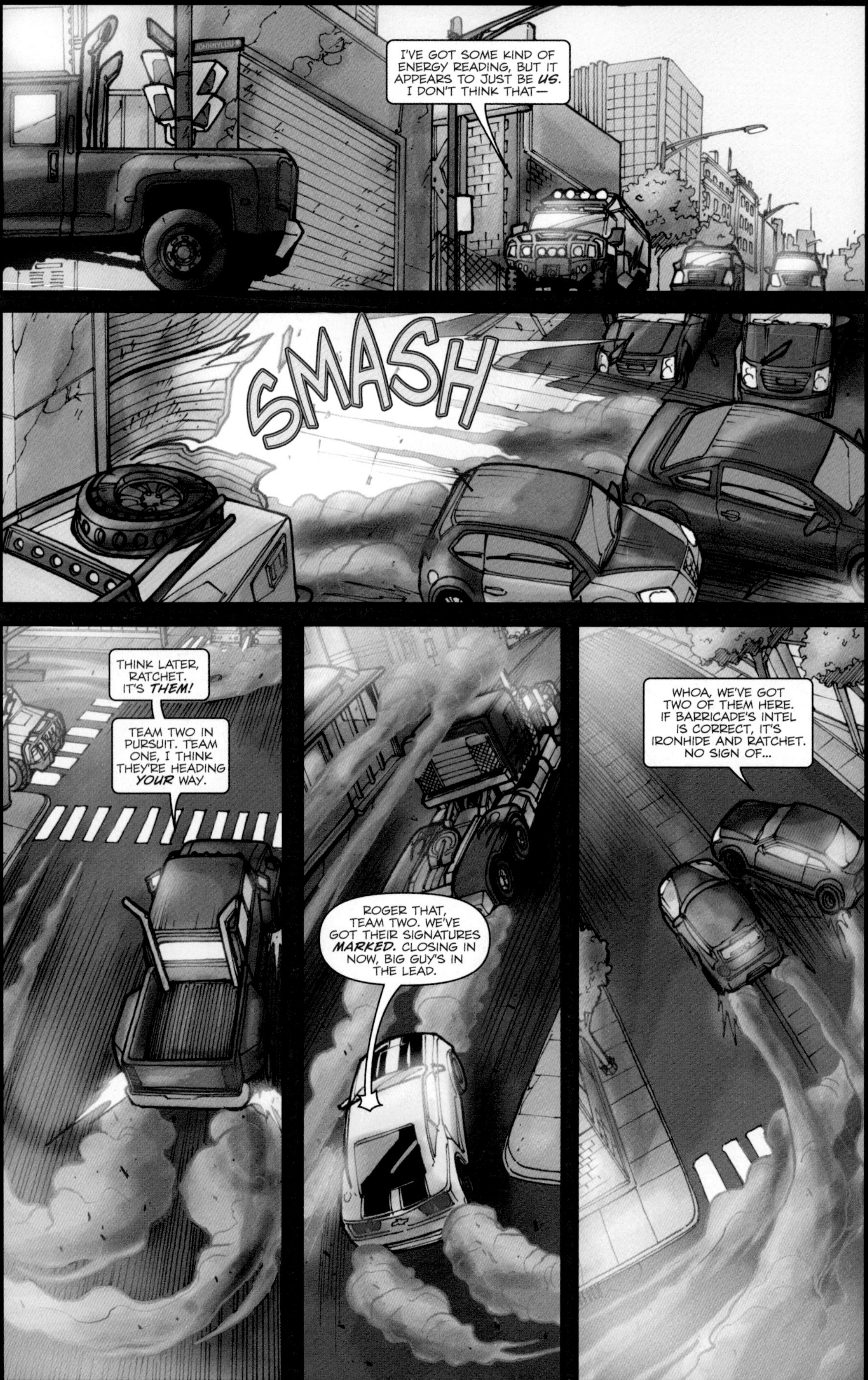
I'VE GOT SOME KIND OF ENERGY READING, BUT IT APPEARS TO JUST BE US. I DON'T THINK THAT—
SMASH
THINK LATER, RATCHET. IT'S THEM!
TEAM TWO IN PURSUIT. TEAM ONE, I THINK THEY'RE HEADING YOUR WAY.
ROGER THAT, TEAM TWO. WE'VE GOT THEIR SIGNATURES MARKED. CLOSING IN NOW, BIG GUY'S IN THE LEAD.
WHOA, WE'VE GOT TWO OF THEM HERE. IF BARRICADE'S INTEL IS CORRECT, IT'S IRONHIDE AND RATCHET. NO SIGN OF...

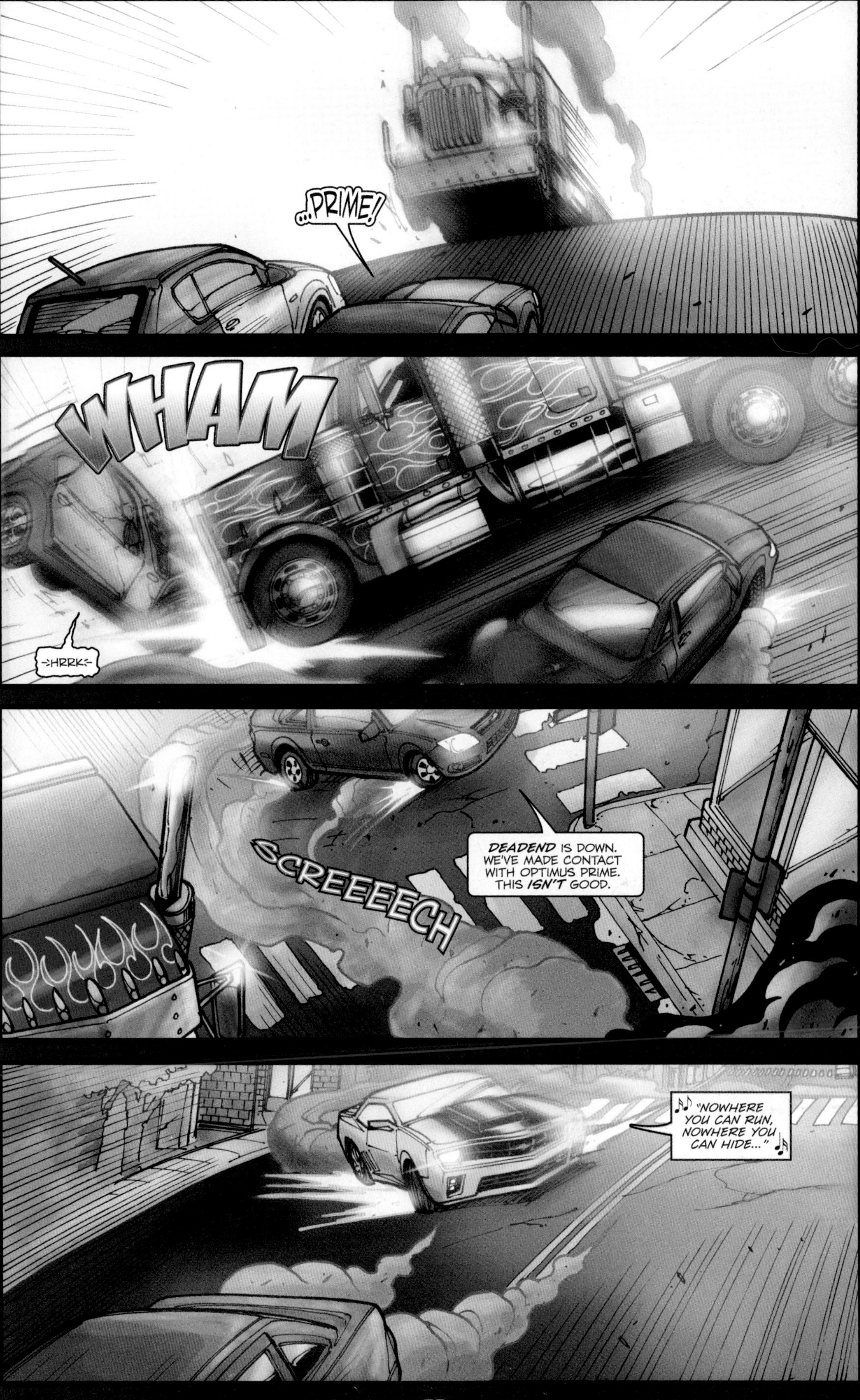
...PRIME!
WHAM
-HRRK-
SCREEEEECH
DEADEND IS DOWN. WE'VE MADE CONTACT WITH OPTIMUS PRIME. THIS ISN'T GOOD.
"NOWHERE YOU CAN RUN, NOWHERE YOU CAN HIDE..."

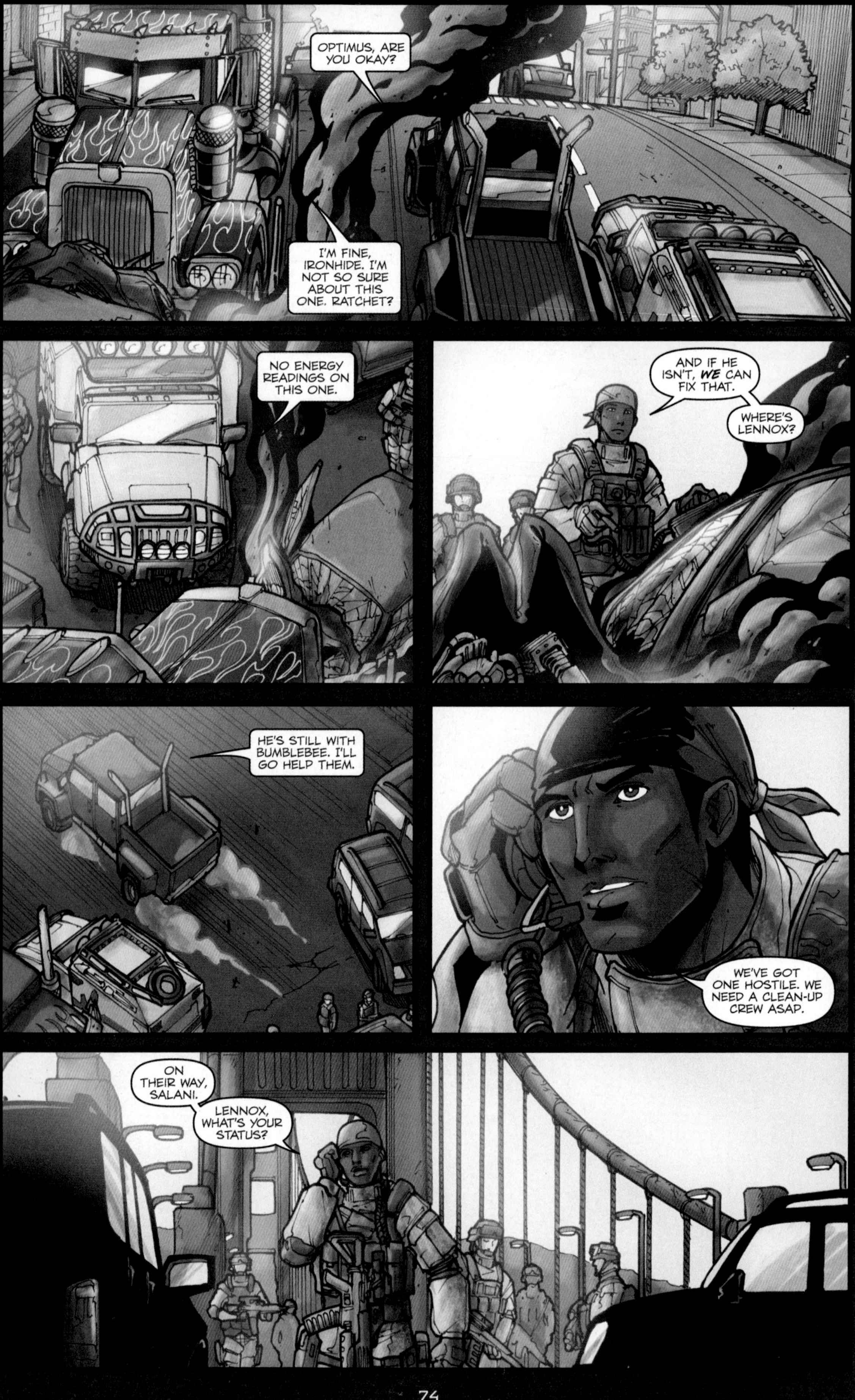
OPTIMUS, ARE YOU OKAY?
I'M FINE, IRONHIDE. I'M NOT SO SURE ABOUT THIS ONE. RATCHET?
NO ENERGY READINGS ON THIS ONE.
AND IF HE ISN'T, *WE* CAN FIX THAT.
WHERE'S LENNOX?
HE'S STILL WITH BUMBLEBEE. I'LL GO HELP THEM.
WE'VE GOT ONE HOSTILE. WE NEED A CLEAN-UP CREW ASAP.
ON THEIR WAY, SALANI.
LENNOX, WHAT'S YOUR STATUS?

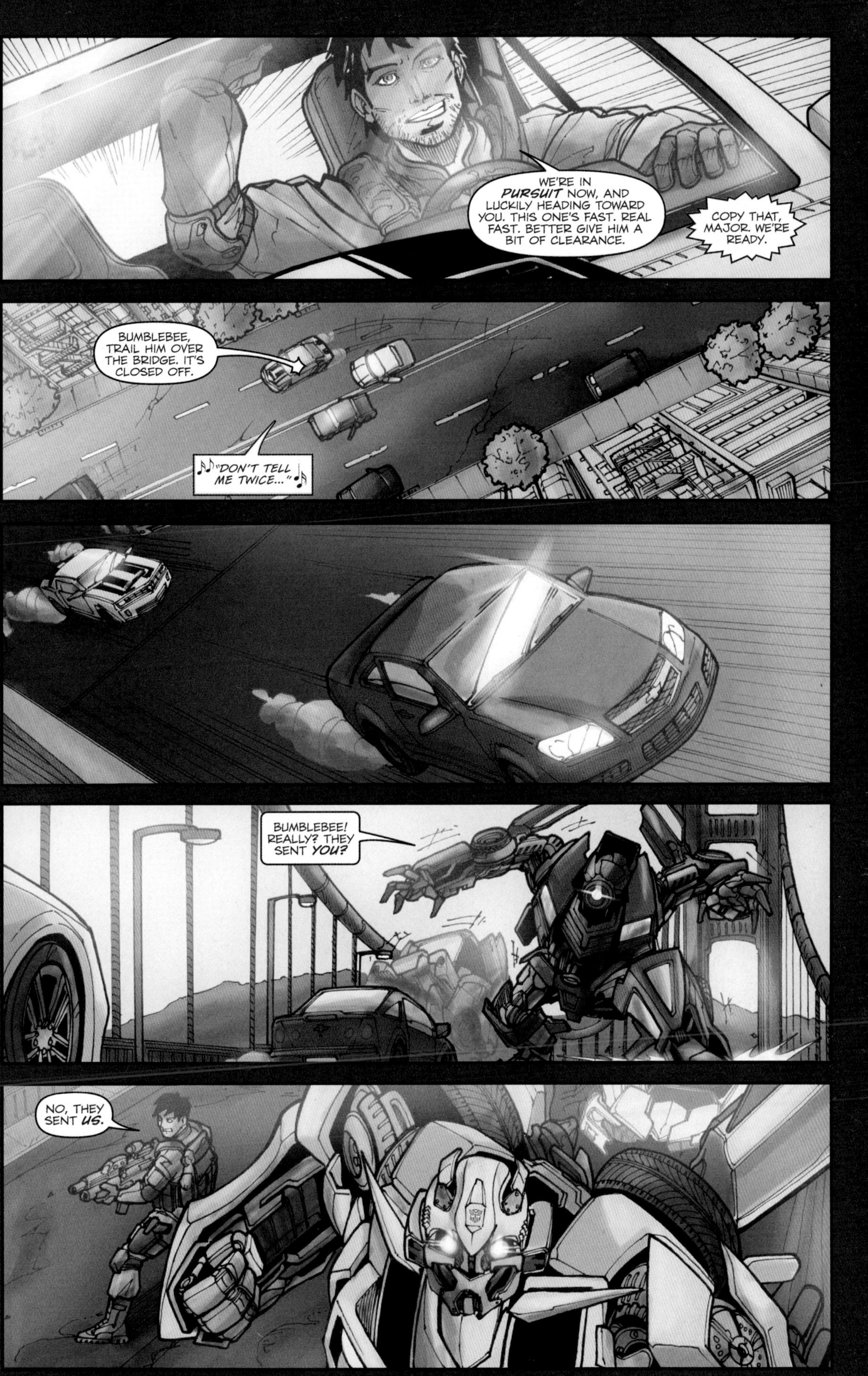
WE'RE IN PURSUIT NOW, AND LUCKILY HEADING TOWARD YOU. THIS ONE'S FAST. REAL FAST. BETTER GIVE HIM A BIT OF CLEARANCE.
COPY THAT, MAJOR. WE'RE READY.
BUMBLEBEE, TRAIL HIM OVER THE BRIDGE. IT'S CLOSED OFF.
"DON'T TELL ME TWICE..."
BUMBLEBEE! REALLY? THEY SENT YOU?
NO, THEY SENT US.

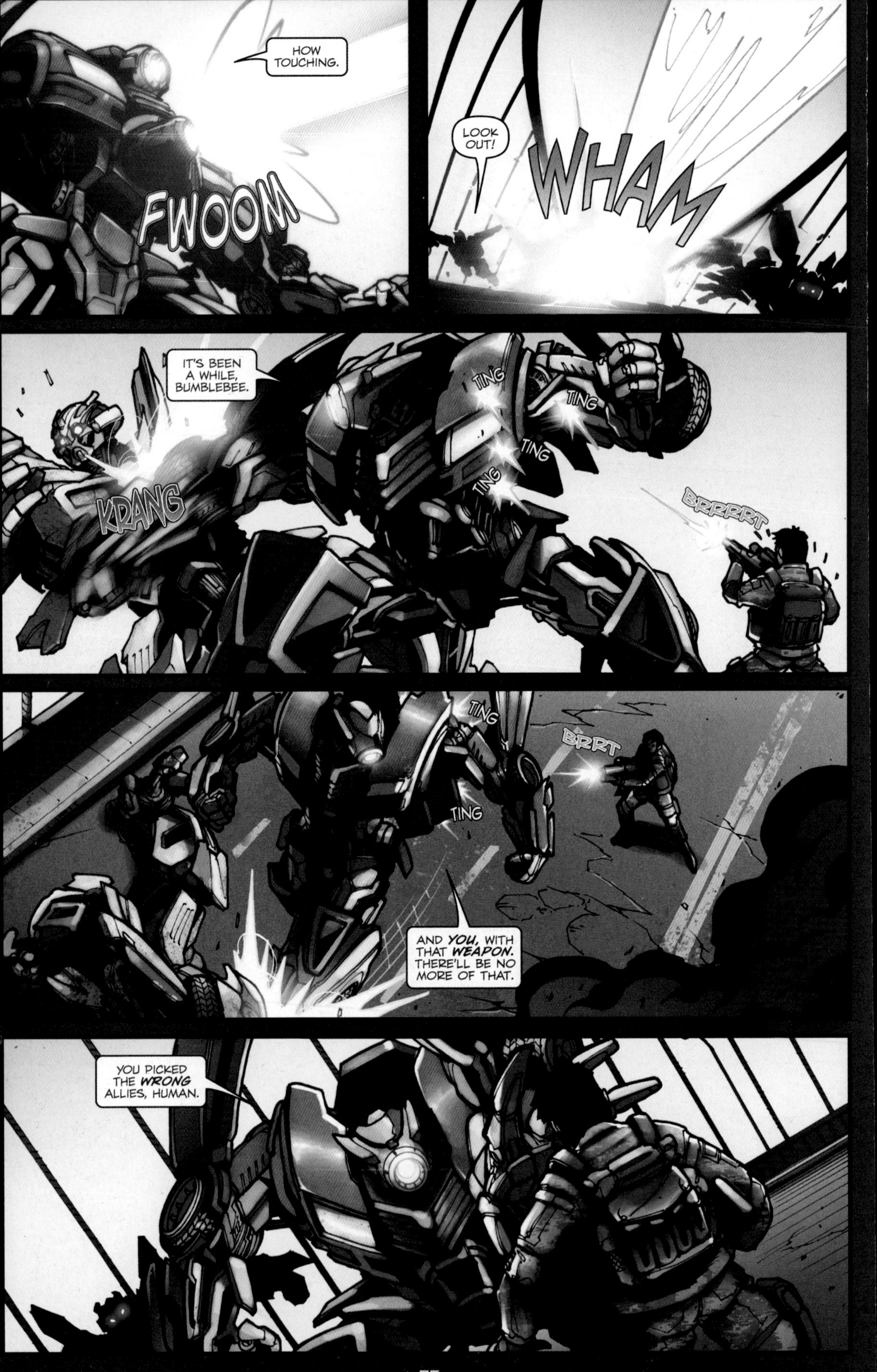
HOW TOUCHING.
FWOOM
LOOK OUT!
WHAM
IT'S BEEN A WHILE, BUMBLEBEE.
KRANG
TING
TING
TING
TING
BRRRRT
TING
BRRT
TING
AND YOU, WITH THAT WEAPON. THERE'LL BE NO MORE OF THAT.
YOU PICKED THE WRONG ALLIES, HUMAN.

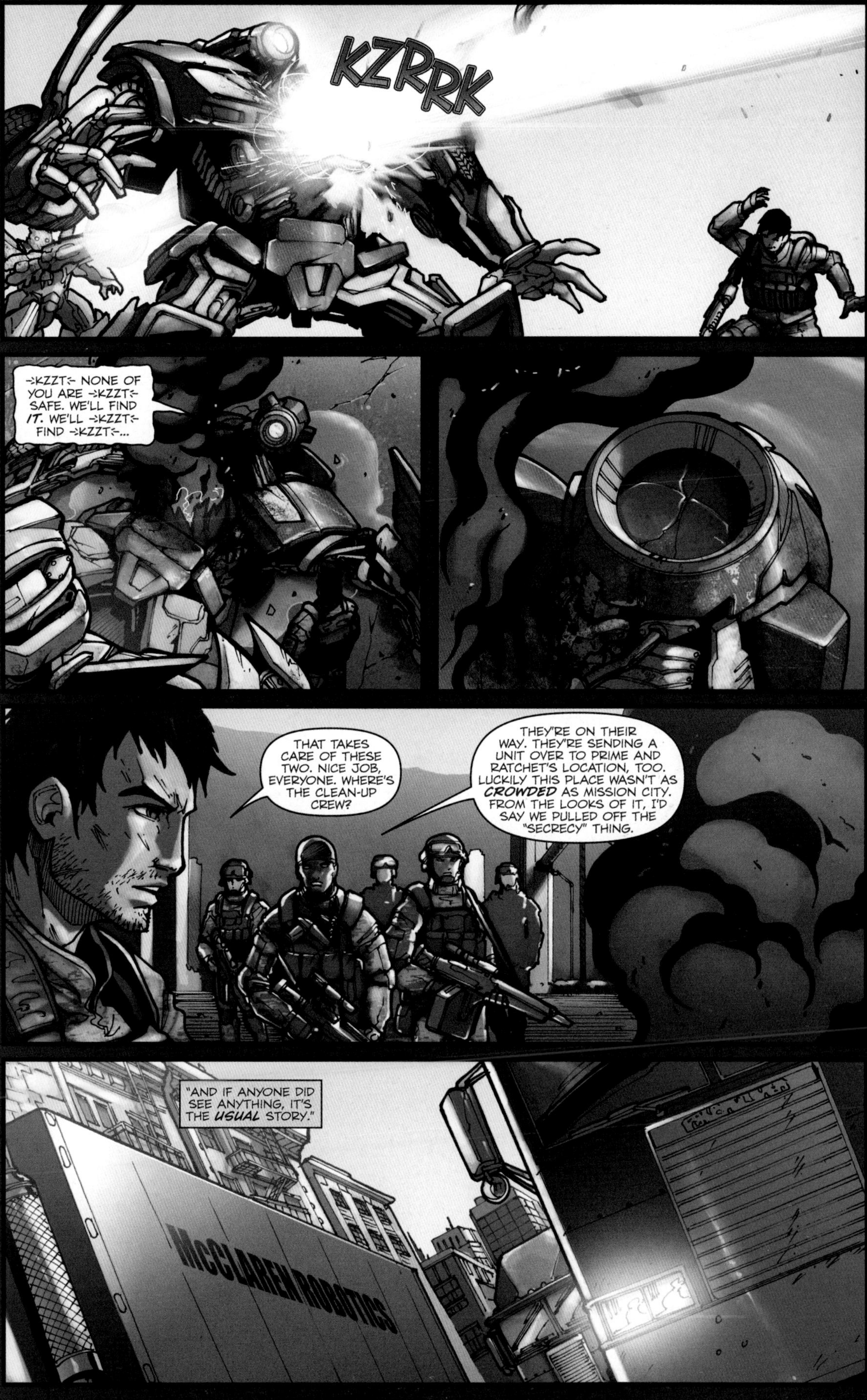
KZRRK
-KZZT- NONE OF YOU ARE -KZZT- SAFE. WE'LL FIND *IT.* WE'LL -KZZT- FIND -KZZT-...
THAT TAKES CARE OF THESE TWO. NICE JOB, EVERYONE. WHERE'S THE CLEAN-UP CREW?
THEY'RE ON THEIR WAY. THEY'RE SENDING A UNIT OVER TO PRIME AND RATCHET'S LOCATION, TOO. LUCKILY THIS PLACE WASN'T AS *CROWDED* AS MISSION CITY. FROM THE LOOKS OF IT, I'D SAY WE PULLED OFF THE "SECRECY" THING.
"AND IF ANYONE DID SEE ANYTHING, IT'S THE *USUAL* STORY."
McCLAREN ROBOTICS

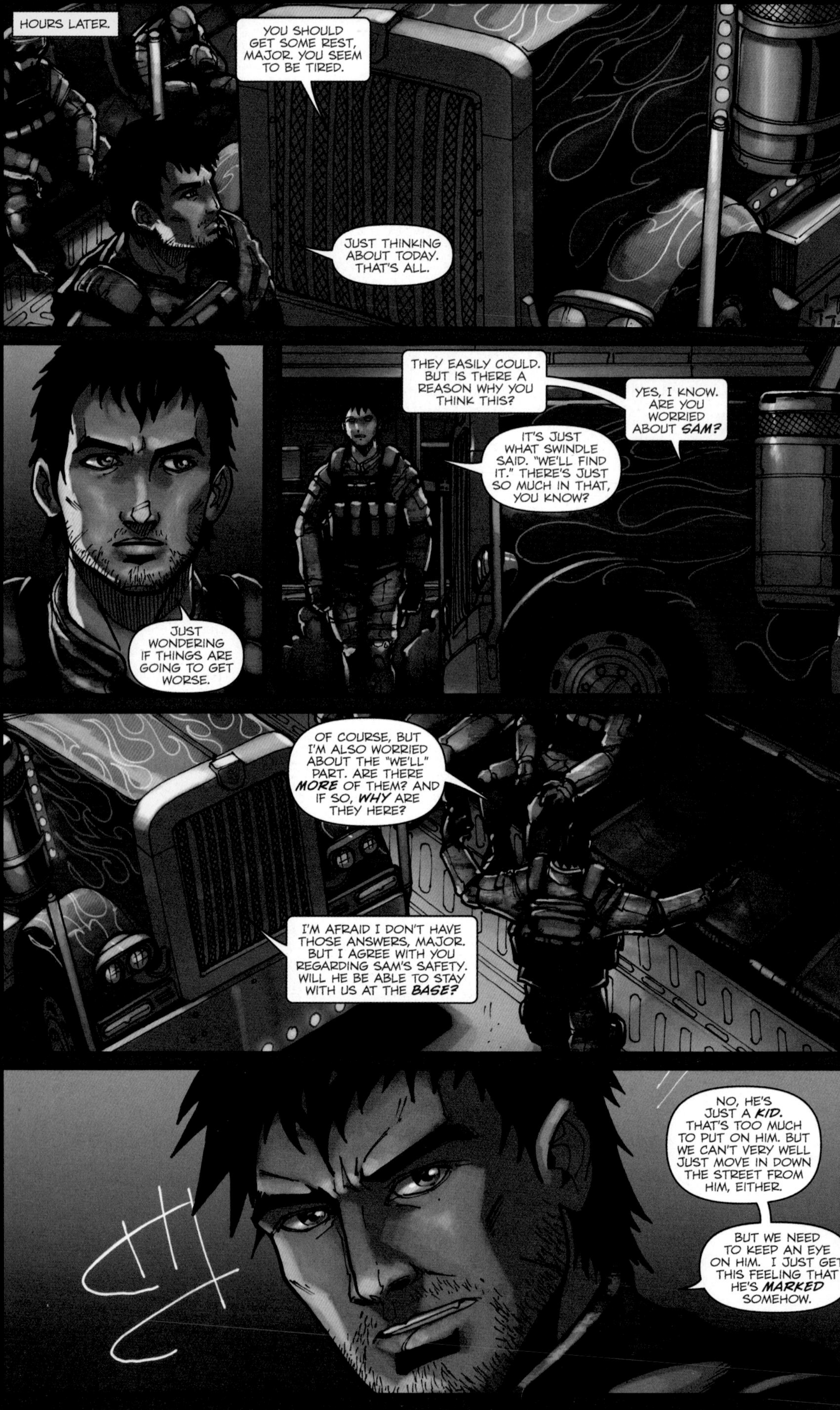
HOURS LATER.
YOU SHOULD GET SOME REST, MAJOR. YOU SEEM TO BE TIRED.
JUST THINKING ABOUT TODAY. THAT'S ALL.
YES, I KNOW. ARE YOU WORRIED ABOUT SAM?
JUST WONDERING IF THINGS ARE GOING TO GET WORSE.
THEY EASILY COULD. BUT IS THERE A REASON WHY YOU THINK THIS?
IT'S JUST WHAT SWINDLE SAID. "WE'LL FIND IT." THERE'S JUST SO MUCH IN THAT, YOU KNOW?
OF COURSE, BUT I'M ALSO WORRIED ABOUT THE "WE'LL" PART. ARE THERE MORE OF THEM? AND IF SO, WHY ARE THEY HERE?
I'M AFRAID I DON'T HAVE THOSE ANSWERS, MAJOR. BUT I AGREE WITH YOU REGARDING SAM'S SAFETY. WILL HE BE ABLE TO STAY WITH US AT THE BASE?
NO, HE'S JUST A KID. THAT'S TOO MUCH TO PUT ON HIM. BUT WE CAN'T VERY WELL JUST MOVE IN DOWN THE STREET FROM HIM, EITHER.
BUT WE NEED TO KEEP AN EYE ON HIM. I JUST GET THIS FEELING THAT HE'S MARKED SOMEHOW.

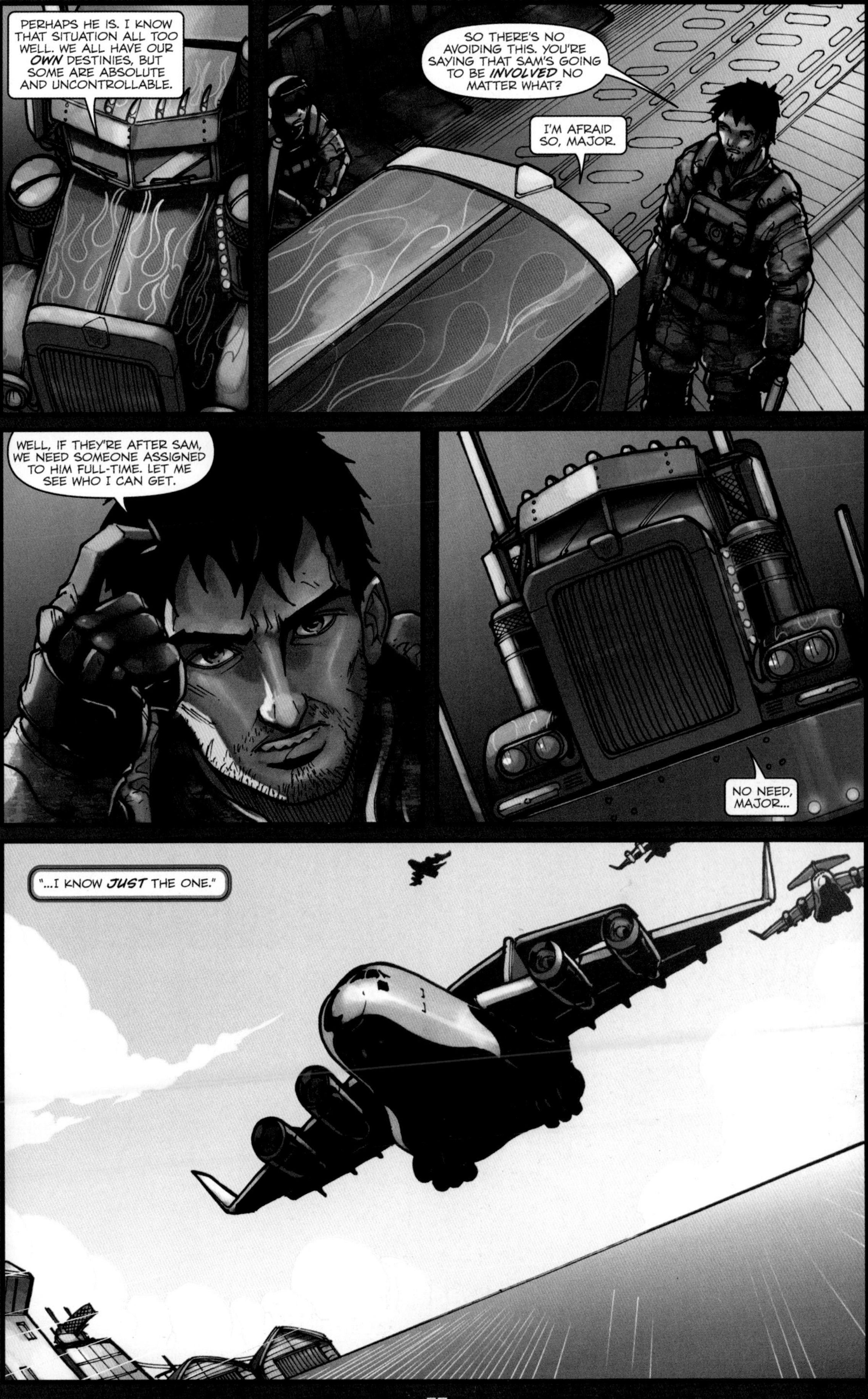
PERHAPS HE IS. I KNOW THAT SITUATION ALL TOO WELL. WE ALL HAVE OUR *OWN* DESTINIES, BUT SOME ARE ABSOLUTE AND UNCONTROLLABLE.
SO THERE'S NO AVOIDING THIS. YOU'RE SAYING THAT SAM'S GOING TO BE *INVOLVED* NO MATTER WHAT?
I'M AFRAID SO, MAJOR.
WELL, IF THEY'RE AFTER SAM, WE NEED SOMEONE ASSIGNED TO HIM FULL-TIME. LET ME SEE WHO I CAN GET.
NO NEED, MAJOR...
"...I KNOW *JUST* THE ONE."

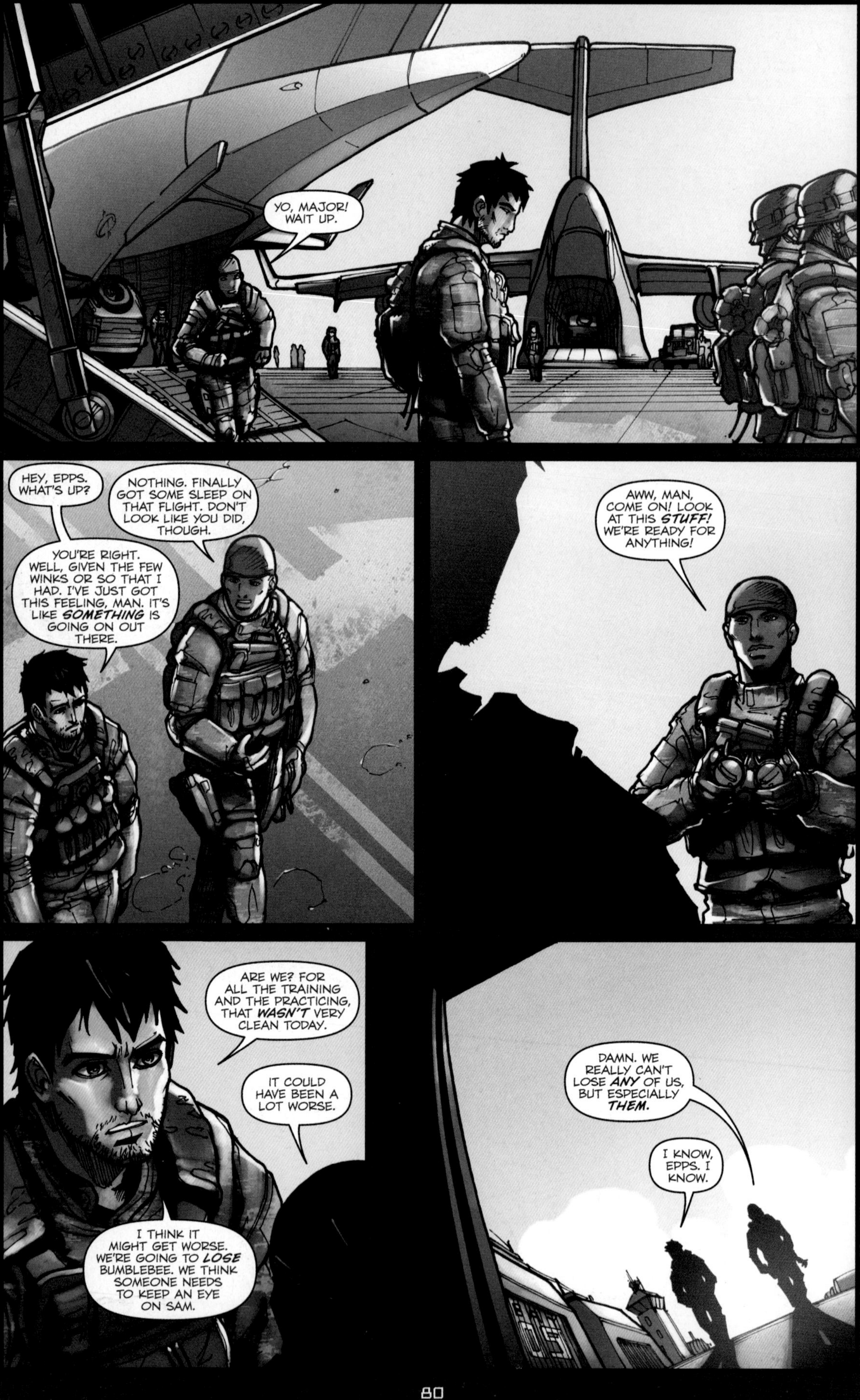
YO, MAJOR! WAIT UP.
HEY, EPPS. WHAT'S UP?
NOTHING. FINALLY GOT SOME SLEEP ON THAT FLIGHT. DON'T LOOK LIKE YOU DID, THOUGH.
YOU'RE RIGHT. WELL, GIVEN THE FEW WINKS OR SO THAT I HAD. I'VE JUST GOT THIS FEELING, MAN. IT'S LIKE SOMETHING IS GOING ON OUT THERE.
AWW, MAN, COME ON! LOOK AT THIS STUFF! WE'RE READY FOR ANYTHING!
ARE WE? FOR ALL THE TRAINING AND THE PRACTICING, THAT WASN'T VERY CLEAN TODAY.
IT COULD HAVE BEEN A LOT WORSE.
I THINK IT MIGHT GET WORSE. WE'RE GOING TO LOSE BUMBLEBEE. WE THINK SOMEONE NEEDS TO KEEP AN EYE ON SAM.
DAMN. WE REALLY CAN'T LOSE ANY OF US, BUT ESPECIALLY THEM.
I KNOW, EPPS. I KNOW.

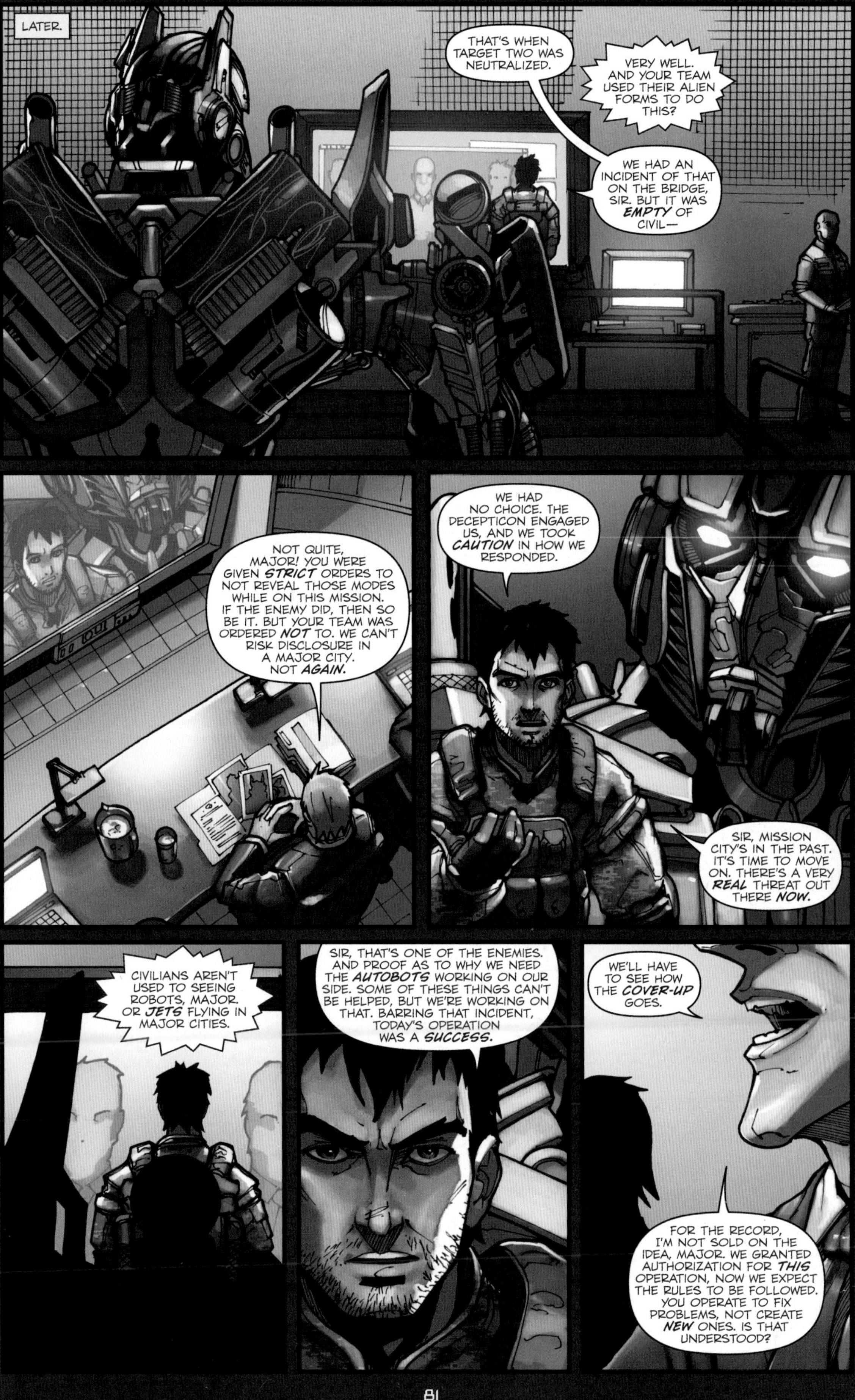

LATER.
THAT'S WHEN TARGET TWO WAS NEUTRALIZED.
VERY WELL. AND YOUR TEAM USED THEIR ALIEN FORMS TO DO THIS?
WE HAD AN INCIDENT OF THAT ON THE BRIDGE, SIR. BUT IT WAS EMPTY OF CIVIL—
NOT QUITE, MAJOR! YOU WERE GIVEN STRICT ORDERS TO NOT REVEAL THOSE MODES WHILE ON THIS MISSION. IF THE ENEMY DID, THEN SO BE IT. BUT YOUR TEAM WAS ORDERED NOT TO. WE CAN'T RISK DISCLOSURE IN A MAJOR CITY. NOT AGAIN.
WE HAD NO CHOICE. THE DECEPTICON ENGAGED US, AND WE TOOK CAUTION IN HOW WE RESPONDED.
SIR, MISSION CITY'S IN THE PAST. IT'S TIME TO MOVE ON. THERE'S A VERY REAL THREAT OUT THERE NOW.
CIVILIANS AREN'T USED TO SEEING ROBOTS, MAJOR. OR JETS FLYING IN MAJOR CITIES.
SIR, THAT'S ONE OF THE ENEMIES. AND PROOF AS TO WHY WE NEED THE AUTOBOTS WORKING ON OUR SIDE. SOME OF THESE THINGS CAN'T BE HELPED, BUT WE'RE WORKING ON THAT. BARRING THAT INCIDENT, TODAY'S OPERATION WAS A SUCCESS.
WE'LL HAVE TO SEE HOW THE COVER-UP GOES.
FOR THE RECORD, I'M NOT SOLD ON THE IDEA, MAJOR. WE GRANTED AUTHORIZATION FOR THIS OPERATION, NOW WE EXPECT THE RULES TO BE FOLLOWED. YOU OPERATE TO FIX PROBLEMS, NOT CREATE NEW ONES. IS THAT UNDERSTOOD?

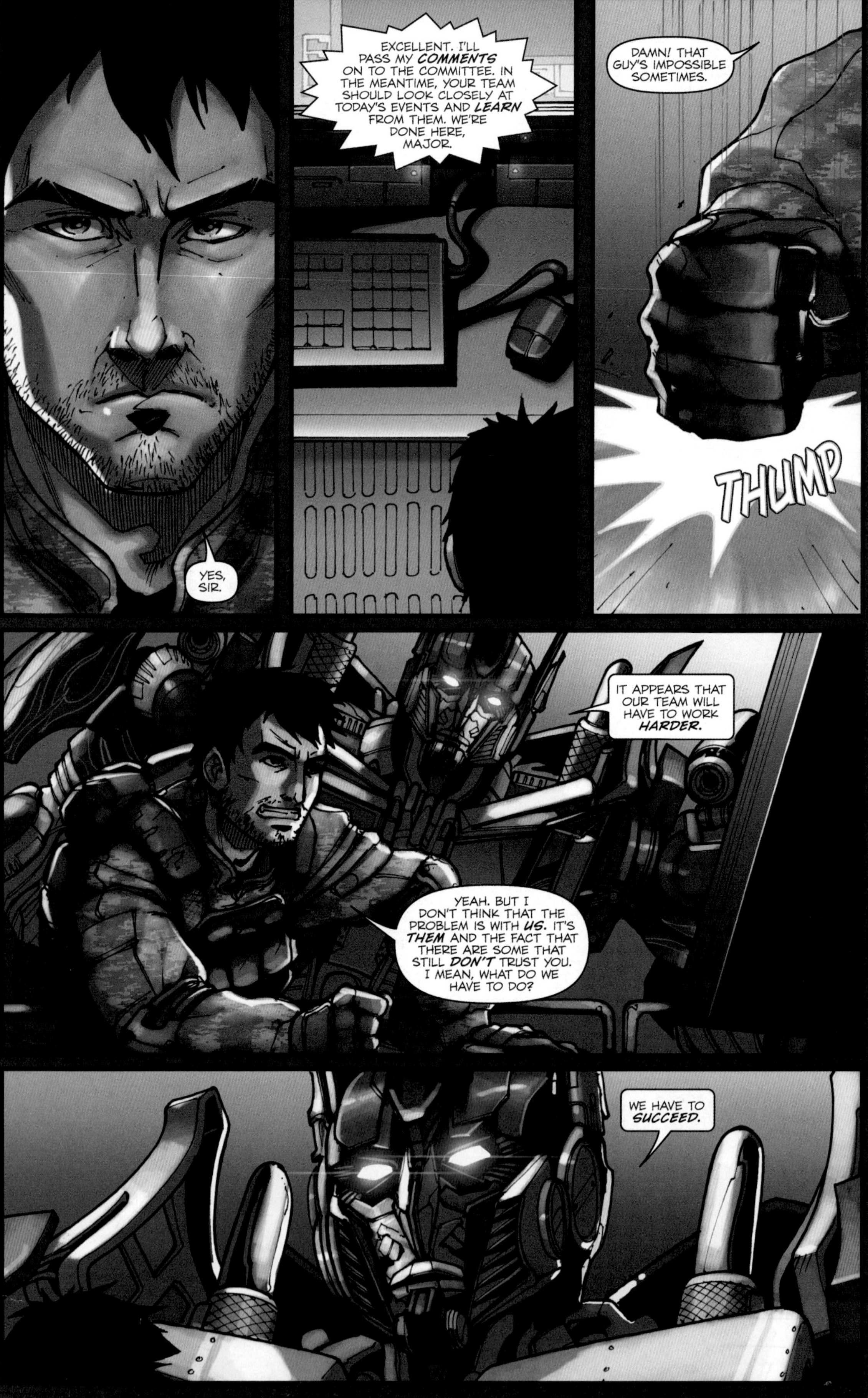
EXCELLENT. I'LL PASS MY COMMENTS ON TO THE COMMITTEE. IN THE MEANTIME, YOUR TEAM SHOULD LOOK CLOSELY AT TODAY'S EVENTS AND LEARN FROM THEM. WE'RE DONE HERE, MAJOR.
YES, SIR.
DAMN! THAT GUY'S IMPOSSIBLE SOMETIMES.
THUMP
IT APPEARS THAT OUR TEAM WILL HAVE TO WORK HARDER.
YEAH. BUT I DON'T THINK THAT THE PROBLEM IS WITH US. IT'S THEM AND THE FACT THAT THERE ARE SOME THAT STILL DON'T TRUST YOU. I MEAN, WHAT DO WE HAVE TO DO?
WE HAVE TO SUCCEED.

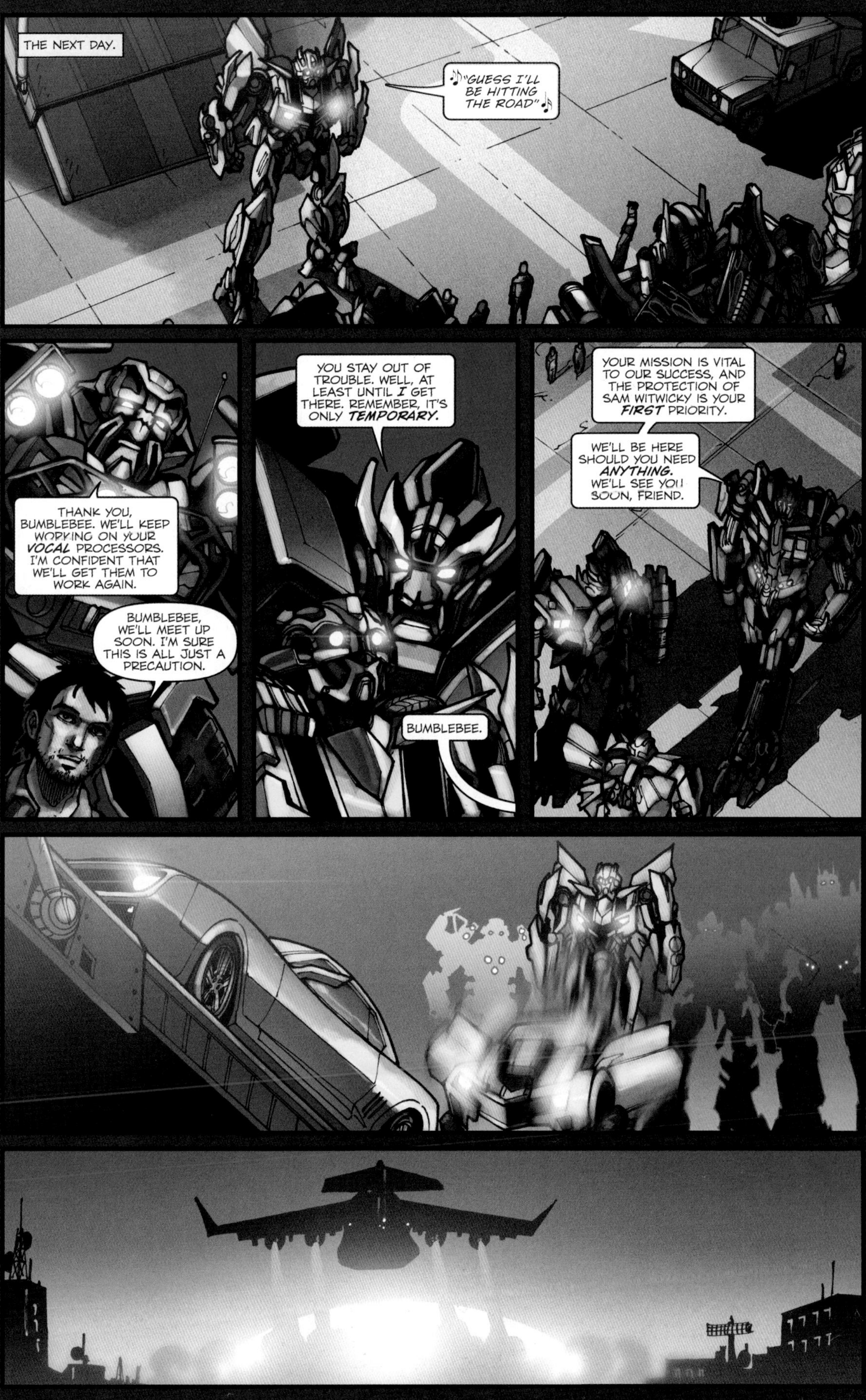
THE NEXT DAY.
♪"GUESS I'LL BE HITTING THE ROAD"♪
THANK YOU, BUMBLEBEE. WE'LL KEEP WORKING ON YOUR VOCAL PROCESSORS. I'M CONFIDENT THAT WE'LL GET THEM TO WORK AGAIN.
BUMBLEBEE, WE'LL MEET UP SOON. I'M SURE THIS IS ALL JUST A PRECAUTION.
YOU STAY OUT OF TROUBLE. WELL, AT LEAST UNTIL I GET THERE. REMEMBER, IT'S ONLY TEMPORARY.
BUMBLEBEE.
YOUR MISSION IS VITAL TO OUR SUCCESS, AND THE PROTECTION OF SAM WITWICKY IS YOUR FIRST PRIORITY.
WE'LL BE HERE SHOULD YOU NEED ANYTHING. WE'LL SEE YOU SOON, FRIEND.

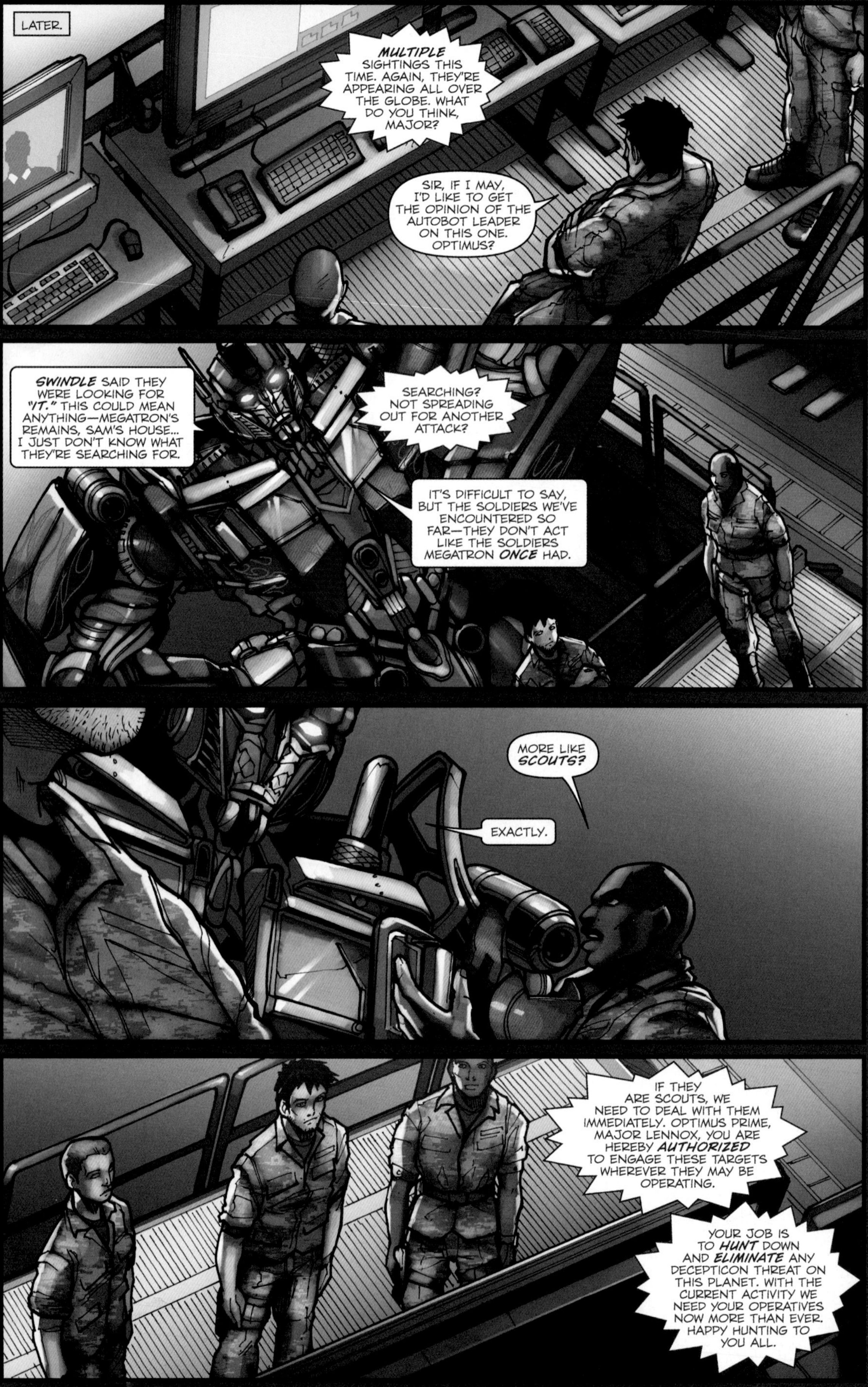
LATER.
MULTIPLE SIGHTINGS THIS TIME. AGAIN, THEY'RE APPEARING ALL OVER THE GLOBE. WHAT DO YOU THINK, MAJOR?
SIR, IF I MAY, I'D LIKE TO GET THE OPINION OF THE AUTOBOT LEADER ON THIS ONE. OPTIMUS?
SWINDLE SAID THEY WERE LOOKING FOR "IT." THIS COULD MEAN ANYTHING—MEGATRON'S REMAINS, SAM'S HOUSE... I JUST DON'T KNOW WHAT THEY'RE SEARCHING FOR.
SEARCHING? NOT SPREADING OUT FOR ANOTHER ATTACK?
IT'S DIFFICULT TO SAY, BUT THE SOLDIERS WE'VE ENCOUNTERED SO FAR—THEY DON'T ACT LIKE THE SOLDIERS MEGATRON ONCE HAD.
MORE LIKE SCOUTS?
EXACTLY.
IF THEY ARE SCOUTS, WE NEED TO DEAL WITH THEM IMMEDIATELY. OPTIMUS PRIME, MAJOR LENNOX, YOU ARE HEREBY AUTHORIZED TO ENGAGE THESE TARGETS WHEREVER THEY MAY BE OPERATING.
YOUR JOB IS TO HUNT DOWN AND ELIMINATE ANY DECEPTICON THREAT ON THIS PLANET. WITH THE CURRENT ACTIVITY WE NEED YOUR OPERATIVES NOW MORE THAN EVER. HAPPY HUNTING TO YOU ALL.

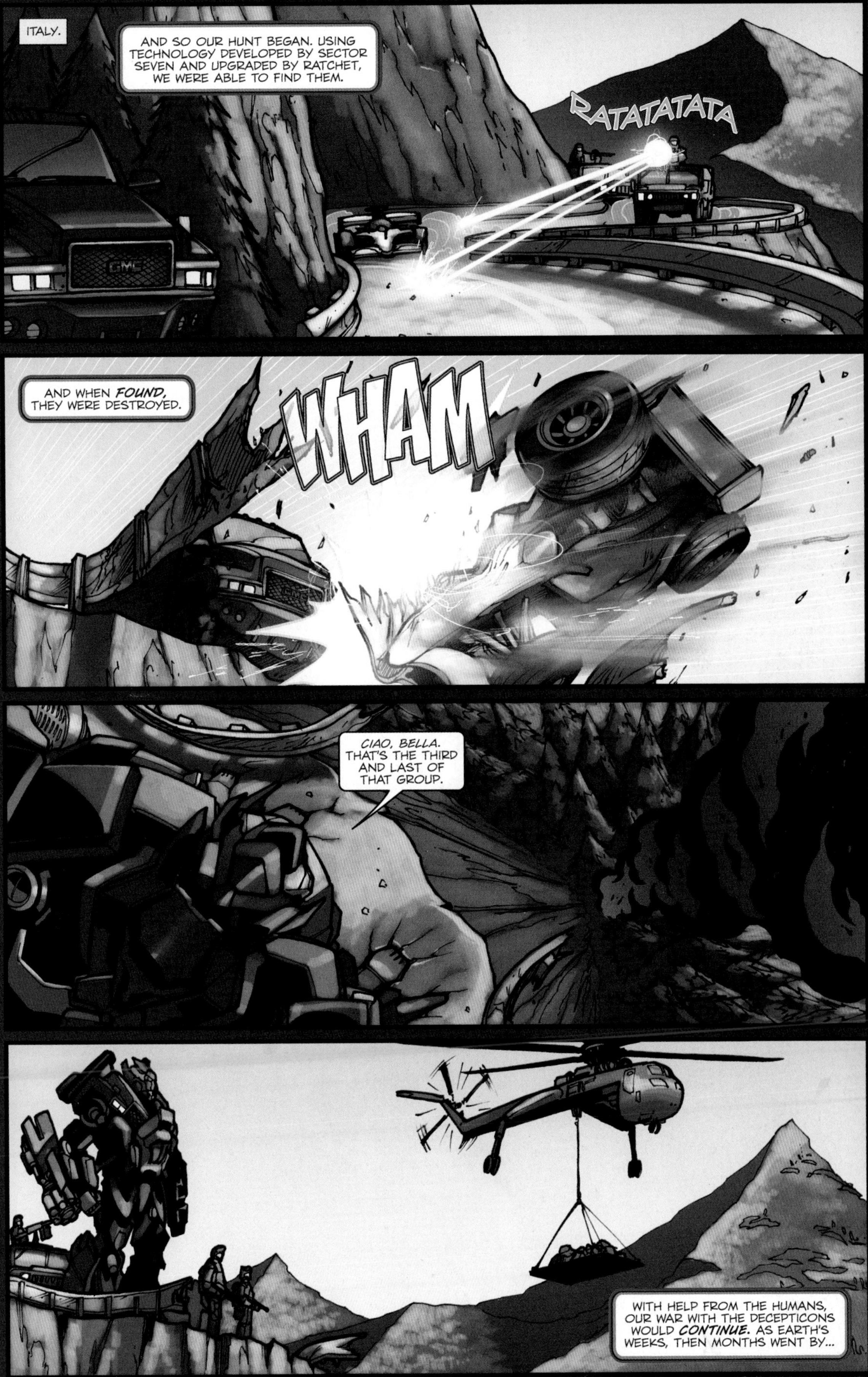
ITALY.
AND SO OUR HUNT BEGAN. USING TECHNOLOGY DEVELOPED BY SECTOR SEVEN AND UPGRADED BY RATCHET, WE WERE ABLE TO FIND THEM.
RATATATATA
AND WHEN *FOUND*, THEY WERE DESTROYED.
WHAM
CIAO, BELLA. THAT'S THE THIRD AND LAST OF THAT GROUP.
WITH HELP FROM THE HUMANS, OUR WAR WITH THE DECEPTICONS WOULD ***CONTINUE.*** AS EARTH'S WEEKS, THEN MONTHS WENT BY...

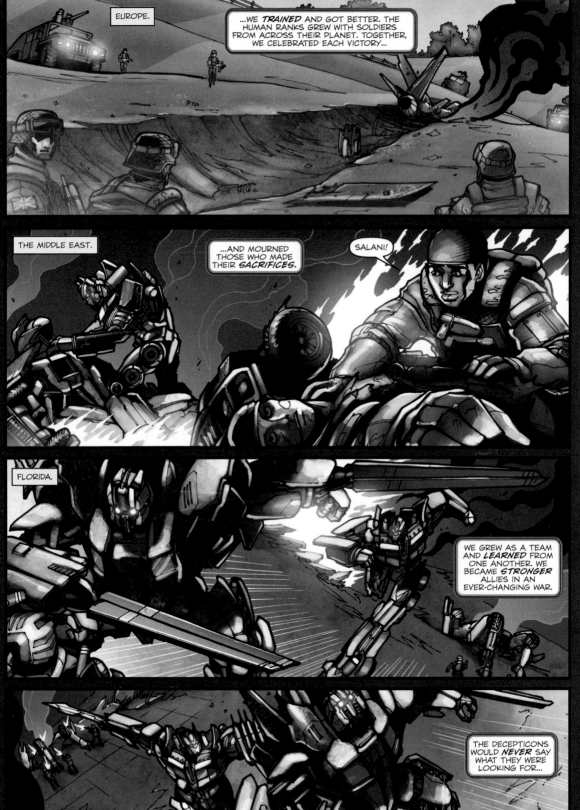

EUROPE.

...WE *TRAINED* AND GOT BETTER. THE HUMAN RANKS GREW WITH SOLDIERS FROM ACROSS THEIR PLANET. TOGETHER, WE CELEBRATED EACH VICTORY...

THE MIDDLE EAST.

...AND MOURNED THOSE WHO MADE THEIR *SACRIFICES*.

SALANI!

FLORIDA.

WE GREW AS A TEAM AND *LEARNED* FROM ONE ANOTHER. WE BECAME *STRONGER* ALLIES IN AN EVER-CHANGING WAR.

THE DECEPTICONS WOULD *NEVER* SAY WHAT THEY WERE LOOKING FOR...

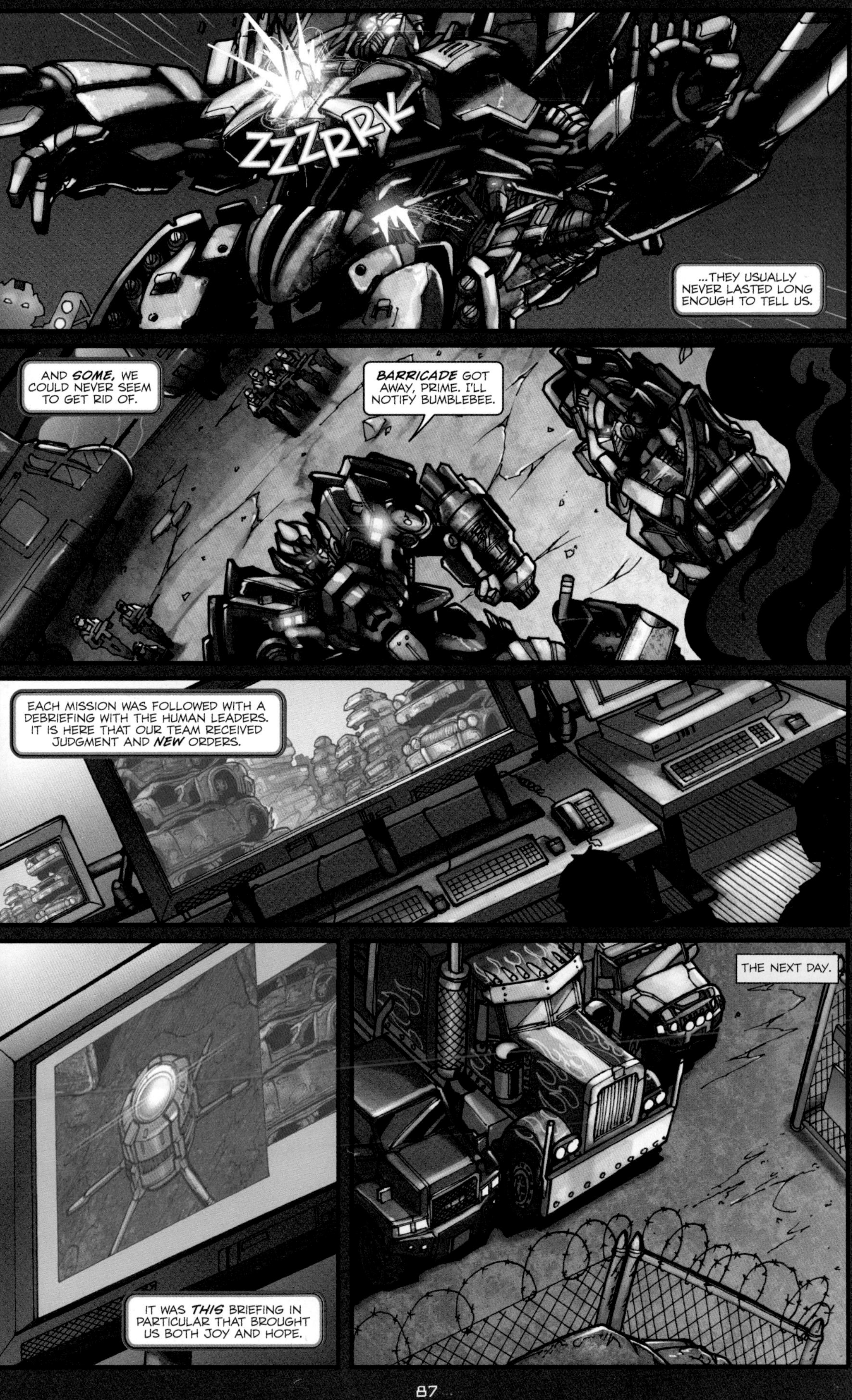
ZZZRRK
...THEY USUALLY NEVER LASTED LONG ENOUGH TO TELL US.
AND SOME, WE COULD NEVER SEEM TO GET RID OF.
BARRICADE GOT AWAY, PRIME. I'LL NOTIFY BUMBLEBEE.
EACH MISSION WAS FOLLOWED WITH A DEBRIEFING WITH THE HUMAN LEADERS. IT IS HERE THAT OUR TEAM RECEIVED JUDGMENT AND NEW ORDERS.
IT WAS THIS BRIEFING IN PARTICULAR THAT BROUGHT US BOTH JOY AND HOPE.
THE NEXT DAY.

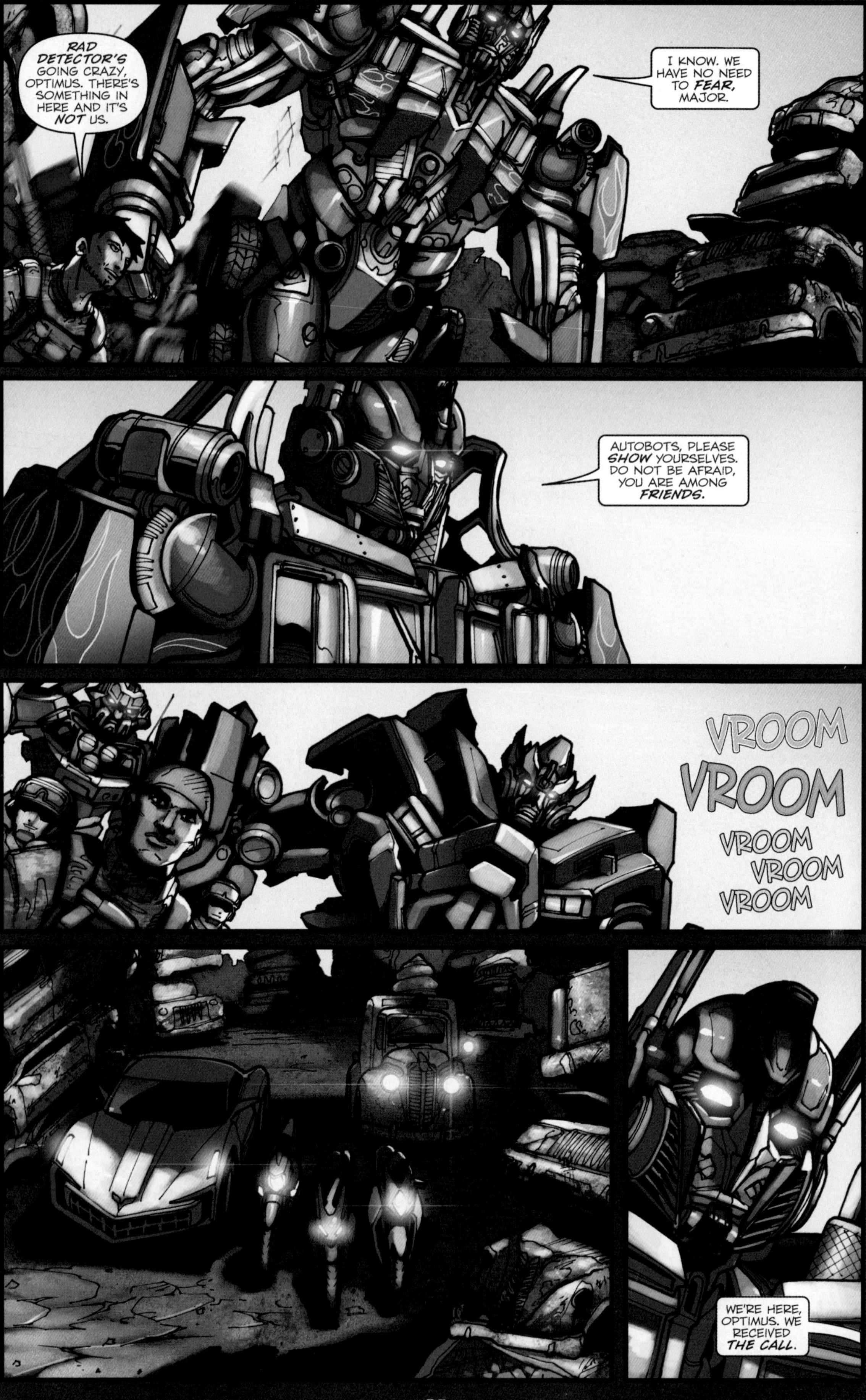
RAD DETECTOR'S GOING CRAZY, OPTIMUS. THERE'S SOMETHING IN HERE AND IT'S NOT US.
I KNOW. WE HAVE NO NEED TO FEAR, MAJOR.
AUTOBOTS, PLEASE SHOW YOURSELVES. DO NOT BE AFRAID, YOU ARE AMONG FRIENDS.
VROOM
VROOM
VROOM
VROOM
VROOM
WE'RE HERE, OPTIMUS. WE RECEIVED THE CALL.

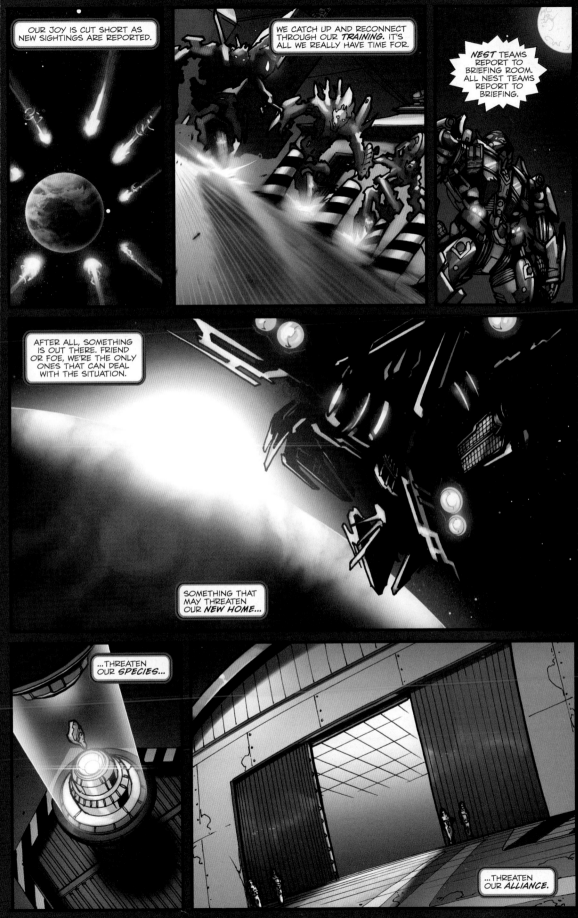

OUR JOY IS CUT SHORT AS NEW SIGHTINGS ARE REPORTED.

WE CATCH UP AND RECONNECT THROUGH OUR *TRAINING.* IT'S ALL WE REALLY HAVE TIME FOR.

NEST TEAMS REPORT TO BRIEFING ROOM. ALL NEST TEAMS REPORT TO BRIEFING.

AFTER ALL, SOMETHING IS OUT THERE. FRIEND OR FOE, WE'RE THE ONLY ONES THAT CAN DEAL WITH THE SITUATION.

SOMETHING THAT MAY THREATEN OUR *NEW HOME...*

...THREATEN OUR *SPECIES...*

...THREATEN OUR *ALLIANCE.*

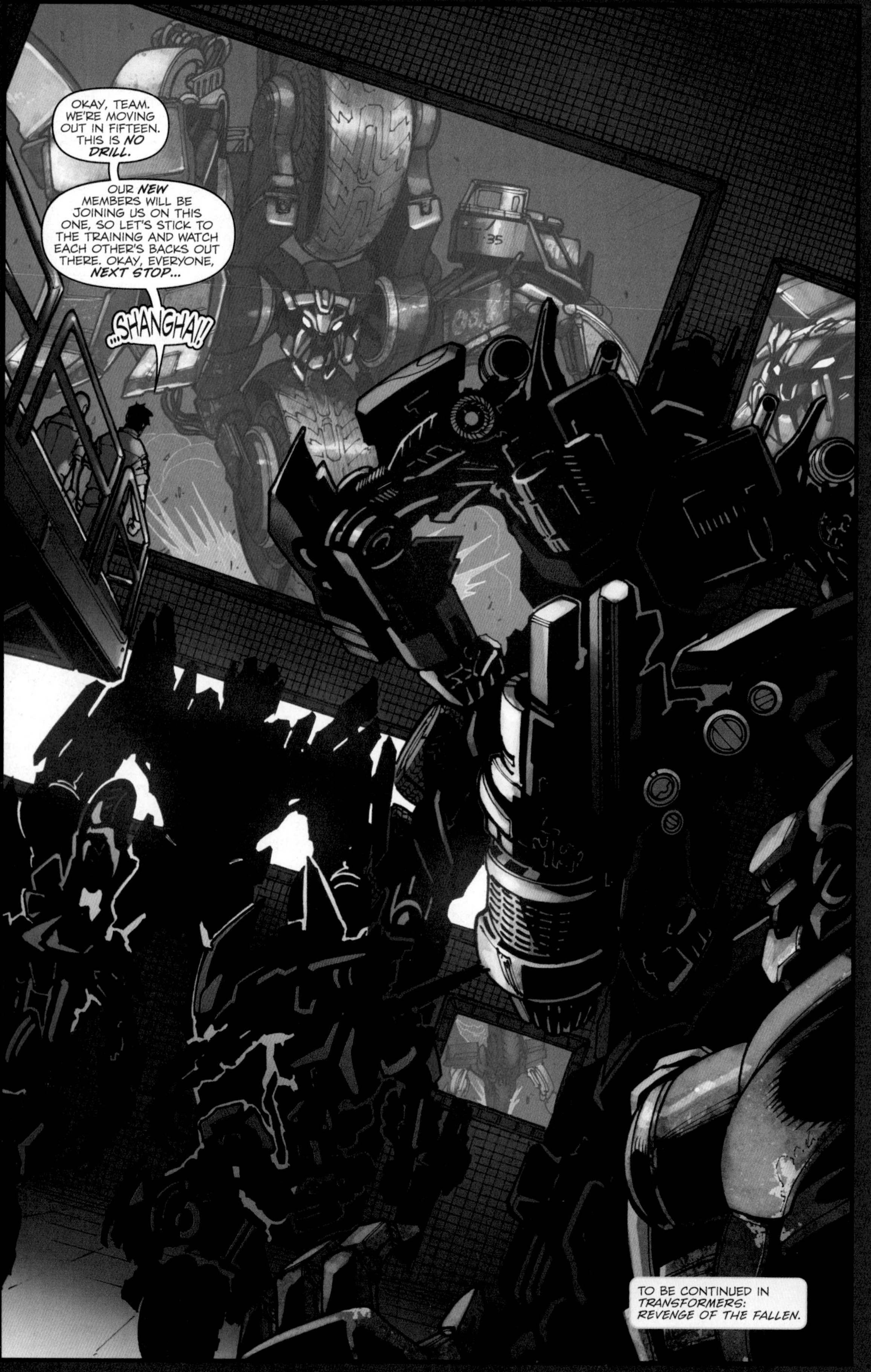
OKAY, TEAM. WE'RE MOVING OUT IN FIFTEEN. THIS IS *NO DRILL.*
OUR *NEW* MEMBERS WILL BE JOINING US ON THIS ONE, SO LET'S STICK TO THE TRAINING AND WATCH EACH OTHER'S BACKS OUT THERE. OKAY, EVERYONE, *NEXT STOP...*
...SHANGHAI!!
TO BE CONTINUED IN *TRANSFORMERS: REVENGE OF THE FALLEN.*

ART

GALLERY

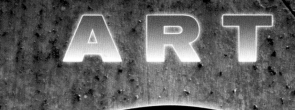

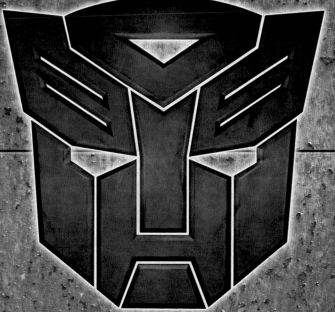

Art by Alex Milne
Colors by Josh Perez

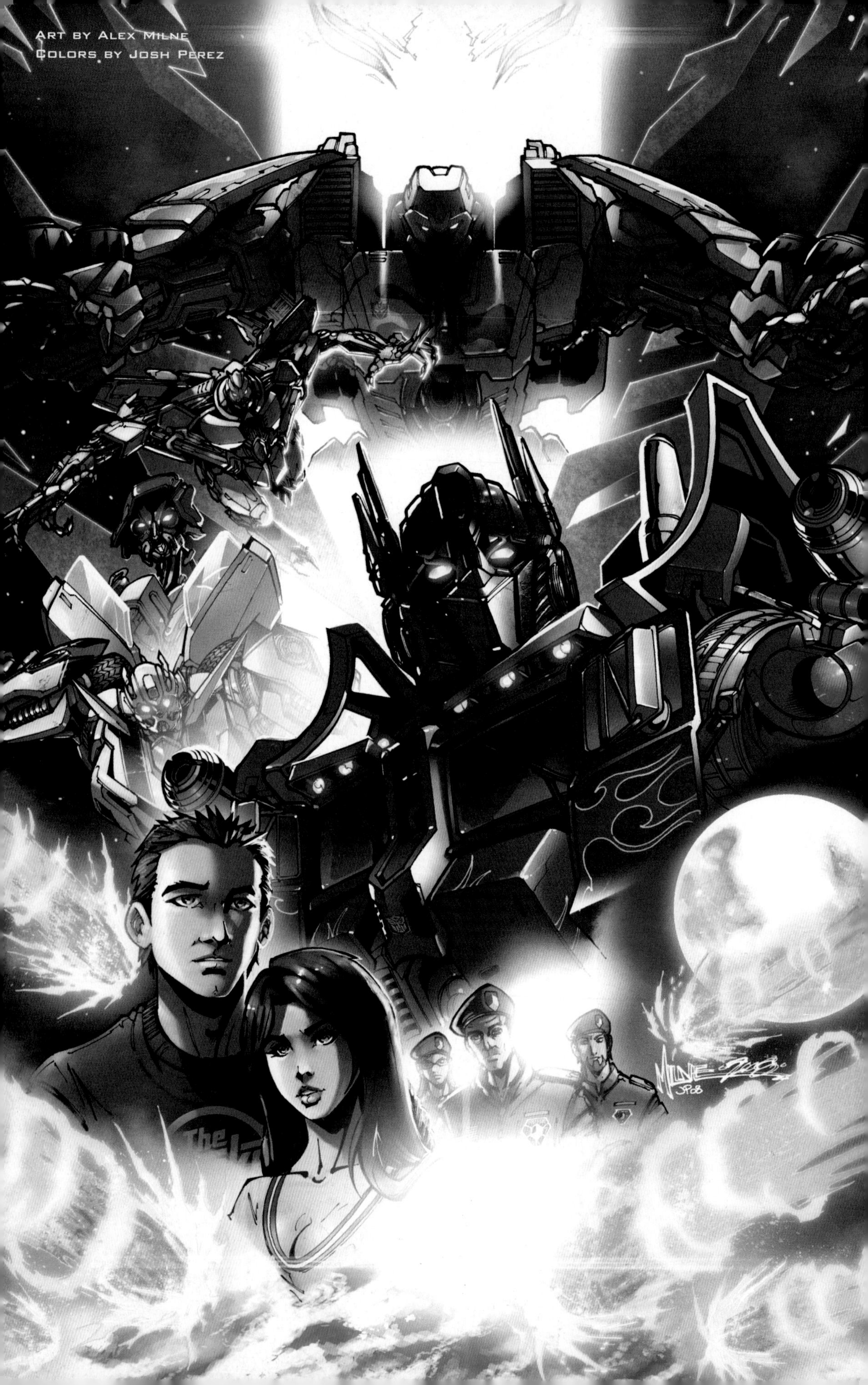

Art by Josh Nizzi

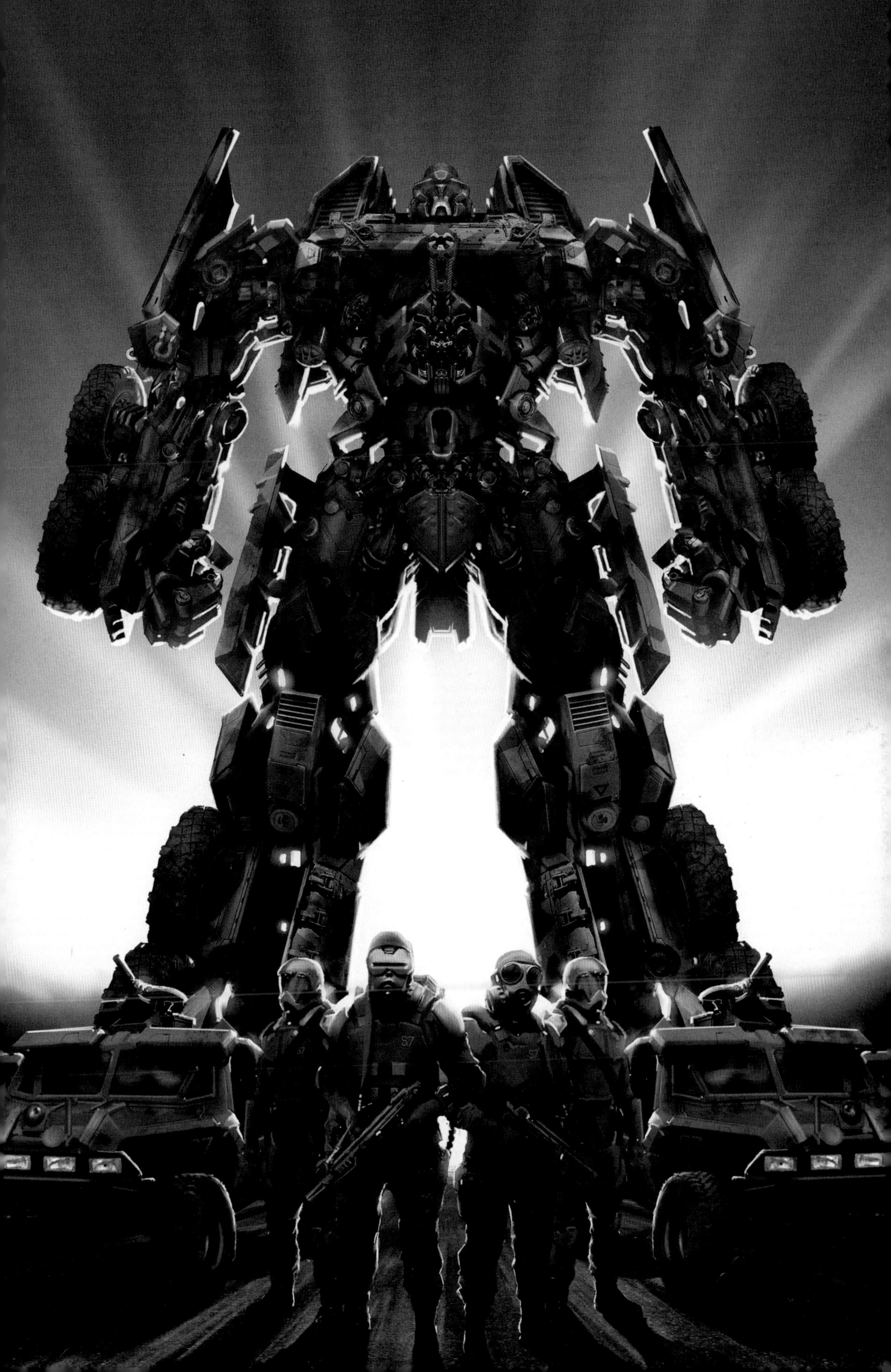

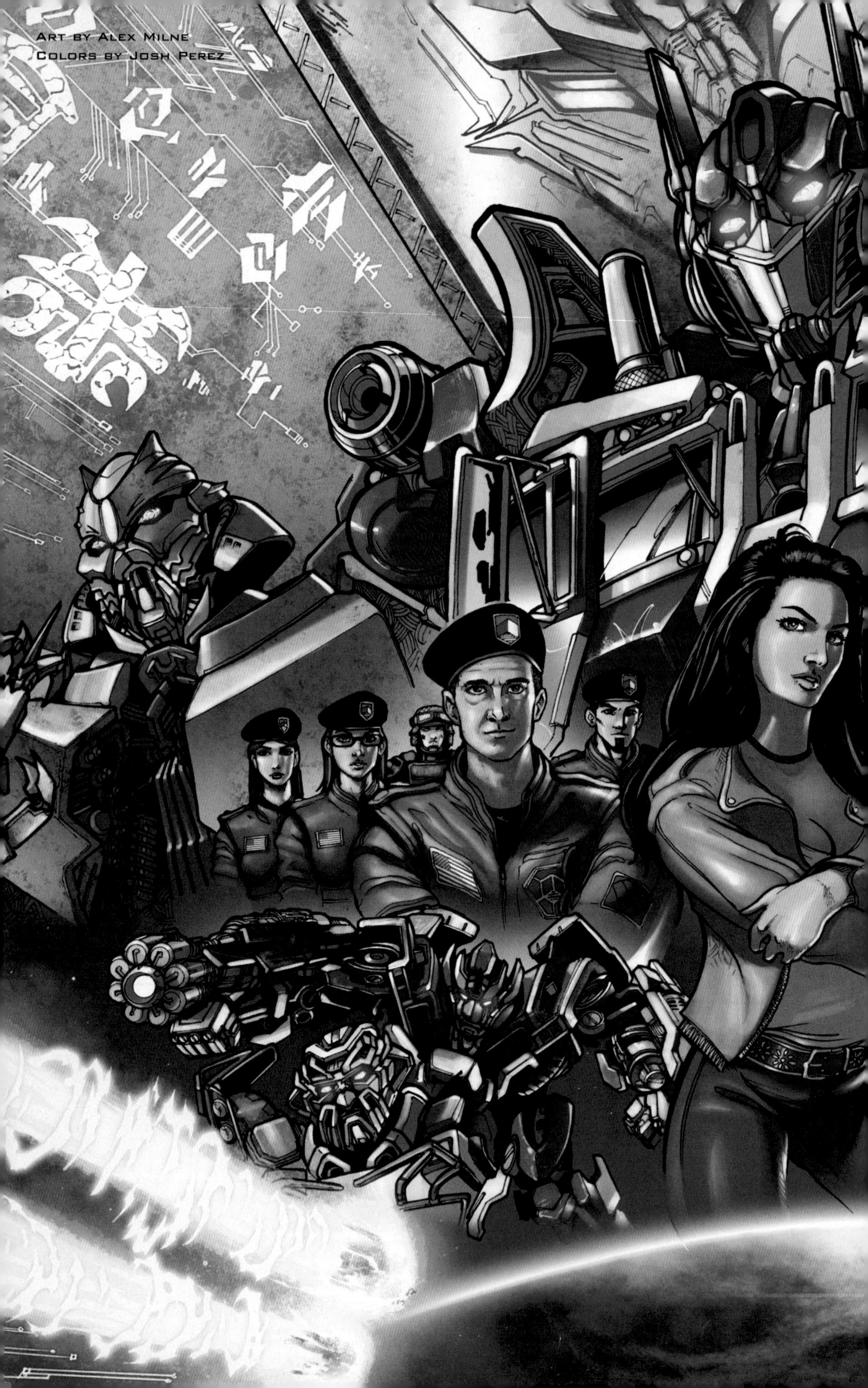
Art by Alex Milne
Colors by Josh Perez

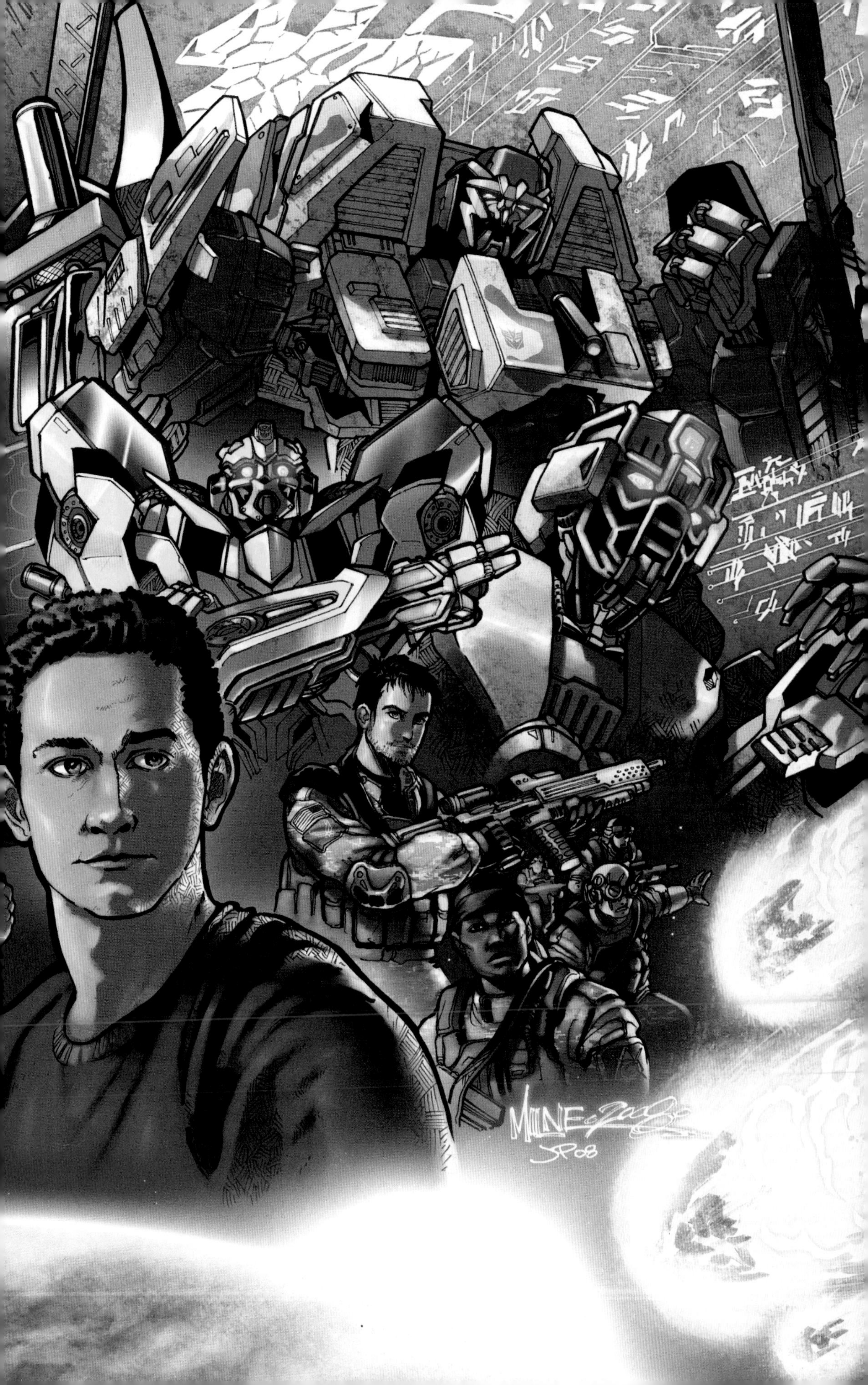
MILNE

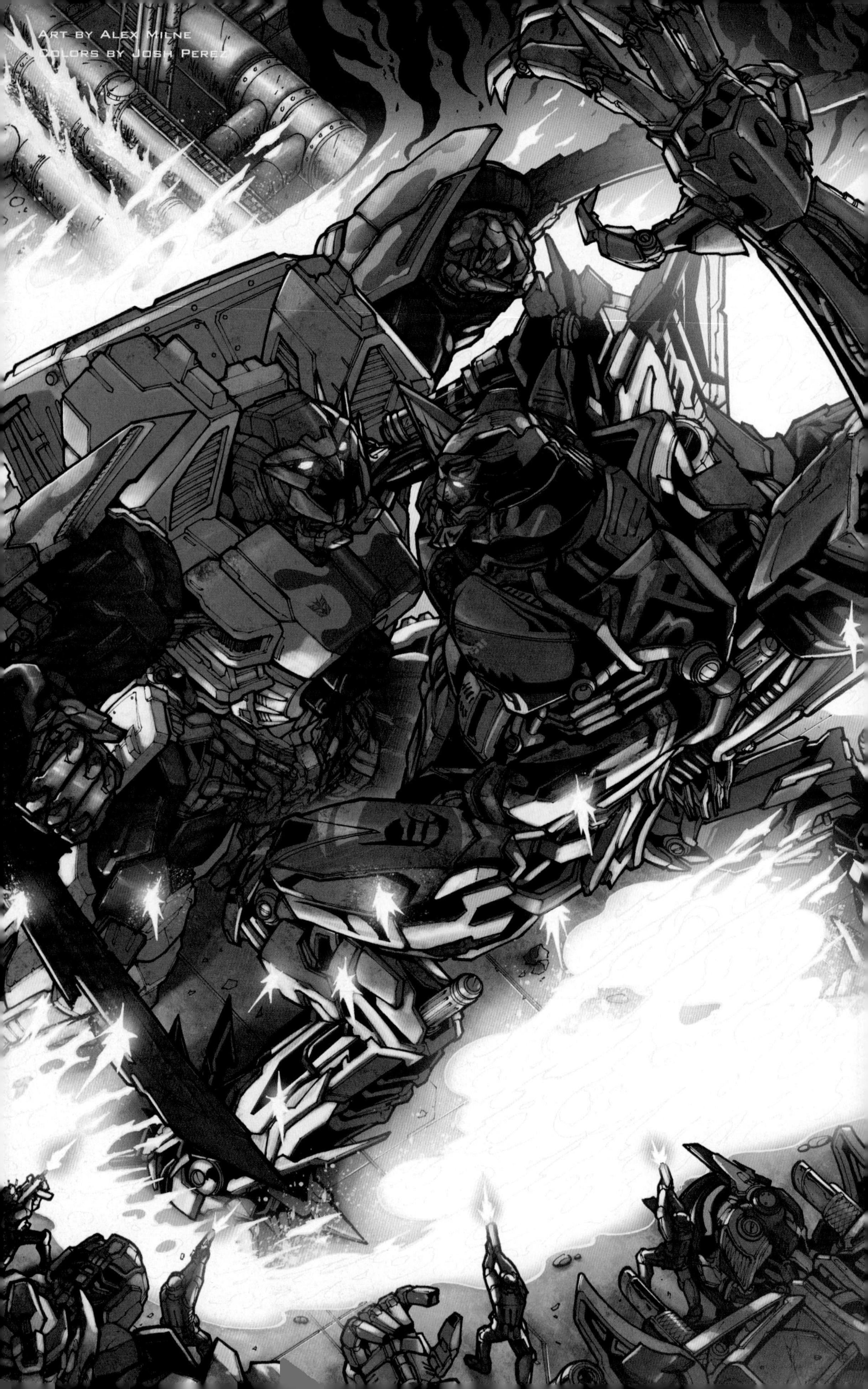
Art by Alex Milne
Colors by Josh Perez

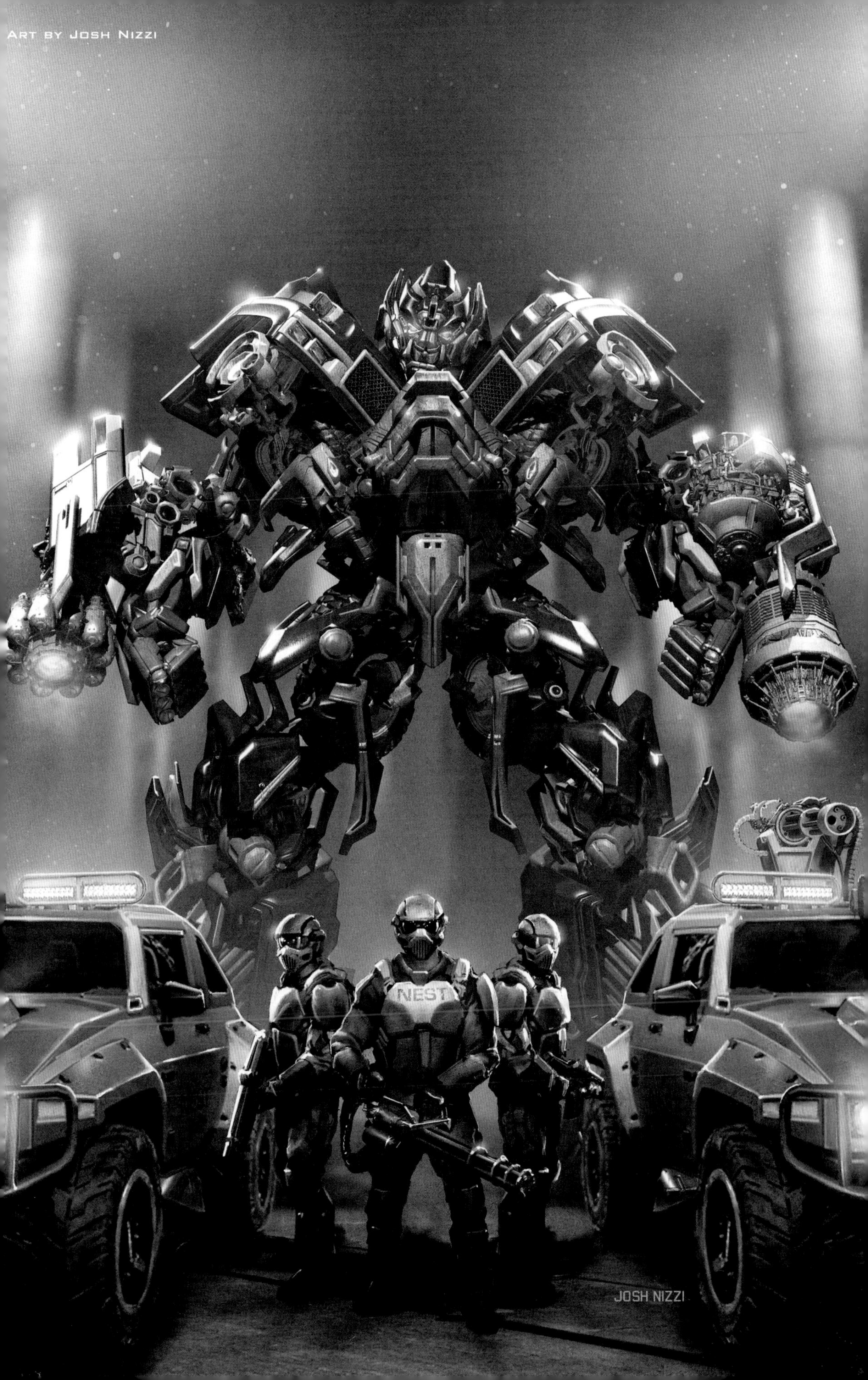
NEST
JOSH NIZZI

Art by Josh Nizzi

Art by Alex Milne
Colors by Josh Perez

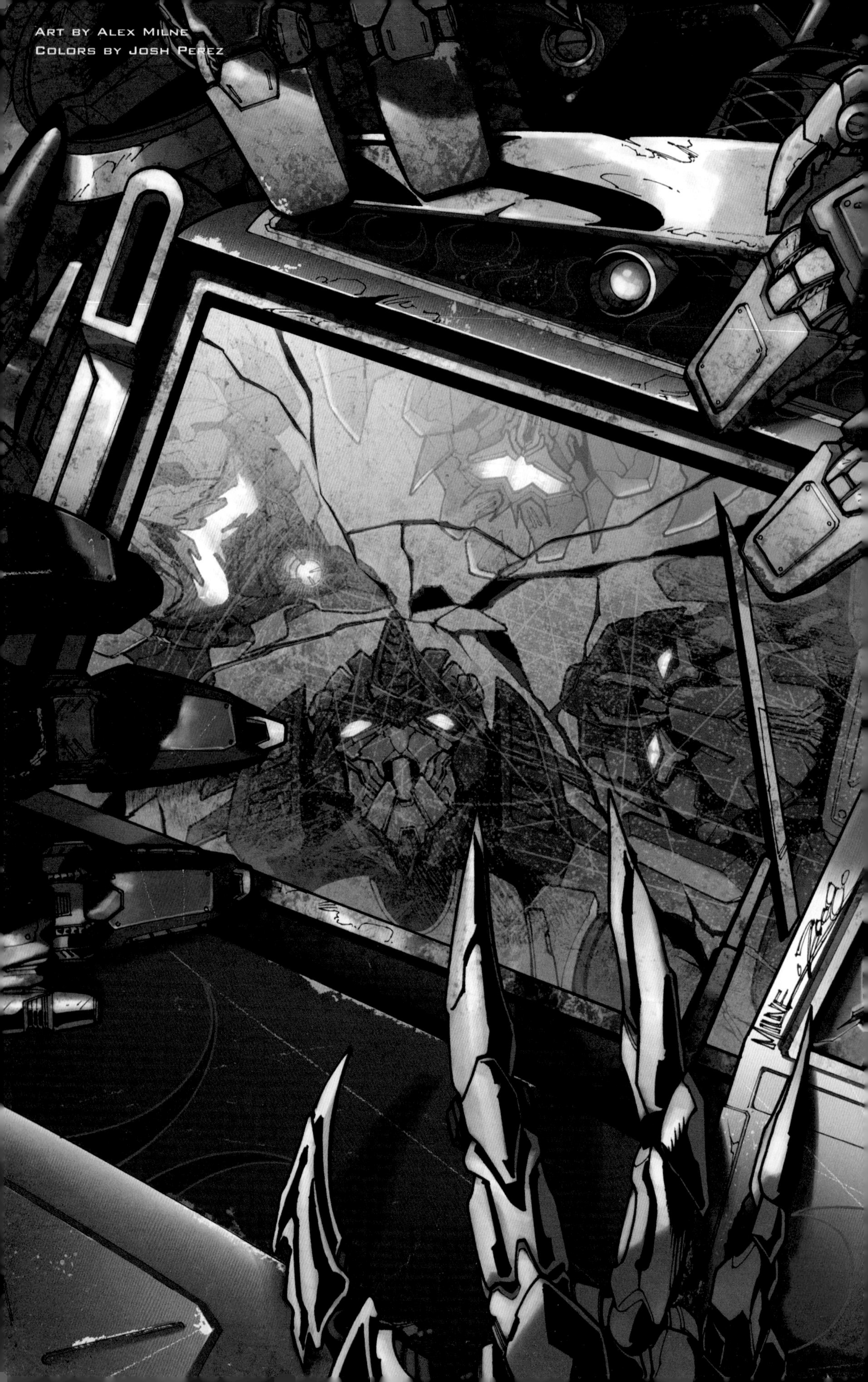

ART BY JOSH NIZZI

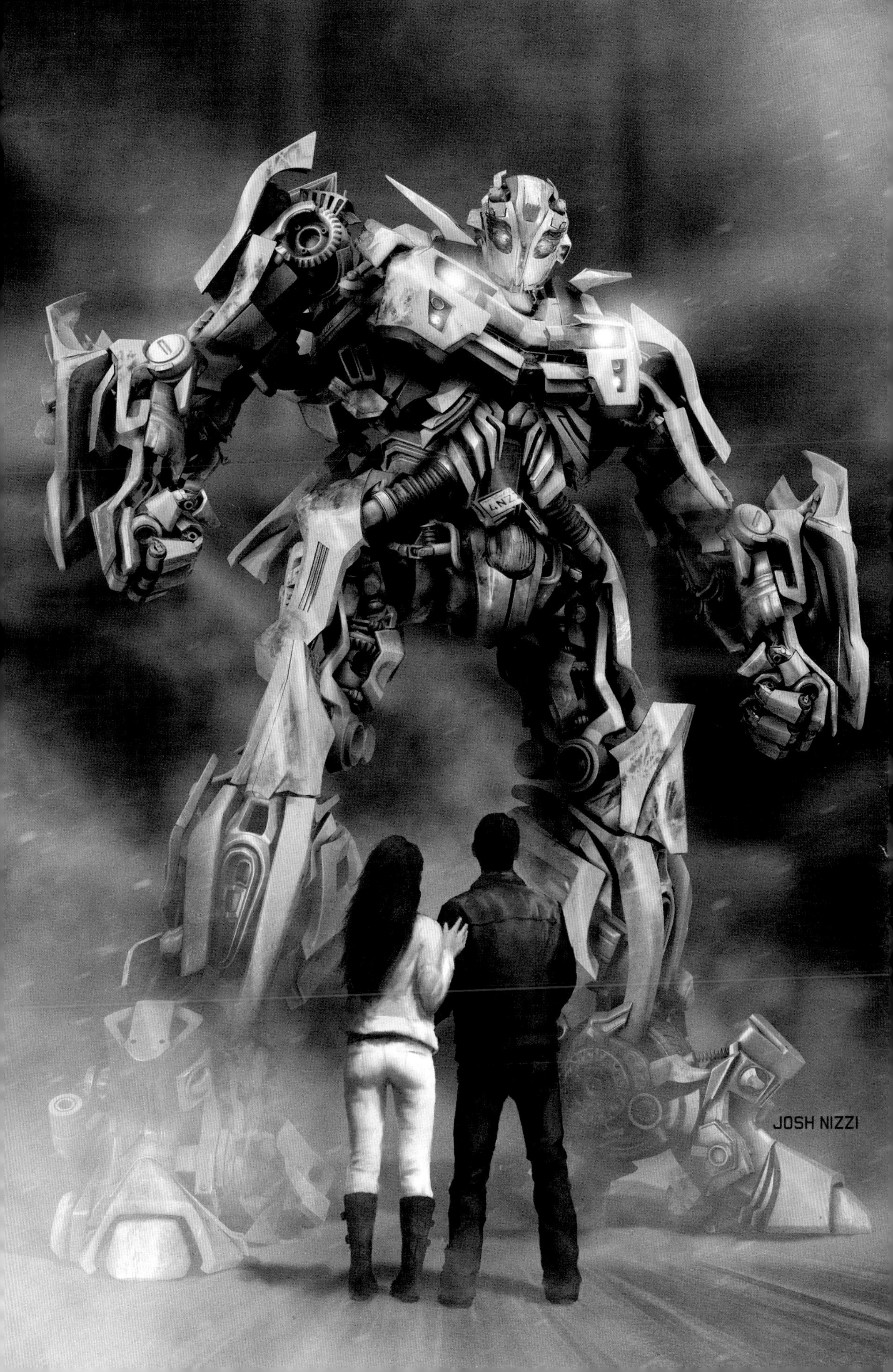
LNZ
JOSH NIZZI

Art by Alex Milne
Colors by Priscilla Tramontano

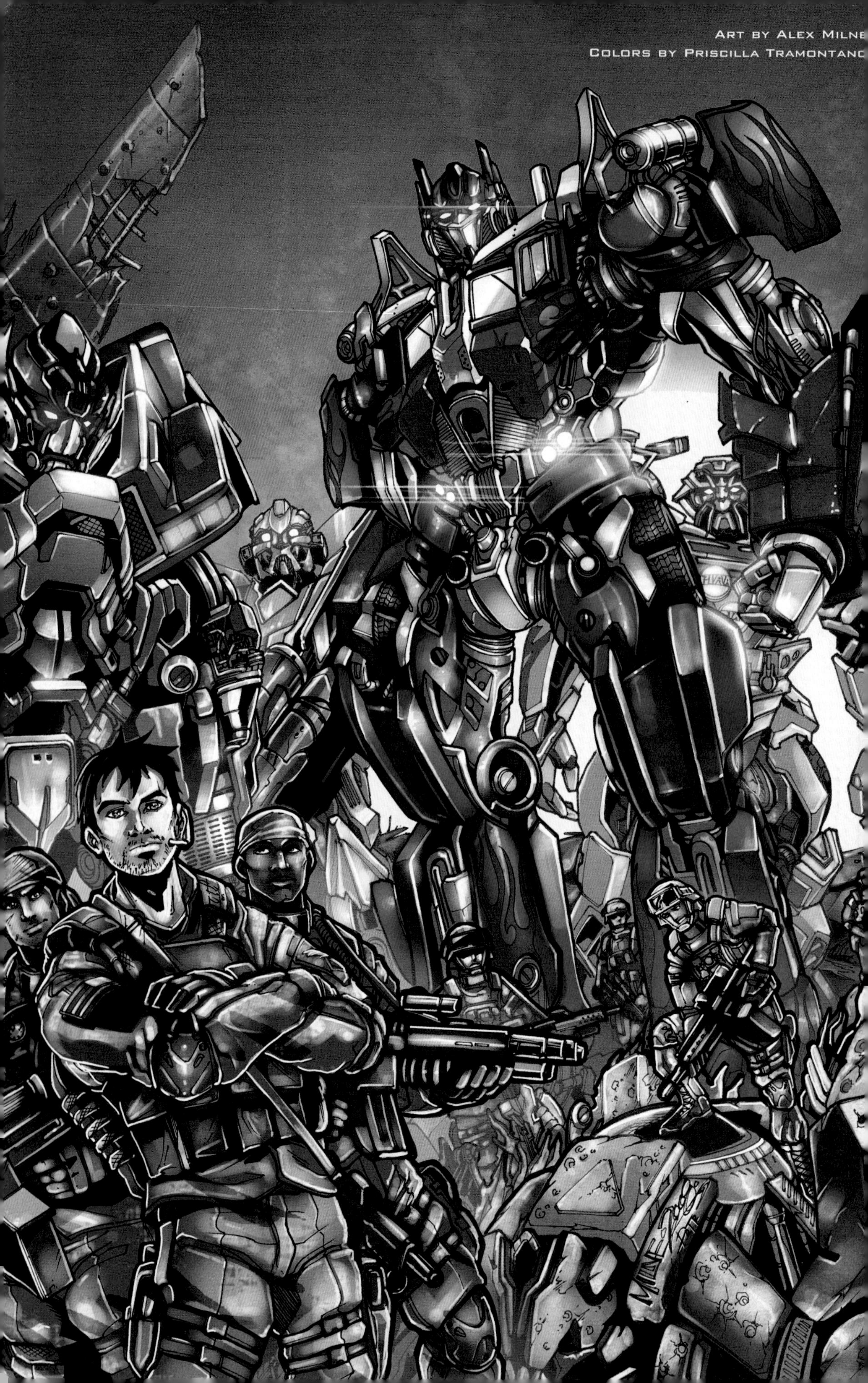

Art by Josh Nizzi

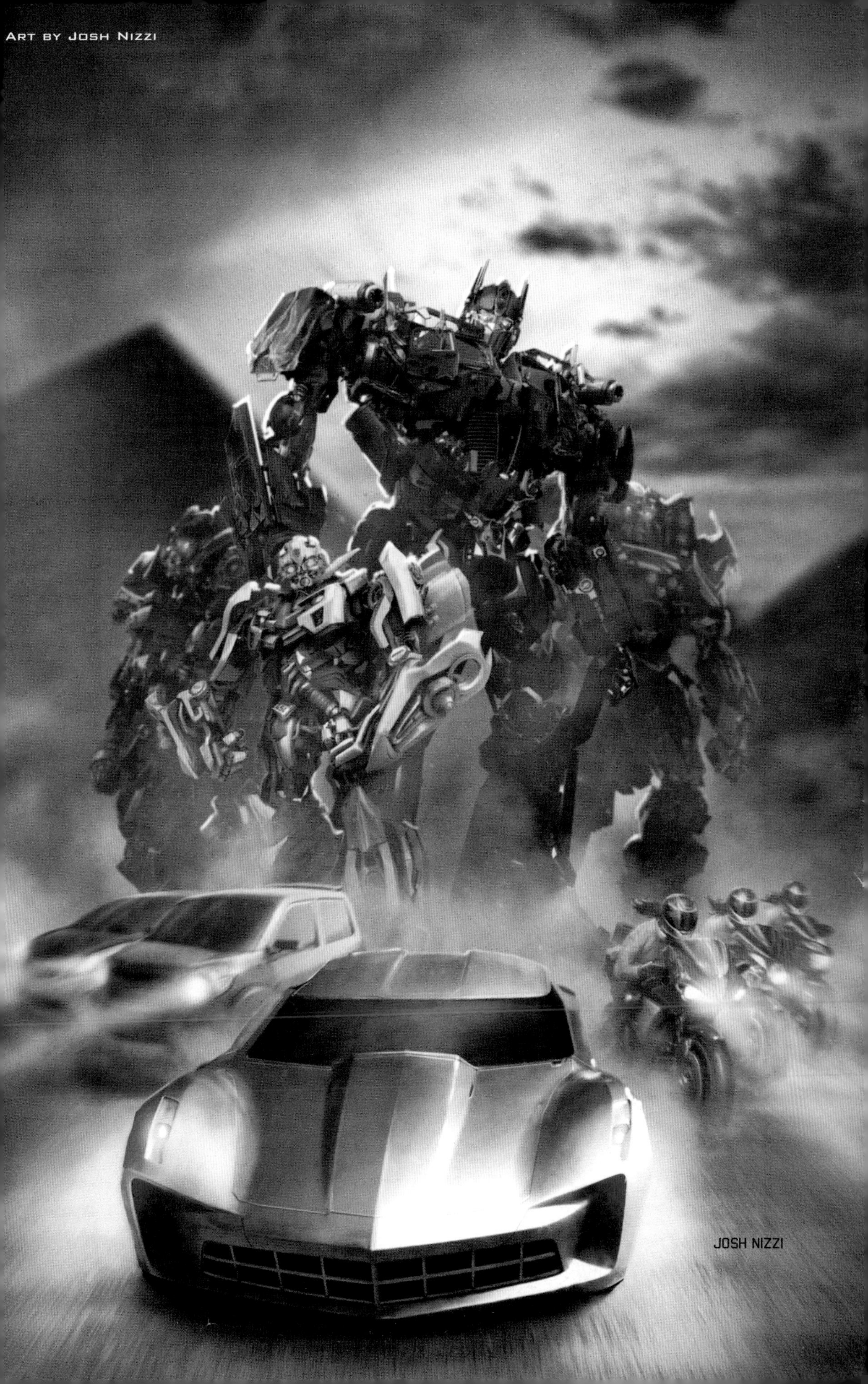
JOSH NIZZI

EXCLUSIVE MATERIAL

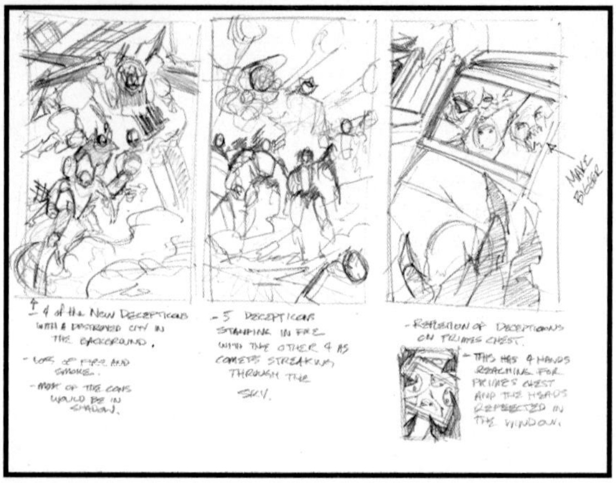

- 5 DECEPTICONS STANDING IN FIRE WITH THE OTHER 4 AS COMETS STREAKING THROUGH THE SKY.
- THIS HAS 4 HANDS REACHING FOR PRIME'S CHEST AND THE HEADS REFLECTED IN THE WINDOW.

Cover design ideas by Alex Milne for Issue Two.

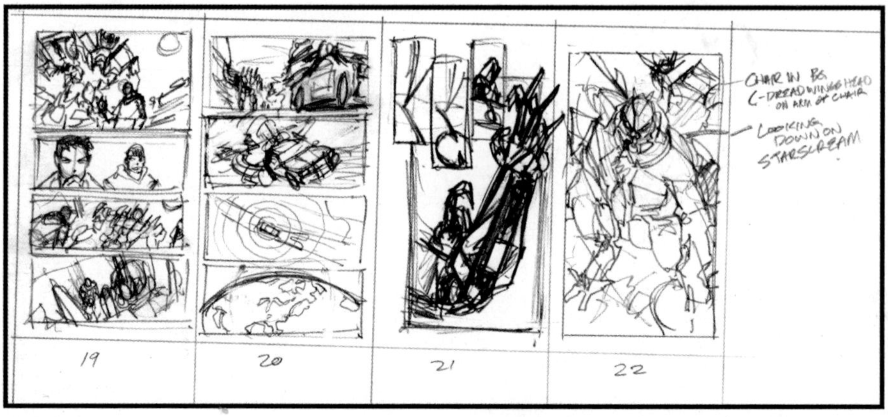

CHAIR IN BG
(-DREADWING HEAD ON ARM OF CHAIR
LOOKING DOWN ON STARSCREAM
19
20
21
22

Thumbnail "roughs" for the last four pages of Issue One.

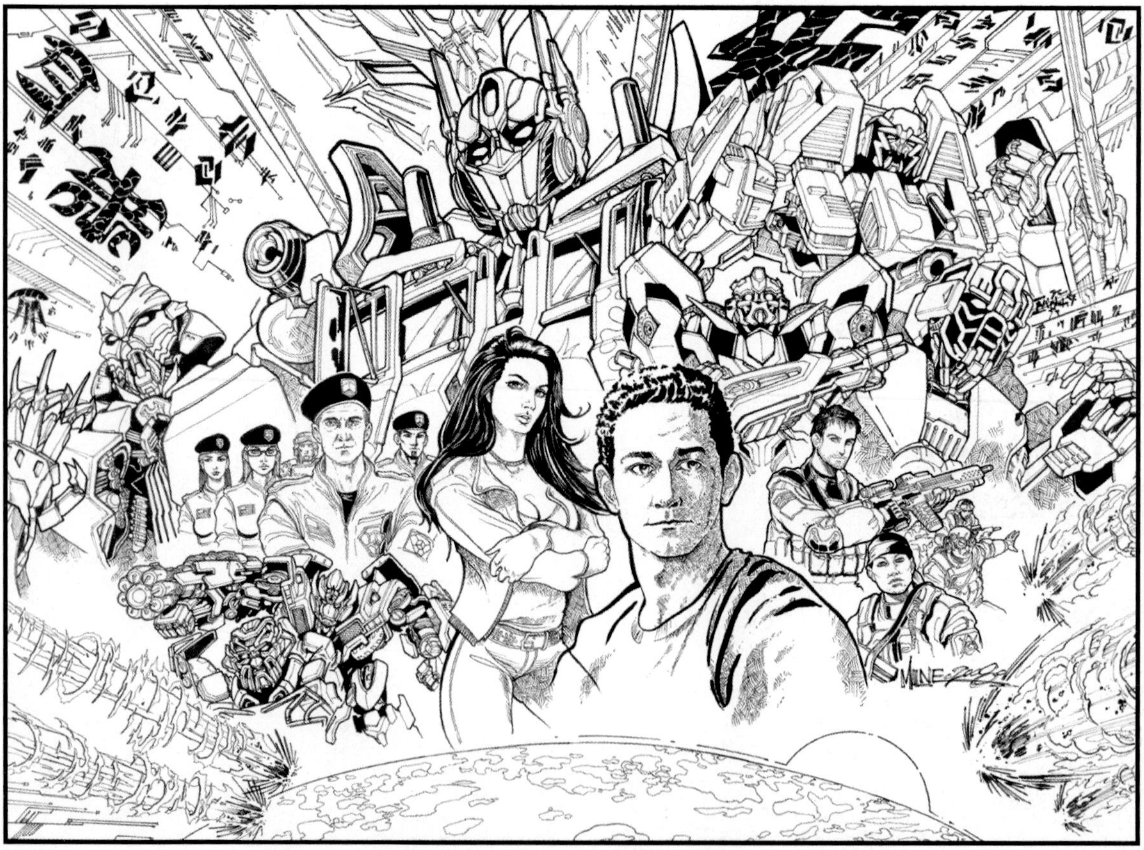

Inks for Alex Milne's incentive cover for Issue One.

Original design sketches made by Alex Milne for *The Reign of Starscream* that were unable to be used at the time. Here for the first time are those sketches.

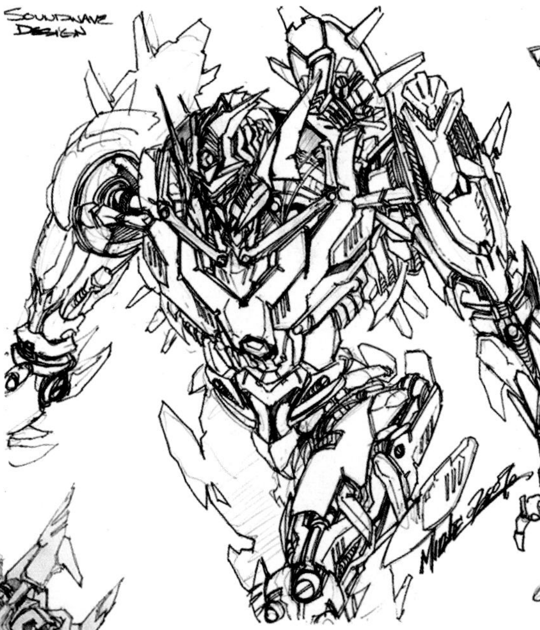
SOUNDWAVE
DESIGN

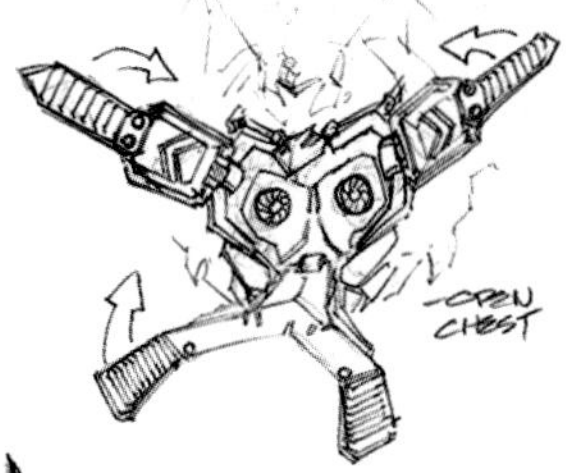
-OPEN
CHEST

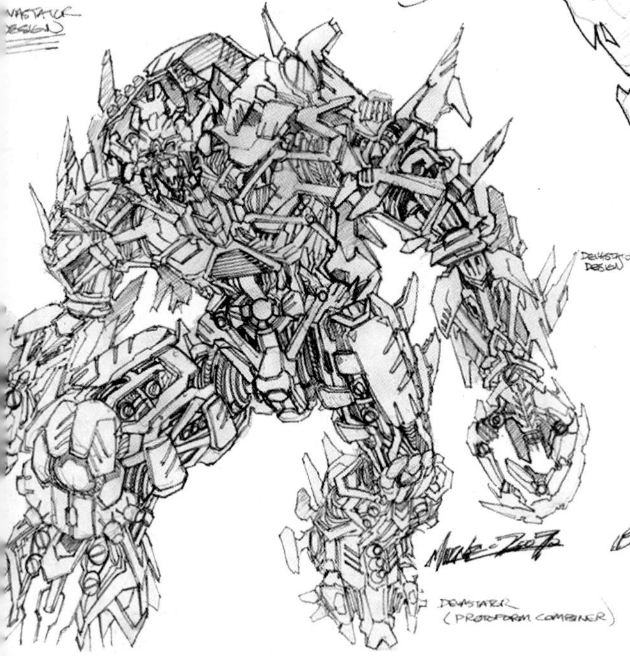
DEVASTATOR
(PROTOFORM COMBINER)

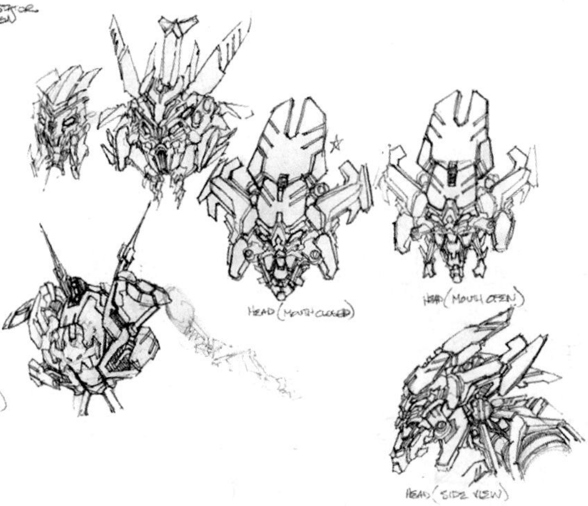
DEVASTATOR
DESIGN
HEAD (MOUTH CLOSED)
HEAD (MOUTH OPEN)
HEAD (SIDE VIEW)

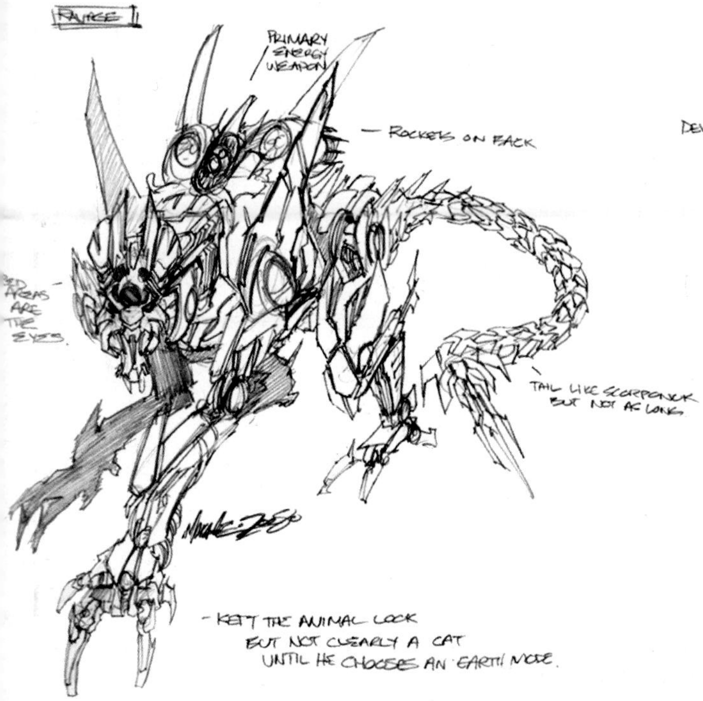
RAVAGE
PRIMARY
ENERGY
WEAPON
- ROCKETS ON BACK
TAIL LIKE SCORPONOK
BUT NOT AS LONG
- KEPT THE ANIMAL LOOK
BUT NOT CLEARLY A CAT
UNTIL HE CHOOSES AN EARTH MODE.

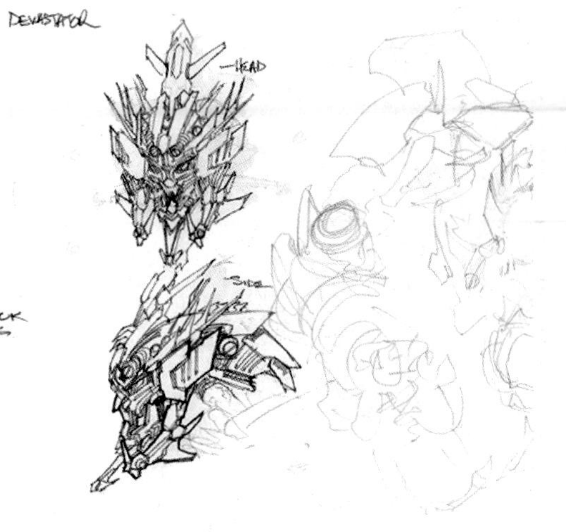
DEVASTATOR
-HEAD
SIDE

ALSO AVAILABLE

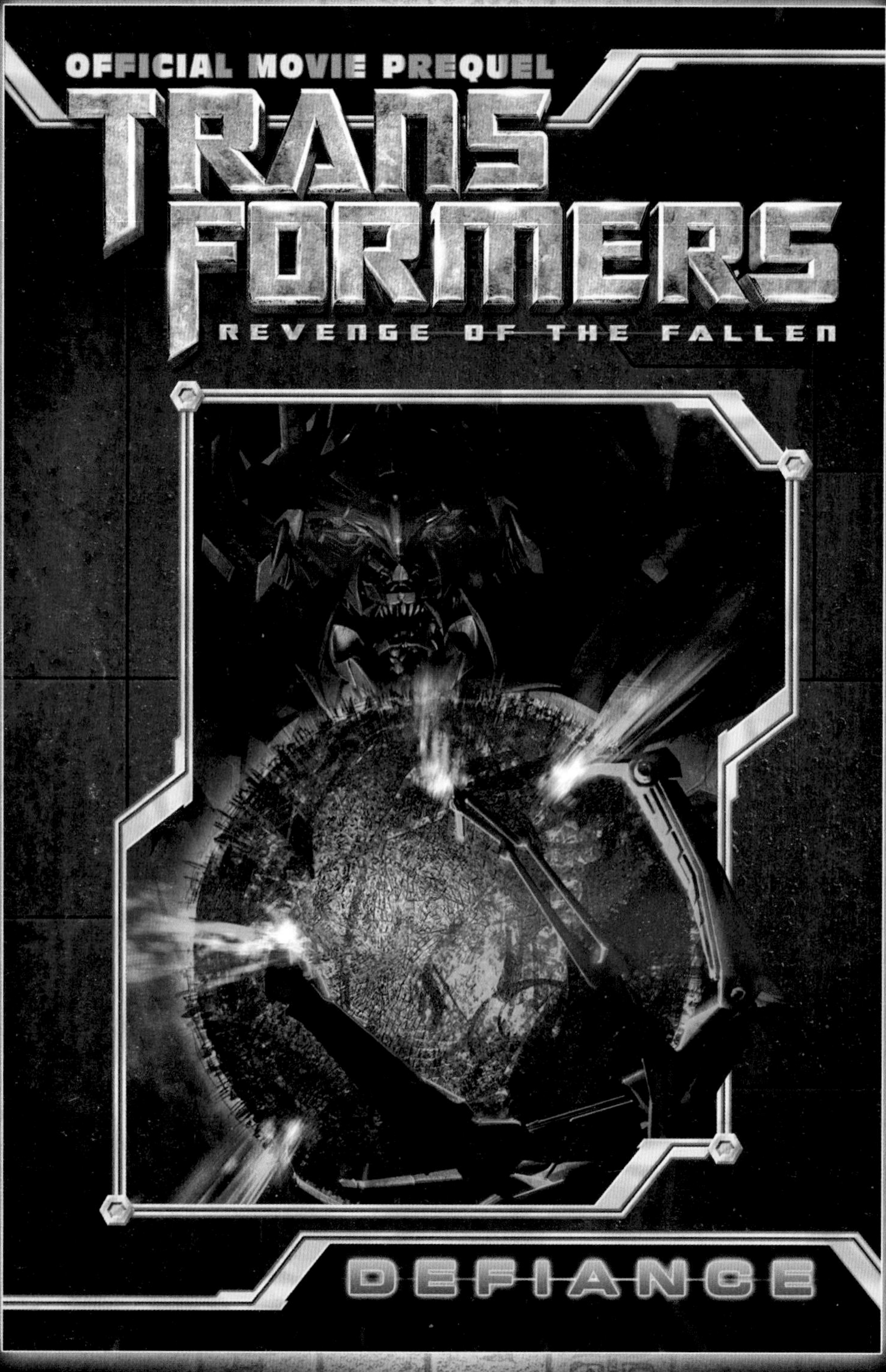
OFFICIAL MOVIE PREQUEL
TRANSFORMERS
REVENGE OF THE FALLEN
DEFIANCE

TRANSFORMERS: REVENGE OF THE FALLEN: DEFIANCE

$17.99 • ISBN: 978-1-60010-457-2 • Full Color • 104 pages